Microsoft Outlook 2016

Student Edition

30 Bird Media
510 Clinton Square
Rochester NY 14604
www.30Bird.com

Microsoft Outlook 2016
Student Edition

CEO, 30 Bird Media: Adam A. Wilcox

Series designed by: Clifford J. Coryea, Donald P. Tremblay, and Adam A Wilcox

Managing Editor: Donald P. Tremblay

Instructional Design Lead: Clifford J. Coryea

Copyeditor: Robert Staeger

Keytester: Kurt J. Specht

Trademarks

Some of the product names and company names used in this book have been used for identification purposes only and may be trademarks or registered trademarks of their respective manufacturers and sellers.

Disclaimer

We reserve the right to revise this publication without notice.

OUTL2016-A1-R10-SCB

Table of Contents

Introduction

Welcome to *Outlook 2016 Complete*. This course will provide both basic and advanced concepts and skills to be productive with Microsoft Outlook 2016: how to communicate via email messages, organize your contacts, arrange your schedule, organize Outlook items, use advanced message properties, and collaborate with others. This course maps to the objectives of the Microsoft Office Specialist exam for Outlook 2016. Objective coverage is marked throughout the course. You can download an objective map for the series from http://www.30bird.com.

You will benefit most from this course if you want to be an expert user of Outlook 2016. If you intend to take a Microsoft Office Specialist exam for Outlook, this course will prepare you for the exam.

After you complete this course, you will know how to:

- Open and interact with Outlook and navigate and view its different areas

- Create email messages, act on those you've received, add content to a message, and use signatures

- Store information about other people using contacts, use contact groups, and use the People pane

- Track your work using tasks, manage existing tasks, and assign tasks to others

- Manage your calendar using appointments, schedule meetings with other people, and navigate the calendar

- Customize options for the ribbon, change interface options, and manage your messages using Quick Steps

- Organize Outlook by managing accounts, folders, and categories; use advanced searching and filtering features, and create Quick Steps

- Manage your inbox by configuring junk mail filters, create rules, and use cleanup tools

- Use advanced email settings such as message properties, delivery options, styles, themes, and stationery

- Organize your work with notes and journal entries

- Use Outlook's collaboration features, such as item and calendar sharing, mail merges, and integrate with social media services

Course setup

To complete this course, each student and instructor will need to have a computer running Outlook 2016 with a working email account. Setup instructions and exercises are written assuming Windows 10; however, with slight modification, the course will work using Windows XP Service Pack 3, Windows Vista Service Pack 1, Windows 7, or Windows 8.x.

Hardware requirements for Windows 10 course setup include:

- 1 GHz or faster processor (32- or 64-bit) or SoC
- 1 GB (32-bit) or 2 GB (64-bit) RAM
- 25 GB total hard drive space (50 GB or more recommended)
- DirectX 9 (or later) video card or integrated graphics, with a minimum of 128 MB of graphics memory
- Monitor with 1280x800 or higher resolution
- Wi-Fi or Ethernet adapter

Software requirements include:

- Windows 10 (or alternative as above)
- Microsoft Outlook 2016 or any Microsoft Office 2016 edition that includes Outlook
- The Outlook 2016 Complete data files and PowerPoint slides, available at http://www.30bird.com

Network requirements include:

- A POP3 or Microsoft Exchange email account for the instructor and each student.

Because the exercises in this course include viewing and changing Outlook defaults as well as creating items and exchanging messages, it's best to begin with a fresh installation of the software and an empty mailbox. Configuring the instructor's computer first will facilitate configuring Outlook on students' computers. Be aware that if you are not using a fresh installation, some exercises might work slightly differently and some screens might look slightly different.

1. Install Windows 10, including all recommended updates and service packs. Use a different computer and user name for each student.
2. Install Microsoft Outlook 2016, using all defaults during installation.
3. Update Outlook or Office using Windows Update.
4. Configure Microsoft Outlook 2016.
   a) Start the application, and follow the onscreen prompts to configure a unique email account for the computer.
   b) From the instructor's computer, send two messages to each student. The first should include "Welcome" in the subject field.
   c) On student computers, verify that the instructor's messages have arrived.
   d) Close Outlook.
5. Install the Outlook 2016 Complete data files in the Documents folder.

Chapter 1: Fundamentals

In this chapter, you'll learn to:

- Explore the Outlook interface
- View Outlook items
- Use Quick Search

Module A: Getting around

It's important to understand the Outlook interface to use it effectively. If you've used other Microsoft Office programs such as Word or Excel, some features will be familiar; others are unique to Outlook. In particular, you can think of Outlook as a tightly integrated suite of applications in itself, and navigating between them as a key skill.

In this module, you'll learn:

- About Outlook
- How to open Outlook
- How to use the ribbon and Backstage view
- How to navigate using the Navigation pane

Introducing Outlook

Outlook is a *personal information manager*, a program you can use to manage your calendar and keep in touch with people. Although its best-known use is for sending and receiving email, you can also use it to store your contacts and tasks or schedule appointments and meetings.

Outlook stores messages, contacts, tasks, and so on as *items*. Instead of being stored as separate files on your computer's hard drive, they're stored in folders in the Outlook database. Each folder holds a particular type of item; for example, the Inbox folder contains email messages, and the Contacts folder contains contacts.

This structure isn't just to help keep you organized, as the Outlook interface itself changes to accommodate the type of content you're viewing. Your calendar and your mailbox both contain Outlook items, yet the available views and commands are very different for each.

Opening Outlook

How you open Outlook depends on your version of Windows. In Windows 10, use the Start menu's **All Apps** command. In Windows 8 or 8.1, find the Microsoft Office group in your Apps list, and click **Outlook 2016**.

1. Click the **Start** button to open the Start menu.
2. Click **All Apps > Outlook 2016**.

The Outlook interface

MOS Outlook Exam Objective(s): 1.1.3

The Outlook window contains several major elements. Some of these are very similar to those found in other Office applications, but others are unique to Outlook.

1. The *Quick Access toolbar* holds a customizable set of commonly used commands. By default, it contains the Send/Receive, Undo, and Customize Quick Access Toolbar buttons.

2. The *ribbon* contains most of Outlook's commands. It's arranged in tabs, each of which contains groups of related command buttons.

3. The *Folder pane* contains folders relevant to the selected area.

4. The *Navigation* options are what you use to access the different parts of Outlook. Use these options to switch between areas: Mail, Calendar, People, or Tasks. The "overflow" option (displayed as three dots) displays a shortcut menu with additional navigation and folder options.

5. The *Item list* shows the contents of the selected folder, in a format appropriate to the type of item it contains.

6. The *Reading pane* previews the contents of the item you've selected. It's available in all views but only displays by default in mail folders and the To-Do list. The Reading pane includes the Item list.

7. The *To-Do bar* displays information related to your schedule, even when you're not viewing your calendar. It includes three tools, or "peeks," that can be displayed/hidden individually: Calendar, People, and Tasks.

Exercise: Exploring Outlook

In this exercise, you'll navigate the Outlook interface.

Do This	How & Why
1. Open Outlook.	In Windows 10, click **Start > All Programs > Outlook 2016**. Outlook opens and displays your inbox.
2. Observe the Outlook window.	From left to right, you can see the Folder pane, with the Navigation options below it; the Reading pane, which includes the Item list, and below which is the People pane; and the To-Do bar.
3. Observe the Folder pane.	It contains a list of folders. The Inbox is selected.
4. Observe the other panes.	The message list shows the email currently in your inbox, and the reading pane shows the contents of the selected message. The To-Do bar shows a calendar and your upcoming appointments and tasks.
5. Observe the ribbon.	The Home tab is displayed. It contains several groups, each with one or more commands.

The ribbon

The *ribbon* holds the most commonly used commands in Outlook and arranges them on multiple levels. It displays one tab of commands at a time. Each tab contains multiple groups, and each group has one or more related command buttons. Some buttons open menu lists; other button groups contain *galleries*, which further consist of buttons you can click directly or display lists of options. Additionally, some groups have a launcher button ![launcher icon], which you use to open a window with additional commands.

The Home tab of the ribbon, while viewing a mail folder

The ribbon displays commands in a flexible format. If the Outlook window is wide enough, most command buttons appear as large icons with text labels. If the window is too small for these to fit, they're replaced by smaller icons. At even smaller sizes, the text might disappear entirely, or the whole group is replaced by a single menu. When an item on the ribbon has a downward pointing arrow on its label, you can click it to show a full menu. You can also click the More button on the lower right of a gallery to show all of its contents.

The ribbon is also context-sensitive. The tabs and their contents change, depending on what view you're in and what sort of item you have selected. This means that the ribbon always contains commands relevant to what you're doing and hides most commands you can't use. For example, in Mail view, the Home tab is filled with message-related commands, while in Calendar view it displays commands related to scheduling.

Backstage view

Clicking most ribbon tabs displays a different set of ribbon commands, while leaving the rest of the window unchanged. The exception is the brightly colored File tab at the far left of the ribbon. Clicking it opens *Backstage* view, a screen that provides access to file management and program options. In Outlook, these include account settings, mailbox cleanup, and options for rules and alerts. Although you can use it to open or save files, you won't likely do this as often as you might in an application such as Word or Excel.

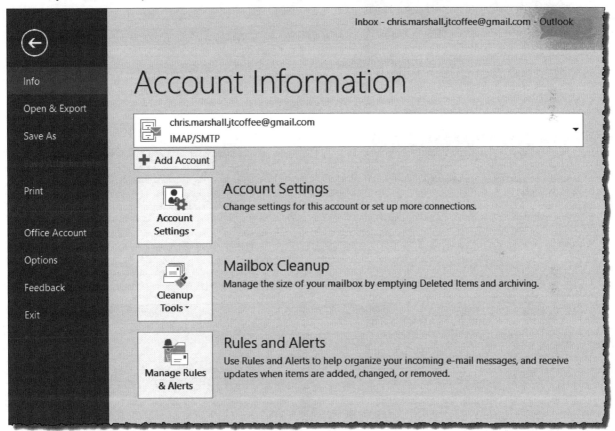

You can return to the regular Outlook window by clicking the back arrow in the upper-left corner of Backstage view.

Getting help

To get help in Outlook 2016, use the Tell Me box.

1. Click **Tell me what you want to do**.
   To the right of the View tab's name.

   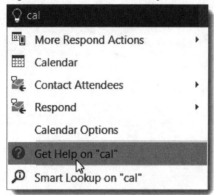

   The insertion point is in the Tell Me box.

2. Begin typing the topic you'd like information for.

3. In the list of context options, click the one that most closely matches your topic.

4. If the options listed aren't what you're looking for, you can always click **Get Help**.

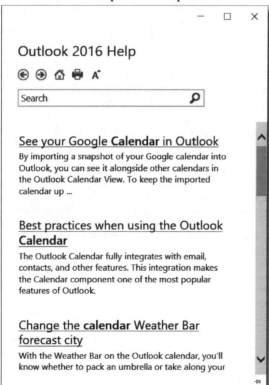

The Outlook 2016 Help window opens with additional information that hopefully matches your topic.

5. Scroll to view the displayed, linked topics, then click to select the desired topic.
   You can also type additional search text in the Search box, then press **Enter** for even more information.

6. When you're finished with your search, close the help window.

Exercise: Using the ribbon

When this exercise begins, you should be in Outlook, viewing the Inbox. You'll explore the ribbon.

Do This	How & Why
1. Observe the Home tab.	It contains eight groups of common mail commands: New, Delete, Respond, Quick Steps, Move, Tags, Find, and Send/Receive.
2. If necessary, enlarge the Outlook window until all icons on the ribbon display legible text labels.	 Drag its lower-right corner to the right. If a window is too small to show the whole ribbon, it will show a more compact version.
3. Click **New Items**.	Some commands are drop-down menus containing more specific options.
4. Click away from the menu.	It closes again.

Do This	How & Why
5. In the Quick Steps group, click the ▣ (Launcher) button.	Typically, the launcher button opens a window with more in-depth tools related to the commands in its group. The Manage Quick Steps window opens.
6. Click **Cancel**.	In the lower-right corner. The window closes.
7. Click the remaining tabs:	
a) Click **Send/Receive**.	This tab holds commands for sending and receiving mail.
b) Click **Folder**.	This tab holds commands for folder management.
c) Click **View**.	This tab holds commands for changing Outlook's appearance and visible information.
d) Click **File**	Backstage view opens, displaying various program options.
8. Click **Home**.	Outlook again displays the inbox.

Navigation and Folder options

Located in the lower left of the main window, the Navigation options provide the primary way to access the different areas of Outlook. These options include Mail, Calendar, People, and Tasks. In addition, the overflow option (shown as three dots) displays a shortcut menu with additional options for Navigation, Notes, Folders, and Shortcuts.

Navigation options, with overflow options expanded

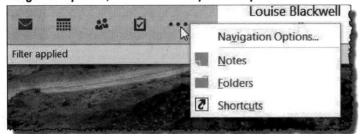

The Folder pane shows folders and shortcuts specific to the view you select; for example, mail folders in Mail view and task folders in Tasks view. Folder List view displays all folders.

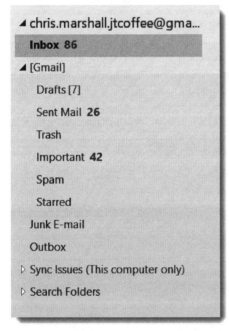

It's easiest to think of using the Navigation and Folder options as a two-part process. First, you choose your Navigation view to change what you want to do, for example, to check email or your calendar. Next, you use the Folder pane in that view to access the information you need.

Resizing panes

You can easily resize panes in the Outlook window by dragging their borders. When desktop space is tight, you can also minimize the Folder and other panes to leave more space for viewing items. Even minimized, some panes have buttons or clickable text you can use to access their usual features.

The minimized Folder pane

- Resize a pane by pointing to its border. When the pointer icon turns to a double-sided arrow, you can resize the pane by dragging to either side.

- Minimize the Folder pane or To-Do bar by clicking ◄ in the upper-right corner of the respective pane.
- Click an option on the minimized pane to access its features.
- To expand a minimized pane to normal view, click the pin icon.

- To display the To-Do bar, click the ribbon's **View** tab; then, in the Layout group, click **To-Do Bar** to display a menu of options, and click the desired option.

- If multiple tools ("peeks") are displayed on the To-Do bar, and you wish to close one of them, click its close button.

  If only one tool is displayed, closing it hides the To-Do bar.

- To hide the To-Do bar, regardless of how many peeks are displayed, in the View tab's Layout group, click **To-Do Bar > Off**.

Exercise: Using panes

In this activity, you'll switch views in the Navigation options and resize the Outlook panes to better view information.

Do This	How & Why
1. In the Navigation options, click **Calendar**.	Outlook switches to Calendar view.
2. Observe Calendar view:	
a) Look at the Navigation pane.	In Calendar view, the Folder pane includes a miniature calendar, and below it a list of calendar options.
b) Look at the ribbon.	The Home tab is still there, but all of its commands have changed to those related to calendars and scheduling.
c) Look at the rest of the window.	The Reading pane and To-Do bar aren't displayed. By default, all that's shown in the item list is today's date and any scheduled events and holidays already in the calendar.
3. Click **People**.	The ribbon, Folder pane, and Item list all change to show contents related to contacts.
4. In the Navigation options, click Folders.	Click the overflow button to display its shortcut menu.
	Navigation Options...
	Notes
	Folders
	Shortcuts
	The full folder list is displayed in the Folder pane. The Contacts folder is still selected, and the ribbons and other panes remain unchanged.

Do This	How & Why
5. In the Folder pane, click **Calendar**.	Don't use the Calendar button.  The resulting view is almost exactly like that of Calendar view. Selecting a folder in Folders view changes the ribbon and other panes to match the contents of a selected folder. Also in the Folder pane, below the miniature calendar, the folders are displayed.
6. Click **Mail**.	Now you're viewing the Inbox again.
7. Point to the line between the Folder pane and message list.	The pointer turns to a double-headed arrow.
8. Drag slightly to the right.	The Folder pane becomes wider.
9. At the top of the Folder pane, click the arrow button.	The pane collapses and the folder list moves left, leaving more space for the Reading pane.
10. Click a folder name in the minimized folder pane.	The contents of that folder are displayed in the Preview pane, but the Folder pane itself remains closed.
11. In the Folder pane, click the **Expand** button.	To expand the pane temporarily.

Do This	How & Why
12. Expand the Folder permanently.	Click the pin icon. 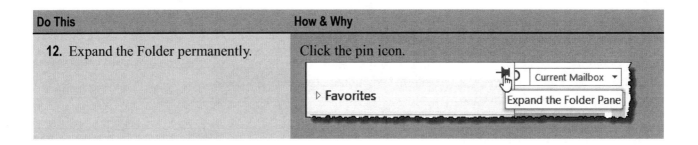

Assessment: Getting Around

1. The _____ replaces the menus and toolbars of older Outlook versions.

    *   Folder pane
    *   To-Do bar
    *   Ribbon
    *   Reading pane

2. The _____ is/are the primary way to access various areas of Outlook.

    *   Navigation options
    *   Quick Access toolbar
    *   Ribbons
    *   Backstage view

3. True or false: You can use the Folder pane normally, even when it's minimized.

    *   True
    *   False

Module B: Viewing Outlook items

Because Outlook is a personal organizer and communication tool rather than a document editor, you'll most often use it just to find and review information. Depending on your exact needs, you might be able to quickly preview items, or you might need to open and even edit them. You'll accumulate a lot of items over time, so you'll also need to know how to arrange them and search for what you need.

In this module, you will learn how to:

- Preview messages
- Open Outlook items
- Change list views
- Use Instant Search

Outlook items

Although items aren't separate documents, in the sense of being individual files on your hard drive, you can still think of each item as a sort of document stored in Outlook's data file, and Outlook itself as the tool you use to view and edit them.

The information in an item may be there primarily as a reference for you, such as a contact or task. It might be communications with others, such as an email message. Or, it might be some of both, such as a meeting you've scheduled with others through Outlook. As a result, Outlook displays each type of item in a different way, and stores each in a different folder.

Previewing messages

The Reading pane makes it quick and easy to view the contents of an item without having to open it. Although you can turn on the Reading pane in any view, it's most commonly used for reading messages.

1. In the Folder pane, select a mail folder, such as your inbox.
2. In the message list, click the message you want to read.

Opening items

You can open any item in its own window to view its full properties. With non-mail items such as contacts or appointments, opening an item also lets you edit it.

When you open an item, the new window has a ribbon corresponding to its item type, while below it displays the item's properties.

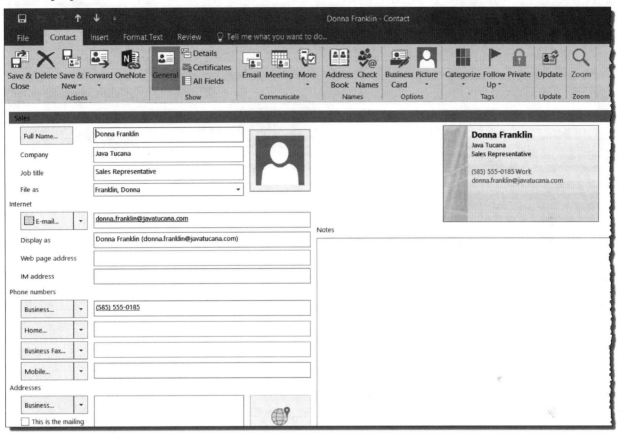

 MOS Outlook Exam Objective(s): 4.1.4

1. Select the folder you want to view.

2. Double-click an item to open it. Note that many items have a Show group in the Home tab, which changes what item details are visible.

3. Optionally, make any changes to the item.

4. If you make any changes, click **Save & Close** to save them; otherwise, close the window to discard them.

Outlook Today

One quick way to view what's going on in Outlook is through the *Outlook Today* screen. Outlook Today is displayed when you click the root folder of your mailbox, which might be your account name, simply "Outlook," or something similar. It displays a summary of your upcoming appointments, open tasks, and messages requiring action.

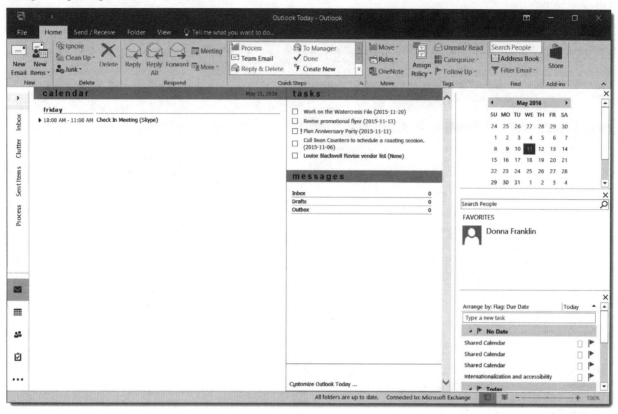

Using groups

By default, most item lists are arranged into *groups*. For example, by default your inbox is arranged by date, but rather than being a simple list it's broken up into chronological groupings: today, past days this week, previous weeks, and so on. Groups aren't listed chronologically, but rather correspond to how you have a folder sorted: you could group by name, message size, contact category, and so on.

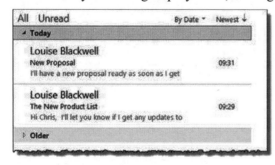

MOS Outlook Exam Objective(s): 2.4.1

Groups help you sort through long lists, and not just by giving visual dividers. You can also minimize a group to get it out of the way.

- To collapse a group, click ◢ next to the group header.

- To expand a group, click ▷
- To collapse all groups, right-click any group header and click **Collapse All Groups**.

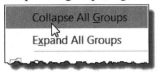

- To expand all groups, right-click any group header and click **Expand All Groups**.

Changing folder views

 MOS Outlook Exam Objective(s): 1.1.4, 2.4.2

You might want to display the items in a folder in different ways—either the same items arranged differently, or sorted in the folder to better find what you need. Options for doing so are found in the View tab for each folder.

The Change View gallery in a mail folder

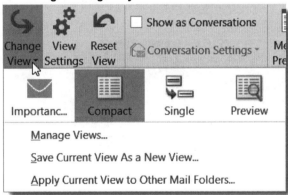

The Arrangement gallery in a mail folder

- To change how a folder's items appear, click **Change View** in the Current View group, and select an option from the gallery. Each type of item has its own views.
- To rearrange or filter a folder's contents, click an option in the Arrangement gallery, located in the Arrangement group. To display the complete gallery, click ▼ (More).

Using Instant Search

Outlook provides a variety of tools for searching, but the most convenient is the Instant Search box located at the top of the item list.

 MOS Outlook Exam Objective(s): 1.3.2, 1.3.4

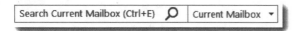

1. Select the folder you want to search.
2. Click inside the Instant Search box, or press **Ctrl**+**E**.
3. Type in the term for which you want to search.

    The item list is filtered, displaying items matching only your search term. By default, an Instant Search applies only to the folder you've selected, but it finds results in which your search term appears as either the item's name or its contents. Additionally, the term itself is highlighted in yellow, making it easy to spot.

4. To clear a search term, click ✕ in the Instant Search box.

When the Instant Search box is active, or when a search term is entered, the Search tab appears on the ribbon. It allows you to specify more detailed options for a search.

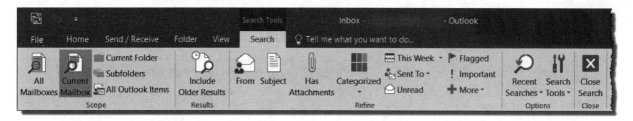

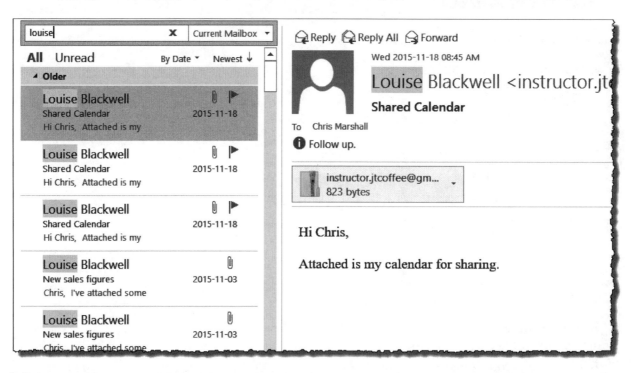

Exercise: Reading your messages

For this exercise, you'll need to have at least two messages from your instructor in your inbox. You'll view the contents of your inbox folder and read the messages in it.

Do This	How & Why
1. Select your Inbox folder.	You should have at least two messages, and one is selected.
2. View the "Welcome" message from your instructor:	
a) Click it.	The contents of the message appear in the Reading pane.
b) Double-click it,	It opens in a separate Message window.
c) Close the message window.	Click ![X] (Close) in the upper-right corner.
3. On the View tab, click **Change View > Preview**.	Each message in your inbox now appears on a single line across the Reading pane.
4. Click **Change View > Hide Message Marked for Deletion**.	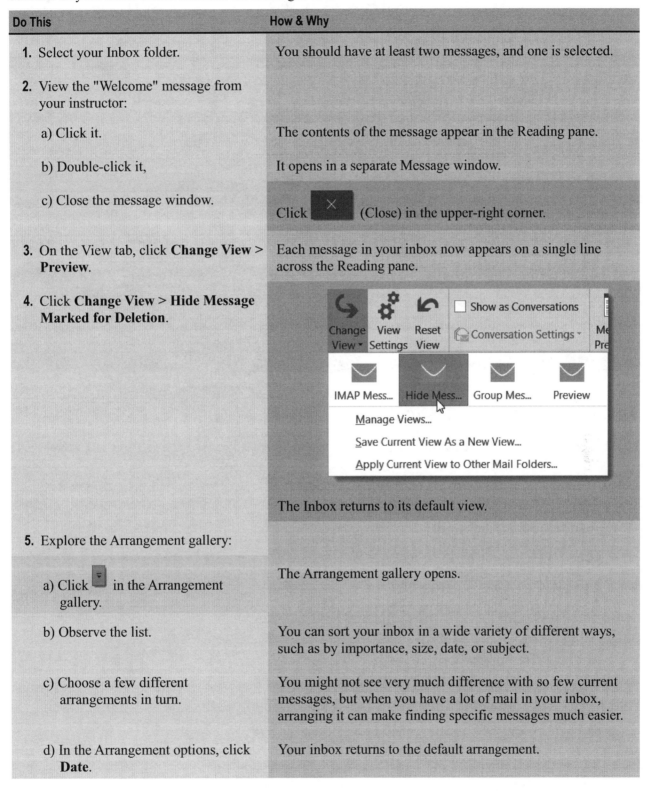
	The Inbox returns to its default view.
5. Explore the Arrangement gallery:	
a) Click ![arrow] in the Arrangement gallery.	The Arrangement gallery opens.
b) Observe the list.	You can sort your inbox in a wide variety of different ways, such as by importance, size, date, or subject.
c) Choose a few different arrangements in turn.	You might not see very much difference with so few current messages, but when you have a lot of mail in your inbox, arranging it can make finding specific messages much easier.
d) In the Arrangement options, click **Date**.	Your inbox returns to the default arrangement.

Do This	How & Why
6. In the Instant Search box, type `welcome`.	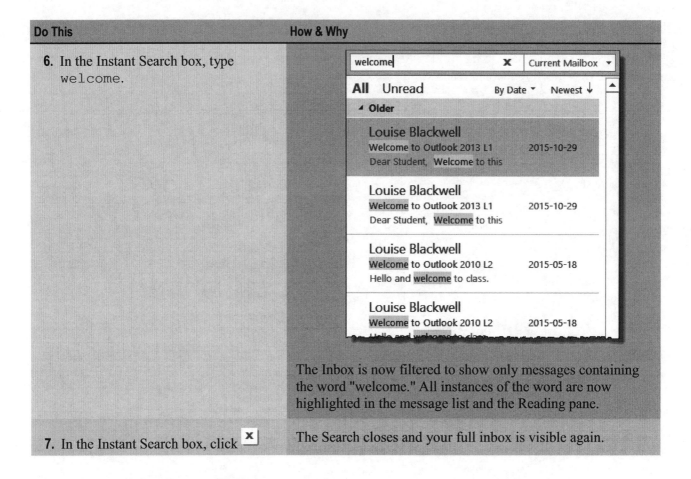 The Inbox is now filtered to show only messages containing the word "welcome." All instances of the word are now highlighted in the message list and the Reading pane.
7. In the Instant Search box, click [x]	The Search closes and your full inbox is visible again.

Assessment: Viewing Outlook items

1. True or false? You can preview any kind of item in the Reading pane.

   - True
   - False

2. Outlook Today is ...

   - A news feed integrated into Outlook.
   - Microsoft's web-based email service.
   - A summary page of Outlook items requiring action.
   - Another name for Folders view.

3. What View tab elements let you change how items appear in a folder?

   - Change View
   - Reading pane
   - Arrangement gallery
   - Reminders window

4. True or false? By default, Instant Search searches all folders for the entered term.

   - True
   - False

Summary: Fundamentals

You should now know how to:

- Navigate the Outlook interface, including the ribbon and navigation pane
- View Outlook items, change folder views, and use the Instant Search function

Synthesis: Fundamentals

In this activity, you'll navigate the Outlook interface and view items.

1. In Folders view, view each folder in turn. Observe how the view and ribbon options change for each folder.

2. In your Contacts folder, change to List view, and then open a contact to view its details. When you're done, change to Business Card view.

3. View the options available to you in Backstage view.

4. Search your Inbox for messages from your instructor.

Chapter 2: Email basics

In this chapter, you'll learn how to:

- Create and format email messages
- Manage email messages
- Attach content to a message
- Create and use signatures

Module A: Creating messages

Creating items is a fairly simple process. Typically, you create a new item using ribbon commands and then enter its properties in a new window. Exactly what the properties are depends on the item's type. The most common items you're likely to create are email messages, which contain not only a message body but additional fields used to control its appearance and delivery.

In this module, you'll learn how to:

- Create a message
- Format message text
- Check message spelling

The Message window

A new Message window comprises several components you can use to create a message:

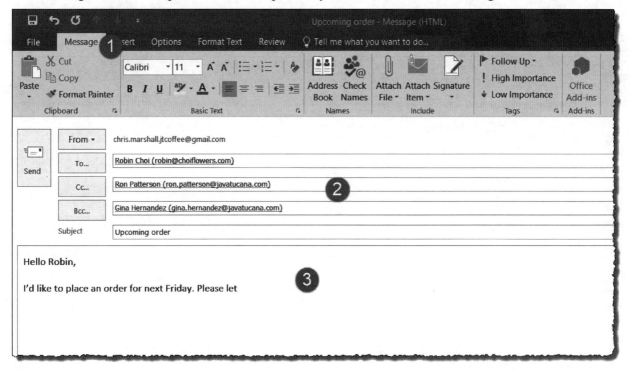

As in most of Outlook, you can perform actions in the Message window by using the ribbon. The *Message tab* in particular is unique to the message window: it contains common commands for formatting, addressing, tagging, and attaching items to your messages.

Header fields are used to address and describe the message. You can use the To, CC, and BCC fields to enter message recipients, and the Subject field to give the message a title.

The *message body* holds the actual message contents. You can type in this area or insert content.

Creating messages

You always compose messages in a message window, but you can open them a number of ways. Most commonly, you do so from your mailbox, but you can also open a message from a task or contact.

 MOS Outlook Exam Objective(s): 2.2.1

1. Click **New Email**.
2. In the To field, enter the recipient's email address. You can type it, or choose it from your address book.
3. In the Subject field, enter the message subject. It should tell the recipient, at a glance, what the message is about.
4. In the message body pane, type the message.
5. Click **Send**.

Exercise: Sending a simple message

For this exercise, you'll need a partner. You'll send a simple message to your partner.

Do This	How & Why
1. On the ribbon, click **New Email**.	You'll first need to be in Mail view. The Message window opens.
2. In the To field, type your partner's email address.	
3. In the Subject field, type Greetings from <Name>.	Use your name.
4. In the message body field, type your message.	

It should look something like this:

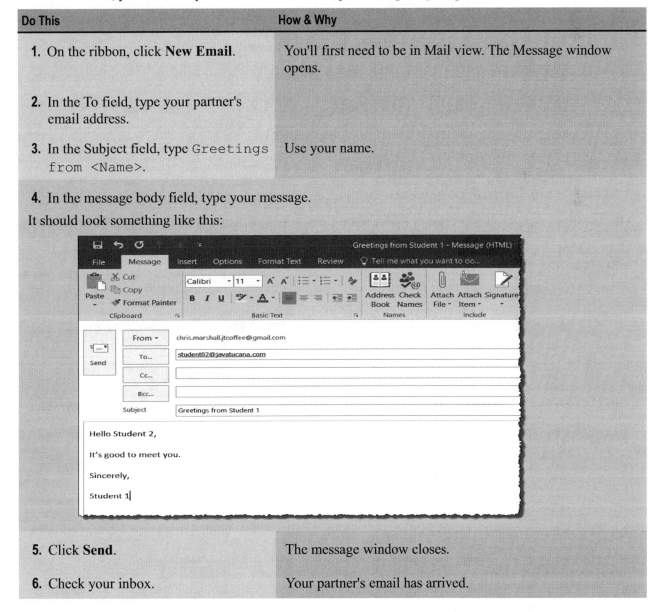

5. Click **Send**.	The message window closes.
6. Check your inbox.	Your partner's email has arrived.

Address fields

A message contains *address fields* named To, Cc, and Bcc. You can enter addresses into any or all of the three, and every one of those recipients will get the same message. Still, each field has a distinct purpose.

MOS Outlook Exam Objective(s): 2.2.3

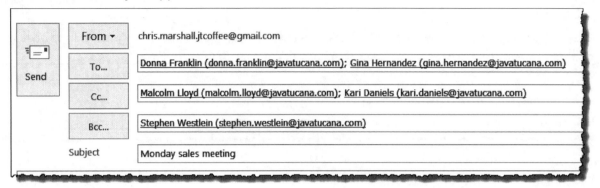

The *To* field is intended for the primary recipient(s) of the message. There must be at least one recipient entered; however, there can be as many as necessary, separated by semicolons.

The *Cc* , or "carbon copy," field draws its name from the days of typewritten letters. All addresses in the Cc field also receive copies of the email. In theory, a Cc is intended for people not directly addressed by the message but still require the information. In practice, this distinction is only one of courtesy: if you receive a message by Cc, you can still reply, like anyone else, should you need to do so.

The *Bcc*, or "blind carbon copy," field is similar to the Cc, but for recipients whose identities are to be hidden from all other recipients. When you receive a message, you see all of the addresses in its To and Cc fields, but only the sender knows who, if anyone, was sent a Bcc. The Bcc field is not displayed by default: you can enable it in the ribbon's Options tab.

The *From* field displays your own address. If you have more than one account, it allows you to specify which account you're sending it from. As with the Bcc, the From field can be enabled on the Options tab.

Adding recipients

You can add recipients by typing them in the address fields, or by selecting recipients from your address book.

When you type in addresses, Outlook will offer to "autocomplete" them according to your current address book entries. If the name you're entering matches one or more of those in your address book, Outlook displays them in a list. You can press **Tab** or **Enter** to choose the first entry on the list, or just keep typing.

If you click any of the buttons (To, Cc, or Bcc), the Select Names window will open; from there, you can choose names from your address book.

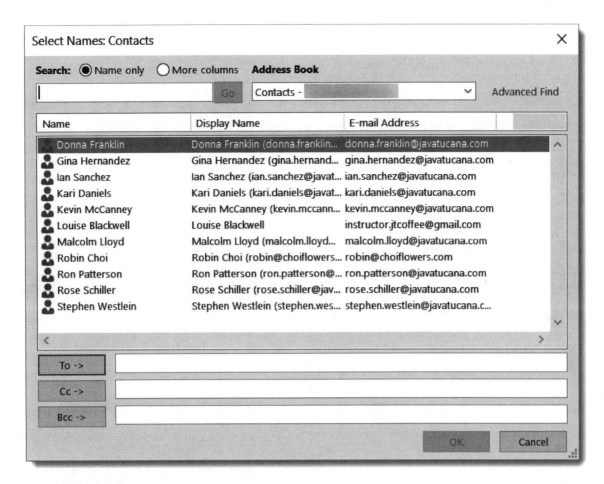

1. Click any of the three buttons.

   It doesn't matter which you click. All three open the same window. You can instead click **Address Book** on the Message tab.

   The Select Names window opens.

2. If necessary, select which address book you want to view.

   If you have multiple email accounts or contact folders, you might have several lists.

3. Click the name you want to add.

   To add multiple addresses, press and hold **Ctrl**.

4. Click the button for the field in which you want to place the address.

   To, Cc, or Bcc.

5. When you've added all the addresses you want, click **OK**.

Exercise: Sending to multiple recipients

You'll need to have two partners for this exercise and your instructor saved as a contact. You'll address an email to two partners and send a copy to your instructor.

Do This	How & Why
1. Open a new message window.	
2. Type a subject, and compose a simple message.	
3. In the To field, type your partner's usual address. Watch to see if it appears in an autocomplete listing before you've finished typing.	If it does appear, you can press **Tab** or **Enter** to automatically complete it.
4. Type ; followed by the address of a third student.	In the To field.
5. Click the **Cc** button.	The Select Names window opens.
6. In the Address Book, click your instructor's name, and then click **Cc**.	If your instructor is not in your contacts, you can type the address in. Your instructor is now added to the Cc field.
7. Click the **Options** tab.	In the Show Fields group. If you needed to display the To and Bcc fields, you could click the **To** and **Bcc** buttons.
8. Click **Send**.	The message is sent to both of your partners. A Cc version is sent to your instructor as well.

Message formatting

You create Outlook messages in the Message window. You can format them as HTML, plain text, or rich text.

 MOS Outlook Exam Objective(s): 2.1.1, 2.3.1

- *HTML* is the default message format. It allows you to create messages formatted like web pages or word processor documents, with your choice of fonts, colors, formatting, and graphics. It's supported by a wide variety of clients and is the most versatile solution.

- *Rich text format* (RTF) is a proprietary Microsoft format and is supported only by Outlook and Exchange clients. Although Outlook uses RTF on Exchange email servers, it automatically converts rich text messages to HTML when you send them to Internet addresses.

- *Plain text format* is the simplest and most streamlined message format. It's supported by all email clients and has the least chance of displaying errors, but it doesn't allow you to apply formatting such as bold, italic, or colored text. You also can't include inline images in a plain text message, though you can still attach them separately.

In HTML or RTF, you can use the ribbon's text formatting commands. If you've used Word or Excel to format text, you'll find Outlook's tools very similar. The ribbon's Basic Text group provides the most common commands, including fonts, colors, paragraph alignment, and bulleted or numbered lists. More complete commands are located on the Format Text tab.

The basic text formatting controls on the Message tab.

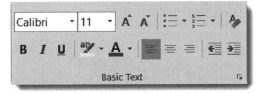

Checking spelling

To spell-check a message, and scan it for both spelling and grammar errors, on the Review tab, click **Spelling & Grammar**.

This opens the Spelling and Grammar window, which suggests replacements and provides additional control.

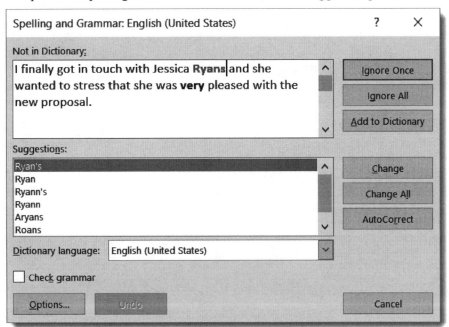

When the window first opens, it will highlight the first suspected problem and show a list of suggested replacements. For each problem, you can choose one of three primary options.

- If the word is correct, click **Ignore Once** to ignore this instance, **Ignore All** to ignore all instances in the message, or **Add to Dictionary** to make sure Outlook always recognizes it in the future.

- If the word is misspelled, click the correct spelling in the Suggestions list. Then click **Change** to change the current instance, **Change All** to change all instances in the message, or **AutoCorrect** to tell Outlook to automatically and globally correct any future instances of this misspelling as you type.

- If the word is misspelled and Outlook didn't suggest a suitable replacement, fix it in the upper pane of the window, then click **Change**, **Change All**, or **AutoCorrect**.

- To check grammar as well, select **Check grammar**.

Exercise: Formatting message text

In this exercise, you'll create a message, format its text, and check it for errors.

 MOS Outlook Exam Objective(s): 2.3.1

Do This	How & Why
1. Open a new message window, and address it to your partner.	
2. Type the message exactly as shown, *including misspellings*:	

> Hello Student 2,
>
> I finally got in touch with Jessica Ryans, and she wanted to sress that she was very pleased with the new proposal.
>
> For Monday, please bring:
> The final logo design
> A preliminary page layout
>
> Thanks,
> Student 1

Do This	How & Why
3. Select the word **very**.	
4. On the Message tab, in the Basic Text group, click **B** (**Bold**).	The word becomes bold.
5. Select the two lines **The final logo design** and **A preliminary page layout**.	You don't need to select all of both lines, as long as you select at least part of each.
6. Click (**Bullets**).	The two lines become a bulleted list.
7. Select your name at the bottom, and apply the following formatting:	Arial Black ▾ 12 ▾ The font and size of the text change.
8. On the Review tab, click **Spelling & Grammar**.	The Spelling & Grammar window opens. The name "Ryans" is highlighted. This is spelled properly, so you'll ignore it.
9. Click **Ignore Once**	The next misspelled word, "sress," is highlighted. You'll change it.
10. Click **Change**.	Outlook informs you that the Spelling check is complete.

Do This	How & Why

11. Click **OK**, and compare your message to the following:

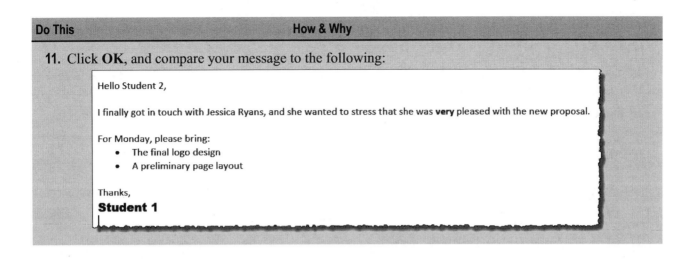

Hello Student 2,

I finally got in touch with Jessica Ryans, and she wanted to stress that she was **very** pleased with the new proposal.

For Monday, please bring:
- The final logo design
- A preliminary page layout

Thanks,
Student 1

Assessment: Creating messages

1. What type of commands won't you find on the Message tab of the ribbon?

   - Formatting text
   - Adding recipients
   - Attaching items
   - Sending messages

2. True or false? Recipients in the To, Cc, and Bcc fields all receive identical messages and can respond to them in the same way.

   - True
   - False

3. What message format is supported by the most email clients?

   - HTML
   - Rich Text
   - Plain Text

4. True or false? If Outlook incorrectly shows a word as a spelling error, you can easily and permanently correct it.

   - True
   - False

Module B: Acting on messages

When you receive messages from others, you'll usually need to do more than just read them. You can respond to them, pass them on to others, print them, or even delete ones you don't need to keep.

In this module, you'll learn how to:

- Reply to a message
- Forward a message
- Print messages
- Delete a message
- Mark messages as read or unread

Message responses

The Respond group—on the Home tab of the mailbox or the Message tab of the Message window—has multiple commands for responding to a message, and it's important to know the differences between them.

 MOS Outlook Exam Objective(s): 1.1.1, 1.1.2, 2.2.5

- *Reply* addresses a new message to the original message sender.
- *Reply All* addresses a message to the sender and to all the other recipients of the original message.
- *Forward* doesn't address the message to anyone automatically; instead, you can choose a recipient.

Additionally, you can respond to a message by requesting a meeting, forward the original message as an attachment, or respond via instant message.

By default, replies and forwards send a copy of the original message along with anything you care to add. In HTML or rich text messages, your reply appears in blue. In plain text, each line of the original message is prefaced with ">." You can change these options on the File tab by clicking **Options**, then clicking **Mail** in the left pane.

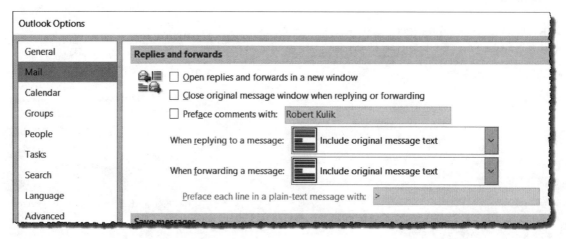

Replying to messages

When you reply to a message, the subject is prefixed by "RE:" so that the recipient can see that it's a reply. Your response is inserted before the previous message. When responding to long messages, or to extended back-and-forth chains of replies, many users consider it polite to delete parts of the message not relevant to your reply.

MOS Outlook Exam Objective(s): 2.2.7

1. Select a message in your mailbox, or open it in a message window.
2. Click **Reply** to respond only to the sender, or click **Reply All** to respond to the sender and all message recipients.

    You'll be able to add or remove recipients just as you would with a new message, if necessary.
3. Type your reply.
4. If you like, delete unnecessary parts of the original message.
5. Click **Send**.

Forwarding messages

When you forward a message, "FW:" precedes its subject. Unlike a reply, a forward is intended for people who never saw the original message. This means no recipients are included by default; instead, you'll need to add them. It also means you should be careful about what you do and don't forward, as a matter of etiquette. You shouldn't pass sensitive information on to people who should not see it, and you should also not remove or change parts of the original message that will distort its original meaning.

1. Select the message in your mailbox, or open it in a Message window.
2. In the Respond group, click **Forward**.
3. Add message recipients.

    You can add to the To, CC, or BCC fields, as you would with any message.
4. Type in any preface or addition you want to make to the forwarded message.
5. Delete any part of the original message you don't want to forward.
6. Click **Send**.

Exercise: Replying to a message

For this exercise, you'll need an existing email from your partner. You'll reply to a message, then forward it.

Do This	How & Why
1. Select a message from your partner.	
2. On the Home tab, click **Reply**.	The new message window has your partner's address in the To field, and the original message quoted. "Re:" precedes the subject.
3. In the message body, type `I'm having a really busy day, but I'll follow up on this tomorrow.`	Your reply appears in blue.

Do This	How & Why
4. Click **Send**.	
5. Select the original message.	If necessary. Click **Forward**. The new message window has the original message quoted, but no recipients. "Fw:" precedes the subject.
6. In the To field, enter another student's address.	
7. In the message body, type I thought you might want to see this.	
8. Click **Send**.	

Message management

Whether or not you need to reply to a message, there are other ways you might want to act on it. You can print a message to have a paper copy, or delete one you don't need. You can even manually mark a message as read or unread.

Marking messages as read or unread

Unread messages are marked as bold in the folder pane and show a closed envelope icon. Additionally, the number of unread messages in your inbox is shown next to the folder name. This helps to signal what messages need your attention. Once a message is read, the bold font is removed, and the icon changes to an open envelope.

 MOS Outlook Exam Objective(s): 2.4.6

Read and unread inbox messages

Because selecting a message displays its contents in the reading pane, Outlook assumes this means you've read it. When you get a lot of email, you might accidentally mark a message as read before you've had a chance to read it, or you might know you don't need to read a particular email. In either case, it's easy to change its status manually.

1. Right-click a message in the folder.

2. In the context menu, click **Mark as Read** or **Mark as Unread**.

Printing messages

Although it's more common to print attached files than messages themselves, printing a message is simple, should you need to do so.

 MOS Outlook Exam Objective(s): 1.2.1

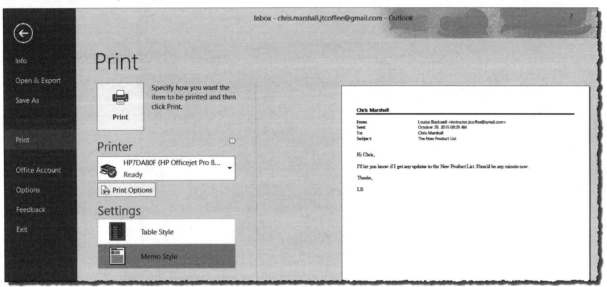

To quickly print a message using the default printer, right-click it, and click **Quick Print**. Alternatively, you can select one or more messages, and access print options in Backstage view.

1. Press **Ctrl+P**, or on the File tab, click **Print**.

   Note that to the right of the printing controls is a preview pane. This shows what the currently selected options will look like when they print.

2. From the Printer list, choose the printer you want to use.

3. From the Settings list, click **Memo Style** to print the currently selected messages, or **Table Style** to print a list of all messages in the current folder.

4. If you like, use the controls below the Print Preview pane to view each page, zoom in closer, or switch the display between one or multiple pages.

5. If you need more advanced options, click **Print Options** to open the Print window.

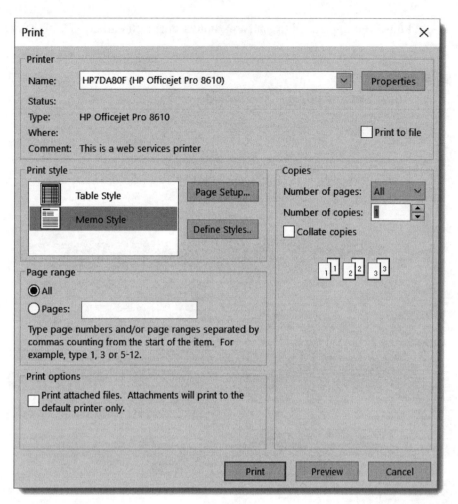

The Print window contains options to change printer settings, the output format, the number of copies, or the page range. You can also set attached files to print automatically.

6. Either in the Print window or on the File tab, click **Print**.

Deleting messages

Outlook won't ask for confirmation when you delete a message. This might seem risky, but they're not actually erased, only moved to the Deleted Items folder. Messages aren't permanently removed until they're deleted from the Deleted Items folder.

 MOS Outlook Exam Objective(s): 2.4.10

1. Select the message.

2. Press **Delete** or **Ctrl+D**; hover the mouse pointer over it in the Item list, and click the ☒ that appears; or click **Delete** on the Home tab.

3. If you want to make sure the message is permanently removed, click the **Deleted Items** folder and repeat the process.

Restoring messages

You might occasionally delete a message by mistake. Fortunately, as long as it's still in your Deleted Items folder, you can recover it. Additionally, if you use a Microsoft Exchange email server, you can even restore "permanently" deleted messages on the Folder tab by clicking Recover Deleted Items.

1. Select the **Deleted Items** folder, and look for the message you want to restore.
2. Drag the message to your Inbox.
    A "ghost" of the message item is dragged along with it until you release the mouse button.

Exercise: Managing a message

In this activity, you'll mark a message as unread, delete a message, then restore it.

Do This	How & Why
1. Click a read message in your inbox.	
2. Right-click the message, and click **Mark as Unread**.	
3. Select any other message.	The original message is now marked bold, and your Inbox shows one more unread message than it did before.
4. In Backstage view, click **Print**.	On the File tab. Outlook displays printing options. The right pane shows a print preview.
5. On the Home tab, click **Delete**.	The message is removed from your inbox.
6. In the folder list, click **Deleted Items**.	The deleted message is shown.
7. Drag the message to your inbox.	
8. Click **Inbox**.	The message appears again in the folder pane.

Assessment: Acting on messages

1. True or false? When a message is part of an extended chain of responses, by default, Reply All includes all previous messages, while Reply includes only the most recent one.

    - True
    - False

2. True or false? Merely selecting a message in your inbox marks it as read.

    - True
    - False

3. Can you recover a message that's been permanently deleted?

    - Yes
    - No
    - Maybe, depending on your account settings.
    - Maybe, depending on how large the message was.

Module C: Adding content

When email was first developed decades ago, it was typically used for typing simple text messages suitable for viewing on terminal screens. Even though a lot of messages today would still fit within those constraints, a modern email client such as Outlook offers much more. You can compose or insert messages with nearly any sort of text or graphics you might find on a web page or Word document. You can even send files for use by other applications.

In this module, you'll learn how to:

- Insert content into a message
- Attach files to a message

Pasting content

If you want a message to include information from another application, you might consider copying it in that application, then pasting it into the message body. This works best with simply formatted text, but can often also work with images, tables, or other content, especially from other Office applications.

Pasting into a message

To paste content into a message:

1. Copy content from another Outlook item or a different application.

    Copying content varies by application, but in Outlook and most other applications, you can first select it, then either click **Copy** or press **Ctrl+C**.

2. Place the cursor where you want to paste the content.

3. Click **Paste** on the Message tab.

    You can also press **Ctrl+V**.

Paste options

When you paste content from another message or application, you can use Outlook's paste options to control exactly how the content is formatted. For example, when you paste content from a Word document into an Outlook message, you might want to preserve the font of the original document, or you might want to keep only the text, without its formatting. Outlook then formats it to match the rest of your message. Exactly what options are available depends on the type of content you're pasting and what application you've copied it from. In general, you have more options (and potential success) pasting content from other Office applications, but you can paste from a web browser or nearly any other application too.

Paste options from a Word document

Some paste options you might use include the following:

Icon	Name	Description
	Use Destination Theme	Formats the pasted content to use the theme defined for the message, including fonts. This makes it match existing message text.
	Keep Source Formatting	Keeps the formatting from the source document or web page, which preserves the original look as closely as possible.
	Merge Formatting	Keeps some formatting elements from the source document, while incorporating it with the destination styles. For example, this preserves bold text but not necessarily the font.
	Keep Text Only	Pastes only the text itself, without the original formatting.
	Paste Special	Opens the Paste Special window, with additional pasting options.
	Set Default Paste	Opens the Editor Options window, with settings for the default behavior of the Paste button.

You can point to each option to see a live preview of the results, so you don't need to experiment blindly. Additionally, immediately after you paste content, a clipboard icon appears next to it. Clicking it, or pressing **Ctrl**, opens the Paste Options menu again, in case you've made a mistake.

Paste special

You can choose **Paste Special** from the paste list to view more options.

The Paste Special window, when pasting from a Word document

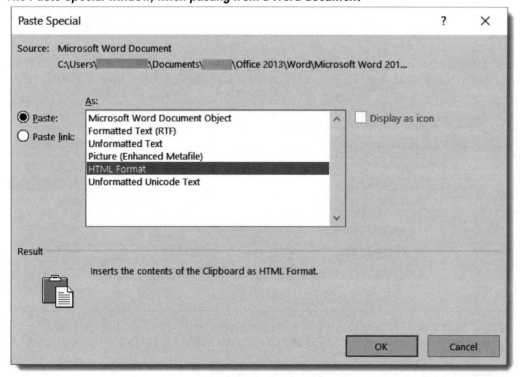

Although the included options vary, depending on what you're pasting, common options include:

- *Microsoft [Office Application] Object*: Place a movable object that's displayed in Outlook but can be opened and edited in its own application.

- *Formatted text (RTF)*: Preserve formatting using Microsoft's Rich Text Format.

- *HTML format*: Preserve formatting using HTML.

- *Unformatted text*: Paste only the text, without formatting.

- *Unformatted Unicode text*: Like unformatted text, but preserving the larger character set of Unicode fonts.

- *Picture (Enhanced Metafile):* Paste the content as a graphic, preserving the appearance of the original content. Note that you can't select or edit text once it's been turned into a picture.

Additionally, when pasting from another document, you can choose the **Paste Link** option. Although this looks the same as standard pasting, pasting as a link means you can update the source document; the changes are then reflected in the message content.

Exercise: Pasting content

In this exercise, you'll practice pasting content from Word into a message.

Do This	How & Why
1. In Word, open `Sales.docx`.	
2. Select the entire document.	You can press **Ctrl+A**.
3. Click the **Copy** button.	
4. In Outlook, create a new message.	
5. Examine the effect of paste options:	
a) Click the arrow beneath the **Paste** button.	The Paste Options list is shown.
b) Point to (Use destination formatting).	The contents of the Word document appear in the message window, but use the message's default theme.
c) Point to (Keep source formatting).	This option keeps the themes of the Word document, including fonts and colors.
d) Point to (Keep text only).	Keeping only the text itself breaks the table formatting and doesn't show the chart at all.
6. Explore Paste Special options:	

Do This	How & Why
a) Click **Paste Special**	The Paste Special window opens.
b) Click each listing in turn, and look the Result field below.	
7. Click **Microsoft Word Document Object**, and click **OK**.	The document contents are pasted into the message as an embedded object.
8. Try to select part of the message.	Because it's an embedded object, you can't select only part of it.
9. Double-click anywhere in the message.	The embedded object opens in Word, where it can be edited or saved. This method isn't very useful if the recipient doesn't have Word installed.
10. Close Word, then close the message window.	If you're asked to save either the document or clipboard content, click **No**.

Inserting content

There are two primary ways to include more than simple text and formatting in a message: by inserting content into the message body, and by attaching items.

In the message body itself, you can add *inline content* such as hyperlinks, graphics, tables, and text formatting. These allow you to give a message almost the full range of content you might see in a web page or Word document. The advantage of this approach is that recipients can easily view all the content in Outlook as a single message. One disadvantage is that inserted content might not appear the same in all email clients. In fact, most are incompatible with plain text messages. Another is that it might be difficult for a recipient to move content from a message into other applications.

You can add inline content by pasting it from another application, or by using the Insert tab in the Message window.

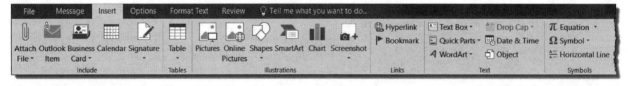

Inserting pictures

You commonly might want to add pictures to your messages. Doing so is as simple as clicking **Pictures** on the Insert tab. You can also click **Online Pictures** to search for clip art files available in Word or on office.com, or **Screenshot** to insert a snapshot of, for example, a window open on your desktop. Inserting most other kinds of content follows a very similar procedure, so once you know the procedure, it's mostly a matter of knowing what you want to add.

 MOS Outlook Exam Objective(s): 2.3.4

Once you've inserted the image, selecting it makes the Format tab appear on the ribbon, with commands specific to formatting images.

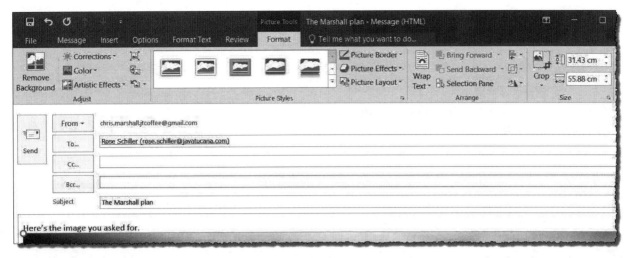

Note that pictures aren't the only inline content with a unique Format tab. For example, drawings, charts, and tables each have one or more tabs with specific commands. All of these are similar to the corresponding tools in other Office applications, if you've used those.

1. On the Insert tab, click **Pictures.**
2. In the Insert Picture window, navigate to the folder containing the image file you want to add.
3. Select the image, and click **Insert**.
4. If necessary, use the Format tab commands to crop, resize, or otherwise edit the image.

Inserting hyperlinks

The **Hyperlink** button on the Insert tab opens the Insert Hyperlink window.

MOS Outlook Exam Objective(s): 2.3.2

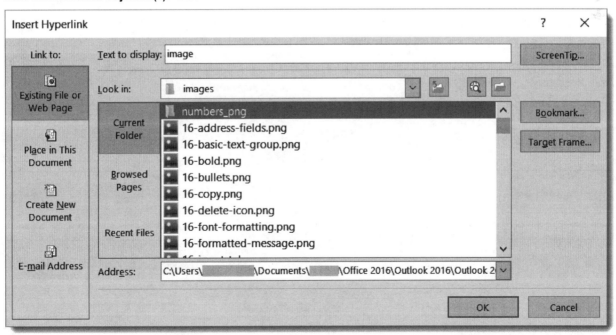

The Insert Hyperlink window allows you to insert a link to an existing file or web page, a place in the current document, a new document, or an email address. Each type of link has its own specific options, but one thing they all have in common is that you can specify both the text displayed by the link, and optionally a ScreenTip that appears when you point to the link.

You can also just type or paste a URL or email address into a message; Outlook recognizes it as a hyperlink. However, doing so isn't as reliable or flexible a method, so it's useful to know how to manually insert a link.

1. Copy the web address from your browser, so you don't risk any mistakes in typing it.

2. In the Message window, on the Insert tab, click **Hyperlink**.

3. In the left pane, click **Existing File or Web Page**.

4. In the Address field, type or paste the web page's URL.

5. In the "Text to display" field, type the link as you would like it to appear in the message text. By default, this will be the same as the address.

6. Optionally, enter a ScreenTip for the link.

    a) Click **ScreenTip**.

    b) Enter the text you want to display when you point to the link.

    c) Click **OK**.

7. Click **OK**.

Exercise: Inserting into a message

In this exercise, you'll insert an image and hyperlink into a message.

Do This	How & Why
1. Create a new message addressed to your partner.	
2. Insert `logo.png`:	
a) On the Insert tab, click **Pictures**.	The Insert Picture window opens.
b) In the current folder, click **logo.png**.	
c) Click **OK**.	The image appears in the message. The Picture Tools | Format tab appears in the ribbon.
d) On the Format tab, click **Artistic effects**.	You can use the controls on this tab to format graphical content.

Do This	How & Why
e) Choose any option from the gallery.	You can point at any option to see it previewed in the message.
3. Place the insertion point below the picture.	You might need to press **Enter.**
4. Insert a hyperlink to a web site:	
a) In your web browser, navigate to a favorite web site.	
b) Right-click the contents of the Address bar, and click **Copy**.	
c) In the message window's Insert tab, click **Hyperlink**.	⊕ Hyperlink The Insert Hyperlink window opens.
d) Paste the copied address into the Address field.	
e) In the "Text to display" field, type the name of the web site.	
f) Click **OK**.	The link now appears in the message. It links to the address you entered and appears as the text you chose for it to display.

Attaching content

Not all content is suitable for inserting inline. Sometimes formatting won't be preserved well inside a message, and sometimes you'll want to send a whole document file or other content designed to be used by another application. You might also want to send pictures or formatted text to someone using a plain-text email client. In these cases, you can use attachments.

Attachments are files included outside the message body. Instead of displaying in the message itself, the recipient can save them to disk or open them in an appropriate application. An attachment can be, for example, a Word or PDF document. It can also be an Outlook item such as a contact or task. Although attachments are less convenient for simple reading, they allow you to effectively transfer files and other information by email without it being altered in either content or layout. You can even attach items to plain-text messages.

Attaching files

You can attach a file to a message from the Insert tab, or by dragging the file from Windows Explorer to the message window.

 MOS Outlook Exam Objective(s): 2.2.2

When a message has attachments, an Attached field appears below the subject. It shows the icon, name, and size for each attachment.

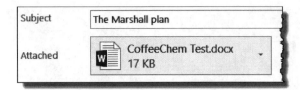

1. On the Insert tab, click **Attach File.**

2. Select the file you wish to attach.

3. Click **Insert**.

Attaching items

Instead of choosing from the files on your computer, when you attach an Outlook item, you'll be selecting from your Outlook folders. You can choose from items such as messages, contacts, or calendar entries.

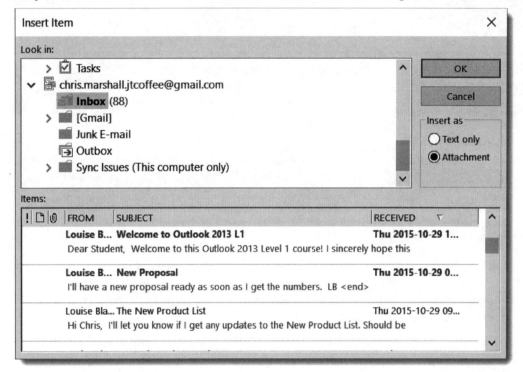

1. On the Insert tab, click **Outlook Item**.

2. In the Insert Item window, choose the folder containing the item you want to attach.

3. Click the item, then click **OK**.

Viewing attachments

When you receive a message with an attachment, you can click the attachment to preview it, or double-click it to open it in another application. You can only preview certain file types in the preview pane, for example, files created in other Office applications. Some attachments you'll need to view in the source application.

 MOS Outlook Exam Objective(s): 1.2.2, 1.2.3

An attachment previewed in the Reading Pane.

Additionally, when you select an attachment, the Attachments tab appears on the ribbon. It offers commands you can use to open, save, remove, or print the attachment.

1. Select the message with the attachment.
2. Take the appropriate action:
   - To preview the attachment in the Preview pane, click its icon.
   - To view the attachment in its source application, double-click it.
   - To save the attachment, on the Attachments tab, click **Save As**.
   - To print the attachment, on the Attachments tab, click **Quick Print**.

Exercise: Sending an attachment

For this exercise, you'll need a partner. You'll exchange message attachments and then view them.

Do This	How & Why
1. Address a message to your partner.	Give it whatever subject text you like.
2. On the Insert tab, click **Attach File**.	
3. Navigate to the data folder.	
4. Click **logo.png**, then click **Insert**.	In the Attached field, the file's name appears.
5. Click **Send**.	
6. Wait for the message from your partner to arrive.	The attachment is displayed just below the message header.
7. In the preview pane, click **logo.png**.	The image itself now appears as a preview.
8. Right-click the image name, and click **Save As**.	The Save As window opens.
9. Save the image as new_logo.png.	

Assessment: Adding content

1. True or false? You can experiment with different paste options without committing to only one at a time.

   - True
   - False

2. Which options might you use to send someone a chart they can open in Microsoft Excel?

   - Unicode Text
   - Attach File
   - Microsoft Office Object
   - Match Styles

3. What part of an inserted web hyperlink do you always have to specify?

   - Address
   - Displayed text
   - Icon
   - ScreenTip

4. True or false? Additional tabs such as Format only appear when you select a picture in a message.

   - True
   - False

5. True or false? If you have an application that can view an Outlook attachment, you can preview the attachment's content in the Reading pane.

   - True
   - False

Module D: Signatures

A *signature* is a personalized identification that's placed at the end of an email message. In addition to identifying the sender, it clearly marks the ending of the message—a feature especially valuable in back-and-forth conversations in which it can be difficult to discern where a quoted message ends and the reply begins. Although you can simply type a signature at the end of each message, it's common practice to create one or more standardized signatures that can be easily placed at the end of all your outgoing messages.

In this module, you'll learn how to:

- Create a signature
- Edit a signature
- Manage multiple signatures

About signatures

Signatures can contain both text and images, but what you should include depends on your needs. Used properly, a signature conveys not only useful information to your messages, but also professionalism and personal identity. In addition to your name and email address, you might want to include other, contact-related information, such as your phone number.

For a personal email account, you might have a favorite quote or small image that might make your messages easily recognizable. For a business account, you could include your company logo, your job title, or a web address. Depending on where you work, organizational policy or local law might require specific information to be included in your business signature, such as company information or a legal disclaimer.

For Monday, please bring:
- The final logo design
- A preliminary page layout

Thanks,

Chris Marshall

Sales Director, Java Tucana
W: 585-555-0185 | chris.marshall@javatucana.com

Creating signatures

You can create a signature by opening the Signatures and Stationery window.

MOS Outlook Exam Objective(s): 2.1.2

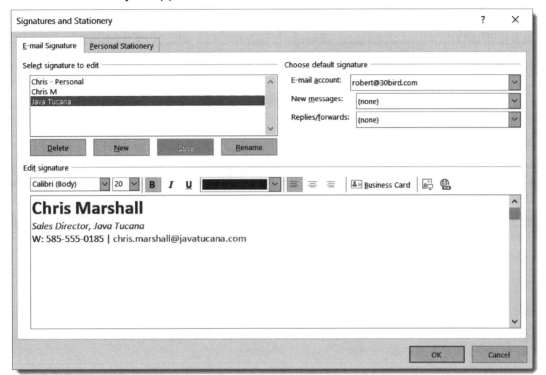

1. Open a message window.

2. Click **Signature > Signatures** to open the Signatures and Stationery window.

3. Click **New**.

    To open the New Signature window.

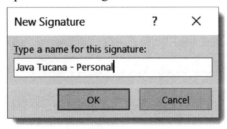

4. Type the name by which you wish to remember the signature, and click **OK**.

5. In the "Edit signature" pane, enter the signature. You can format the text as you like, insert graphics or hyperlinks, or even attach your electronic business card.

6. When you're satisfied with the signature, click **Save**.

7. Click **OK** to close the window.

Managing signatures

You may not want to use the same signature for every message. This is especially true if you use Outlook for multiple email accounts, or use one account for both personal and business correspondence. Fortunately, it's easy to manage multiple signatures and control when they are used.

 MOS Outlook Exam Objective(s): 2.3.5

- To choose a default signature for an account, select it from the **E-mail account** list, then choose the default signature for that account. New messages and replies/forwards each have their own setting.

- To edit a signature, change it in the Edit pane, then click **Save**.

- To rename a signature, select it, and click **Rename**.

- To create a new signature, click **New**.

- To delete a signature, select it, and click **Delete**.

Appending signatures

Once you've defined a signature, it appears in your signatures list and can be appended to any message. Even if you already have a default signature set, you can manually override it to use a different one.

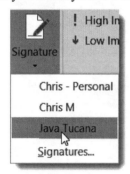

1. On the Insert tab, click **Signature**.

2. Click the signature you wish to use.

3. If you accidentally append the wrong signature, you can select a different one, or select and delete it in the message.

Exercise: Creating a signature

To complete this exercise, you'll need a partner. If you don't have one, just don't send the messages. You'll create a signature and use it in a message.

Do This	How & Why
1. Create a new message addressed to your partner.	Use `Testing My Signature` as the subject, and type something of your choosing into the message body.
2. On the Insert tab, click **Signature** > **Signatures**	The Signatures and Stationery window opens.
3. Create a new workplace signature:	
a) Click **New**.	The New Signature window opens.

Do This	How & Why
b) Type `Java Tucana` and click **OK**.	
c) In the Edit Signature field, type a signature such as the following.	Use your own name and email address. Chris Marshall **Sales Director, Java Tucana** W: 585-555-0185 | chris.marshall@javatucana.com
4. Add some visual interest to the signature:	
a) Using the formatting controls, format the signature to your liking.	It should look more like this: **Chris Marshall** *Sales Director, Java Tucana* W: 585-555-0185 | chris.marshall@javatucana.com
b) Insert a line at the top of the signature, and place the cursor in it.	
c) Click **Pictures**.	The Insert Picture window opens.
d) Click **logo_small.png**, and click **OK**.	The logo is now inserted into the signature.
e) Click **Save**.	The signature is saved.
5. Set both the New Messages and Replies/Forwards lists to **Java Tucana**.	Choose default signature E-mail account: chris.marshall.jtcoffee@gmail.com New messages: Java Tucana Replies/forwards: Java Tucana
6. Click **OK**.	The Signatures and Stationery window closes. Note that the signature isn't included yet, so you'll have to add it manually this time.
7. On the Insert tab, click **Signature > Java Tucana**.	The signature appears beneath the message.
8. Send the message.	
9. Open a new message window.	The default signature is appended only when a new message window is opened.
10. Close the message window.	

Assessment: Signatures

1. True or false? It's a "best practice" to limit a business signature to name and contact information.

    - True

    - False

2. True or false? It's easy to manage multiple signatures in Outlook.

    - True

    - False

3. In Outlook, you use both a personal email address and a business address. You've made both a personal and a business signature. How can you most easily make sure to always use a signature while avoiding using the wrong one?

    - Set Outlook to ask you which signature to use before you send a message.

    - Set the signature for the account you use most as the default, and manually insert the other when you need to.

    - Set a different default signature for each account.

    - Don't set a default signature; instead, manually insert the correct one for each message.

Summary: Email Basics

You should now know how to:

- Create and format messages
- Respond to messages and manage your inbox
- Insert or attach content to a message
- Create and manage your signatures

Synthesis: Email Basics

For this exercise, you'll need to have one primary and one secondary partners.

1. Create a new signature for your personal correspondence. Make sure it's clearly different from your business signature.

2. Send an email to your primary partner using your personal signature. Insert a hyperlink to a favorite web page, with some text from an article and an image you've saved from the site.

3. When you receive your partner's email, forward it to your secondary partner along with a comment, then delete the message.

Chapter 3: Contacts

In this chapter, you'll learn how to:

- Create and manage contacts
- Work with contact groups
- Use the People pane

Module A: Managing contacts

Contacts are how you keep track of people and organizations. They're not just a way to passively store information. Instead, you can use them to help manage your communications and scheduling. This means keeping a detailed contact list can help you in all areas of Outlook.

In this module, you'll learn:

- About contacts
- How to create and update contacts
- How to forward contacts
- How to print contact listings
- How to use electronic business cards

About contacts

In Outlook, *contacts* represent people or organizations you communicate with. A contact is more than just a name and email address, even if those are the parts most commonly used in Outlook itself. Instead, it's a collection of all the information you find important about that contact. You can store a wide variety of information on a contact—anything from an address and telephone number to a birthday, anniversary, and anything else you care to note.

Outlook tightly integrates contacts with other features such as your inbox and calendar, making it easy to use contacts when you create messages or schedule meetings. Additionally, when you open or select a contact, the ribbon displays a Communicate group, in which you can include a contact from an email message, meeting, task, or even a phone call.

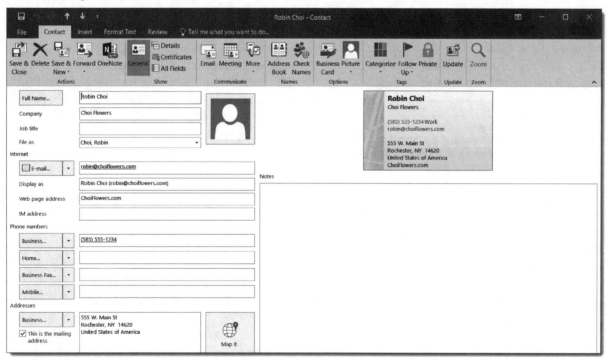

Viewing contacts

You can make use of contacts from most parts of Outlook, but the easiest way to work with them is from your Contacts folder.

- In the Navigation options, click **People**.
- In the folder list, click the **Contacts** folder, if necessary.

Changing contact views

As in other areas of Outlook, you can choose a number of different views for your contacts. Available views include People, Business Card, Card, Phone, and List. You can also click **Manage Views** to set more advanced options.

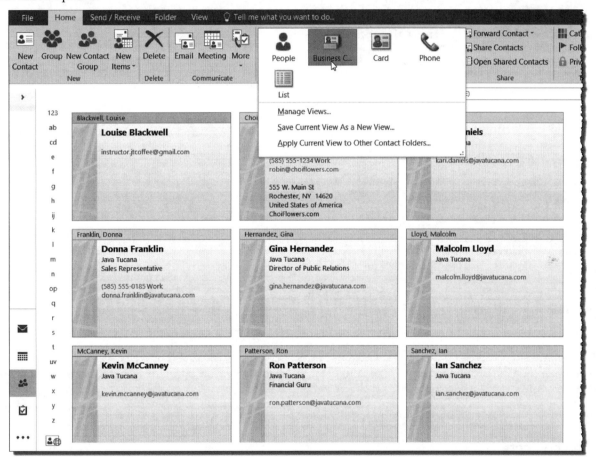

1. On the ribbon, in the Current View gallery, click the view you want to use.

2. If the view you want isn't displayed, or if you want to customize a view, in the Current View gallery, click the **More** button to display all available options.

Creating contacts

Outlook provides multiple ways to create a new contact, or to copy information from an existing one. For any of these methods, you'll be opening a new Contact window.

 MOS Outlook Exam Objective(s): 4.1.1, 4.1.3

- To make a completely new contact, on the ribbon's Home tab, click **New Contact**, then enter the contact's information.

- To create a new contact from the same company as an existing contact, click **New Items > Contact from the Same Company.**

  This method duplicates general company information, such as a website and business phone number, but not person-specific information, such as a job title or email address.

- To add the sender of an email message to your contacts, right-click the sender's address and choose **Add to Outlook Contacts**.

- To add a contact from an *Electronic Business Card* (.vcf) file sent to you, in the message, right-click the business card and choose **Add to Outlook Contacts**.

After you open the Contact window, you'll need to enter all necessary information, then click **Save & Close** to save it to your address book.

Updating contacts

You'll want to update your contacts whenever a contact's information changes, or when you wish to add messages, pictures, or documents to a contact's information. Remember that a contact can be much more than merely a business card.

 MOS Outlook Exam Objective(s): 4.1.2

1. In the contacts list, double-click the contact whose information you wish to edit.

2. Make any necessary changes.
   In the ribbon's Show group, you can click **Details** to see additional properties. To attach files, use the Insert tab.

3. When you're done, click **Save & Close**.

To delete a contact, select the contact, and click **Delete** on the Home tab.

Exercise: Creating a contact

For this exercise, you'll need to have an email from your partner. If you don't have one, you can start by using the **New Contact** button instead. You'll create a contact entry for your partner.

Do This	How & Why
1. In your inbox, select an email from your partner.	Any email will do.
2. In the preview pane, right-click your partner's email address, and click **Add to Outlook Contacts**.	The Contact window opens. Your partner's name and email address is already filled in.
3. Enter the following information:	
a) Company: Java Tucana	
b) Job title: Marketing Director	
c) Phone number: 423-555-6457	
4. On the Insert tab, click **Attach File**.	
5. Select About Us.docx, and click **Insert**.	In the current module data folder. The About Us document is added to the contact.
6. Click **Save & Close**.	On the Contact tab.
7. In the Navigation pane, click **Contacts**.	Your partner now appears in the contact list.

Electronic business cards

Outlook lets you create and share electronic business cards, which display contact information in a format similar to that of a paper business card. It's important to remember that an electronic business card is just a way of presenting contact information, rather than a separate item. Its fields reflect that of the contact. For example, if you change the phone number on the business card, it automatically updates the contact, and vice-versa.

 MOS Outlook Exam Objective(s): 4.1.5

That said, you have a lot of choice as to what information is shown on the electronic business card, as well as what it looks like. The Edit Business Card window lets you arrange the card as you see fit.

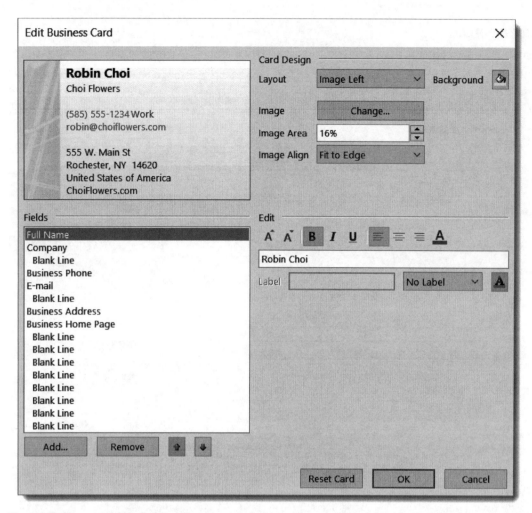

You can choose which fields of a contact's information to include in the business card, and format them how you'd like them to appear. Additionally, you can place a contact image on the card.

Editing business cards

 MOS Outlook Exam Objective(s): 4.1.6

You can open the Edit Business Card window from any open contact. At the top of the dialog box, a preview of the business card reflects any changes you've made. To return to the previous default, click **Reset Card**.

1. On the Contact tab of the ribbon, in the Options group, click **Business Card**.

2. Choose what fields to include on the card by using the **Add** and **Remove** buttons. To change spacing, use the Blank Lines feature.

3. Format each field with the Edit controls. You can show or hide the label for a given field using the Label drop-down box.

   Remember that editing the contents of a field affects the contact itself.

4. Use the Card Design fields to change the rest of the card layout, such as image, image placement, and background color.

Exercise: Editing a business card

For this exercise, you'll need to have a contact entry for your partner. You can instead use any other contact. You'll update your partner's business card.

Do This	How & Why
1. Open the Contact window.	Double-click the contact.
2. On the Contact tab, in the Options group, click **Business Card**.	The Edit Business Card window opens.
3. Click the Layout list, and select **Image Bottom**.	In the Card Design section. The image on the card moves to the bottom.
4. In Fields, select Business Phone.	
5. Click ⬇ (**Move Field Down**).	The field moves downward on the card.
6. Next to Label, click the list, and select **Left**.	The phone number Work label moves left of the number itself.
7. Click **OK**.	The card is saved.

Sharing contacts

You might find yourself wanting to share contact information with others, or even just printing it out for use outside of Outlook. In both cases, Outlook provides simple methods for doing so.

Printing contacts

You can print contacts as you would any other Outlook item. The easiest way to do so is to right-click the contact, and click **Quick Print**, which prints directly to a default printer. You can also print a list of all your contacts in various formats, such as an index card list, phone directory, or contact booklet.

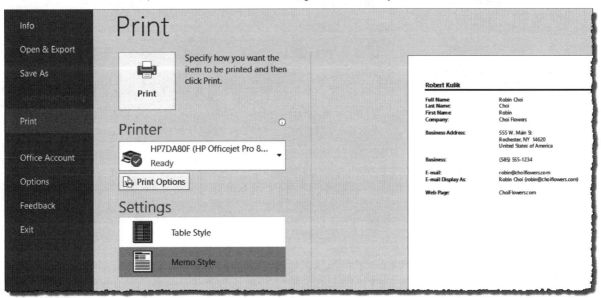

1. Select one or more contacts. If you want to print a list of all contacts, you only need to select one. Or, you can select the Contacts folder itself to display all contacts, or any subfolders you've created, and so on.

2. Press **Ctrl+P**, or on the File tab, click **Print**.

   Note that to the right of the printing controls is a preview pane, showing how the currently selected options will look when printed.

3. If necessary, select the printer you want to use. To display more advanced layout settings and printer options, you can instead click **Print Options** to open the Print window.

4. From the Settings list, select the format in which you want to print. **Memo Style** will print individual contacts you have selected, while the other styles will print a list of your contacts. Use the preview pane to determine which option best suits your needs.

   You may need to click Preview to display multiple items.

5. When you're happy with your selection, click **Print**.

Forwarding contacts

Although it's possible to simply type a contact's info into an email message, it's easier to attach the contact as a file. The recipient can then add the contact to his or her own list.

 MOS Outlook Exam Objective(s): 4.1.7

You can share a contact either as an Outlook item or as an Electronic Business Card (.vcf) file. Saving it as an Outlook item allows you to include any information Outlook stores. However, an Electronic Business Card is a format more compatible with that of other contact management software.

1. Select the contact. Then, on the Home tab, in the Share group, click **Forward Contact > As an Outlook Contact** *or* **Forward Contact > As a Business Card**.

   A new message window opens with the contact attached.

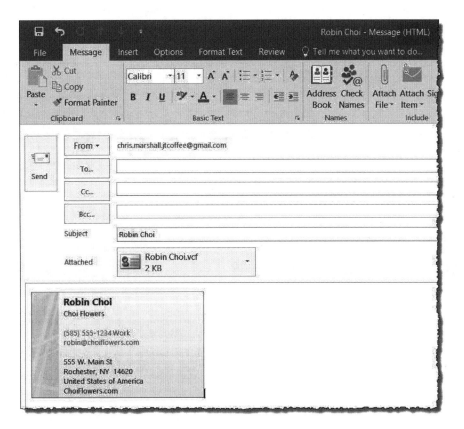

2. In a new Message window, *either* click **Attach Item > Outlook Item**, select the Contacts folder, then select the contact you want to forward; *or* click **Attach Item > Business Card**. You can then select from any contacts you've formatted as business cards, or click **Other Business Cards** to choose from your full contacts list.

Exercise: Forwarding a contact

To complete this exercise, you'll need a partner. You'll forward a contact to your partner, then add a forwarded contact to your own list.

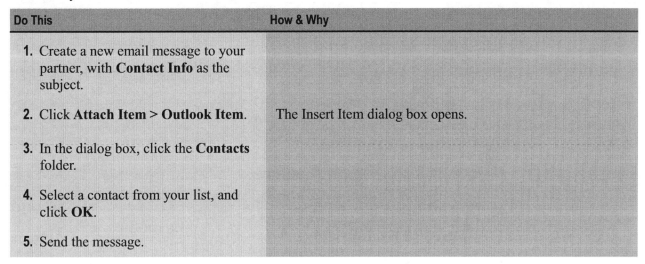

Do This	How & Why
1. Create a new email message to your partner, with **Contact Info** as the subject.	
2. Click **Attach Item > Outlook Item**.	The Insert Item dialog box opens.
3. In the dialog box, click the **Contacts** folder.	
4. Select a contact from your list, and click **OK**.	
5. Send the message.	

Do This	How & Why
6. When your partner's message arrives, double-click the contact icon.	To Chris Marshall Robin Choi.vcf 681 bytes The new contact opens in a Contact window.
7. Click **Save & Close**.	If your list already has a contact with the same information, a Duplicate Contact Window will appear.
8. If necessary, select **Add New Contact**, and click **Add**.	The new contact now appears in your list.

Assessment: Managing contacts

1. When you create a new contact using another contact from the same company, what fields are copied from the existing contact?

    * Business phone number

    * Email address

    * Job title

    * Website

2. True or false? If you change a phone number in an electronic business card, the new number is automatically reflected in the contact item itself.

    * True

    * False

3. Why might you share a contact in .vcf format rather than as an Outlook item?

    * To pass information that can't be included in shared Outlook items.

    * Because Outlook items can only be shared between Microsoft Exchange email users.

    * Because .vcf is more compatible with other email clients.

    * All of the above.

Module B: Using contact groups

Contact groups allow you to treat groups of people as though they were a single contact. This way, you can streamline your interactions with people with whom you commonly communicate into a single procedure.

In this module, you'll learn how to:

- Create contact groups
- Edit contact groups
- Delete contact groups

About contact groups

A *contact group*, also called a *distribution list* in earlier versions of Outlook, is a collection of email addresses that appears as a single contact in your contacts folder. Contact groups are useful when you regularly find yourself communicating with the same group of people, for example, a project team or customer mailing list. Instead of addressing a message to each member of the group, you can simply send it to the group, as if it were a single contact. Similarly, you can include a contact group when you assign tasks or request meetings. You can even place one contact group inside another, larger group.

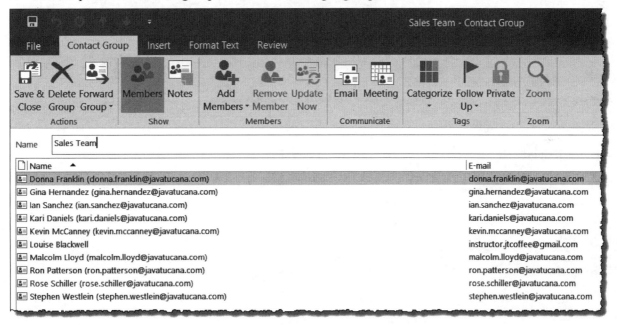

Creating contact groups

You can add members from your Outlook contacts or from your address book. You can also add new email contacts using just a display name and email address.

MOS Outlook Exam Objective(s): 4.2.1, 4.2.2

The Select Members window

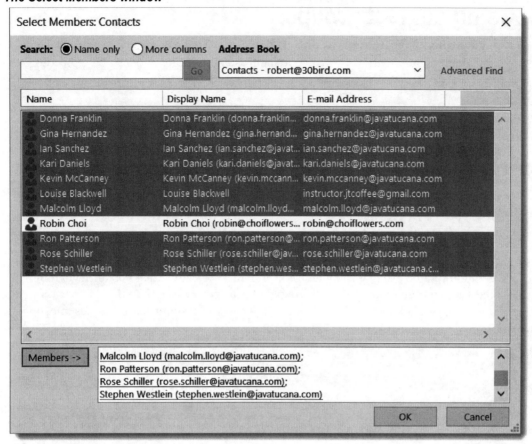

The Add New Member window

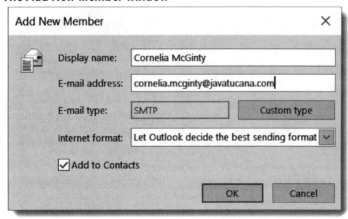

1. On the ribbon's Home tab, click **New Contact Group**.

2. To add members already in your Contacts folder or Address Book, click **Add Members > From Outlook Contacts** *or* **Add Members > From Address Book**.

a) In the Select Members window, click the name you want to enter, or press and hold **Ctrl** and click multiple names.

b) Click **Members** to add your selection to the list.

c) Click **OK**.

3. To add members that aren't in your address book, click **Add Members** > **New E-mail Contact**,

a) In the New Member window, enter the member's display name and email address.

b) If you don't want to add the new member to your list of contacts, clear **Add to Contacts**.

c) Click **OK**.

4. When you've added all the members you need, on the Contact Group tab, click **Save & Close**.

Expanding contact groups

The chief benefit of contact groups is that you can use them just like single contacts when you send a message or meeting request. They appear as one entry in the address fields of the message, but each individual member receives the message just as if you'd added them all separately. You can also add the contact group, then expand it to its individual members, for example, if you want to exclude some members of the group from a particular message without removing them from the group entirely.

1. From the Address Book, add a contact group to the To, Cc, or Bcc field.

2. To the left of the contact group name, click ⊞ .

The Expand List window opens.

3. Click **OK** to confirm your action.

Managing contact groups

You can double-click a contact group in your contact lists to open it, then select the Contact Group tab to access various options.

MOS Outlook Exam Objective(s): 4.2.3, 4.2.4, 4.2.5, 4.2.6

Some commands for contact groups are very much like those for individual contacts. You can save the group, delete it, or forward it to other people; you can tag the group like other Outlook items; and you can send the entire group a message or meeting request. Additionally, there are some commands specific to contact groups.

*   To view or add notes about the group as a whole, click **Notes**. You can return to the member list by clicking **Members**.

*   To add new members, click **Add Members**, then specify whether you're adding existing contacts or creating a new one.

*   To remove members, select them and click **Remove Member**. You can press **Ctrl** while clicking to select multiple members.

*   If you've changed the contact address of an individual group member, click **Update Now** to update the group with the new address.

*   To delete the selected group, click **Delete Group**.

Exercise: Creating a contact group

For this exercise, you'll need at least two pre-defined contacts. You'll create a contact group.

Do This	How & Why
1. In Contacts view, click **New Contact Group**.	The Contact Group window opens.
2. In the Name field, type **My Project Team**.	
3. Click **Add Members > From Outlook Contacts**.	The Select Members window opens.
4. Press and hold **Ctrl** and click at least two contacts in your list.	
5. Click **Members**, then click **OK**.	The new members now appear in the list.
6. Click **Save & Close**.	My Project Team is now listed with the rest of your contacts.
7. Send a message to My Project Team.	Add it just like you would a single contact.

Assessment: Using contact groups

1. Contact lists allow you to:

   - Organize lists of names without making them all contacts.

   - Address a group of people with the convenience of a single name.

   - Send group messages without the complexity of distribution lists.

   - Organize your contacts into categories.

2. True or false? Members of a contact group don't have to be taken from your existing contacts.

   - True

   - False

3. What can't you do from the Contact Group tab?

   - Add notes for the group as a whole.

   - Automatically remove inactive email addresses.

   - Automatically update list information for changed contacts.

   - Schedule a meeting with the group.

Module C: Using the People pane

Outlook provides additional tools for accessing contact information. One is the Outlook Social Connector displayed in message and contact items. The other is the Contact Card window, which appears when you point to a name in any address field. Although each tool has different functions, both let you easily view and act on contact information while doing other tasks.

In this module, you'll learn how to:

- Use the Outlook Social Connector
- Use contact cards

The Outlook Social Connector

Using the *Outlook Social Connector*, you can follow the activities of your contacts, both within your own network and on social networks you share on the Internet. For example, you can use it to connect to your company's SharePoint Server sites, or to social media sites like Facebook and LinkedIn.

Connecting to an external network requires you to install an add-in specific to that network. These add-ins are not included with Outlook, so you'll need to download them for whatever services you want to use. Even without any services installed, however, you can use the Outlook Social Connector to display information about, and correspondence with, your contacts.

The Outlook Social Connector appears as the *People pane*, which by default is displayed at the bottom of the reading pane in Mail view, and the bottom of the message pane in the Message window. You can click the chevron at the far right to expand or minimize it.

The minimized People pane

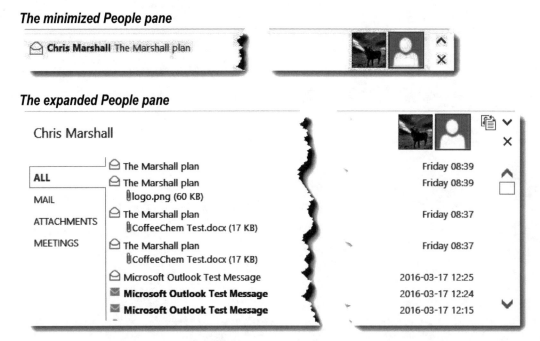

The expanded People pane

When minimized, the People pane shows the name of the sender, and an icon for the sender and each recipient of the message. When you expand it, it shows a larger picture of the sender, if available, and tabs for All Items, Activities, Mail, Attachments, Meetings, and Status updates. You can click any displayed item to open it.

Exercise: Using the People pane

In this exercise, you'll examine the features in the People pane.

Do This	How & Why
1. Open a message in your inbox.	Ideally, choose a message from someone you've communicated with a number of times, such as your partner.
2. Click ⌃ (**Expand**).	The People pane expands.
3. Observe the People pane.	A list of messages from that contact is shown.
4. Click a message in the list.	It opens in a new Message window.
5. Close the message.	To return to the original one.
6. Click the tabs to the left of the People pane to view each category.	Activities, Mail, Attachments, Meetings, and Status Updates.
7. Close the window.	

Contact cards

A *contact card* appears when you point to a sender's name in the preview pane or Message window. As with the People pane, you can use contact cards to quickly view information about a contact and to get in touch by email or meeting request. If you have an instant messaging program integrated with Outlook, you can also send instant messages (IMs) or make phone calls to the contact.

A contact card

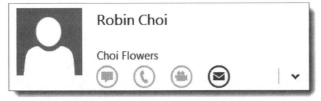

When you first point to the contact, the contact card displays in a compact format, with the contact's identity and a row of icons. By clicking the chevron to the right, you can expand it to show more complete contact details, and a link to open the contact in its own window.

A contact card closes when you move the mouse away from it. If you want it to stay open, click the pin icon in the upper-right corner. Once it's pinned, you can drag the card wherever you like.

Exercise: Examining a contact card

In this exercise, you'll examine a contact card.

Do This	How & Why
1. In any message, point to the sender's name in the preview pane.	The contact card for the sender appears.
2. Click ⌄ (**Expand**).	The contact card is expanded and the contact's info is displayed.
3. Observe the icons in the Contact Card toolbar.	Provided that you have the necessary information for the contact and have the right clients set up, you can send an email message, IM, voice call, or meeting request to the contact. You can also open the contact or save it as a new contact.
4. Click 📌.	To pin the card to the desktop. You can now drag the card around or point away from it, and it stays open.
5. Close the contact card.	

Assessment: Using the People pane

1. True or false? Contact cards and the People pane only differ in where they appear in Outlook.

   - True
   - False

2. True or false? You need to install an add-in to use the Outlook Social Connector with your social network.

   - True
   - False

3. What can't you do from a contact card?

   - Look the contact up on LinkedIn.
   - Make a phone call to the contact.
   - Open the full Contact window.
   - Schedule a meeting with the contact.

Summary: Contacts

You should now know how to:

- Create, edit, and share contacts
- Create contact groups and manage their membership
- Use the People pane in the Outlook Social Connector and contact cards

Synthesis: Contacts

You'll need a partner to complete this exercise, but only to forward your final results.

In this exercise, you'll use contacts to manage a store remodeling project.

1. Create several contacts representing people involved in the project.
   Contacts might be company employees, contractors, or suppliers. Names and email addresses don't have to be real.

2. Create a contact group for people involved in the project. Add at least one member not already in your contacts.

3. Customize your own contact information, including the format of your electronic business card.

4. Send both your contact group and your own contact to your partner.

Chapter 4: Tasks

In this chapter, you'll learn how to:

- Create tasks
- Manage tasks
- Assign tasks to others

Module A: Creating tasks

When you have an activity or project that you need to track to completion, you can do so by creating an Outlook task item. A *Task* is an activity you need to keep track of until its completion, but which doesn't necessarily reserve a space on your calendar. For example, a doctor's appointment that you must attend at a certain time is not a task, but a report you need to hand in by the end of the month is. Additionally, tasks by default are flagged as To-Do items, which means that they appear in your To-Do list and To-Do bar as items needing follow-up.

In this module, you'll learn:

- About task views
- How to create tasks
- How to edit tasks

About tasks

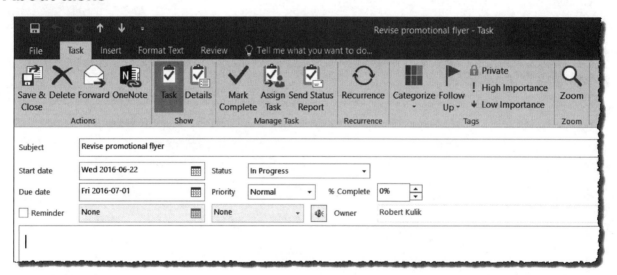

Each task has several properties you can use to define it and track its progress, though not every task must have all properties set. Common properties include:

Subject   The task's name

Start date   When work on the task is expected to begin

Due date   When the task is expected to be completed

Status   Can be set to Not Started, In Progress, Completed, Waiting on someone else, or Deferred

Priority   Can be set to Low, Normal, or High

% Complete   Can be set at any value from 0% to 100%, the latter marking the task as completed

Body   As with the body of a message, can be used to add a description, attach items, and so on

Tasks view

To view your current tasks, you can click the Navigation pane's **Tasks** button, or in the Folders list, open the **My Tasks** folder. Either method opens the Tasks folder, displaying a list of available tasks and their properties. It also changes the ribbon to display commands suitable for task management.

The Tasks folder, in Simple List view

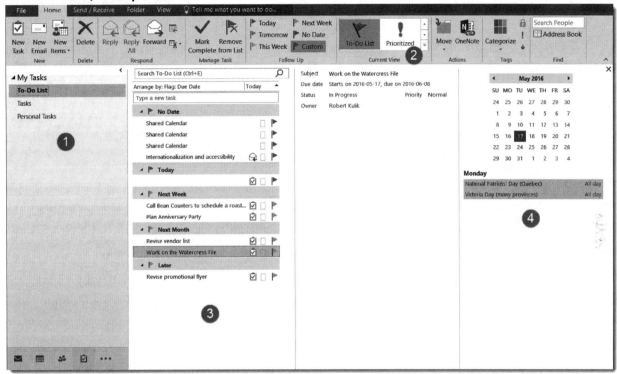

① Your *Tasks folder list* shows your To-Do list, the Tasks folder, and any other custom folders you've created for task items.

② The ribbon's *Current View list* lets you choose how your tasks are displayed. Each option has different information and filtering settings.

③ The *task list* in the contents pane displays your chosen view. Completed tasks, if shown, are crossed out. You can also quickly enter a task here.

④ The *To-Do bar*, accessible from the View tab's Layout group, allows you to display Calendar, People, and/or Tasks peeks. However, in Tasks view, you most likely wouldn't display the Tasks peek, which simply repeats the task list.

Changing task views

You can change task views by clicking any entry in the Home tab's Current View gallery. Each view provides a different way of displaying your tasks. Some differ in the details displayed, while others sort or filter tasks according to different properties. For example, Prioritized view sorts tasks by importance, and Assigned view shows only those tasks that have been assigned to you by others.

The Home tab's Current View gallery also provides advanced options, such creating or modifying views, saving a customized view to the list, or applying a view to multiple task folders.

1. In the Current View group, click the **More** button.
   On the ribbon's Home tab.

2. Click the view you wish to display.

3. If none of the views suit your needs, click **Manage Views** and customize a view to your liking.

Creating new tasks

It's important to remember that only new tasks created from the ribbon automatically open the Task window. Otherwise, the task is created with default properties, which you'll need to edit later.

 MOS Outlook Exam Objective(s): 3.4.1

1. On the Home tab, click **New Task**.

2. Edit the task's properties.

3. Click **Save & Close.**

Quickly adding tasks

Although this method doesn't let you immediately set all the task properties in the same step as creating it, if you just want to quickly mark down a task and fill the details in later, it's quick and convenient. In fact, you can enter a new task directly in Tasks view, or in the To-Do bar's Tasks peek, if it's displayed.

Tasks view's Tasks list

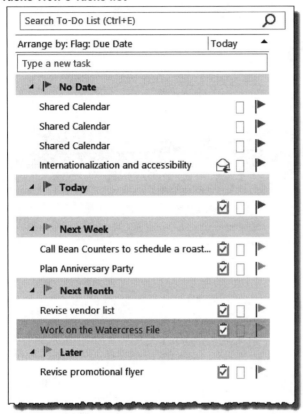

1. Switch to Tasks view.

    Click **Tasks** in the Navigation options.

2. Click in the **Type a new task** field.

3. Type the name of your task, and press **Enter**.

    A new task is added to the list. By default, both its start and due dates are set for today, its Priority is normal, and its Status is Not Started.

Editing tasks

However it was originally created, you can edit any existing task in the Task window.

1. Double-click the task to open it.

2. Edit the task's properties.

3. Click **Save & Close**.

Exercise: Creating a task

In this exercise, you'll create and edit a task.

Do This	How & Why
1. In Tasks view, in the "Type a new task" field, type a task name, then press **Enter**.	Choose a descriptive name, such as `Plan Anniversary Party`. A task is created in your Tasks folder.
2. Open the Tasks folder.	
3. Double-click the new task.	
4. Set the task's properties:	

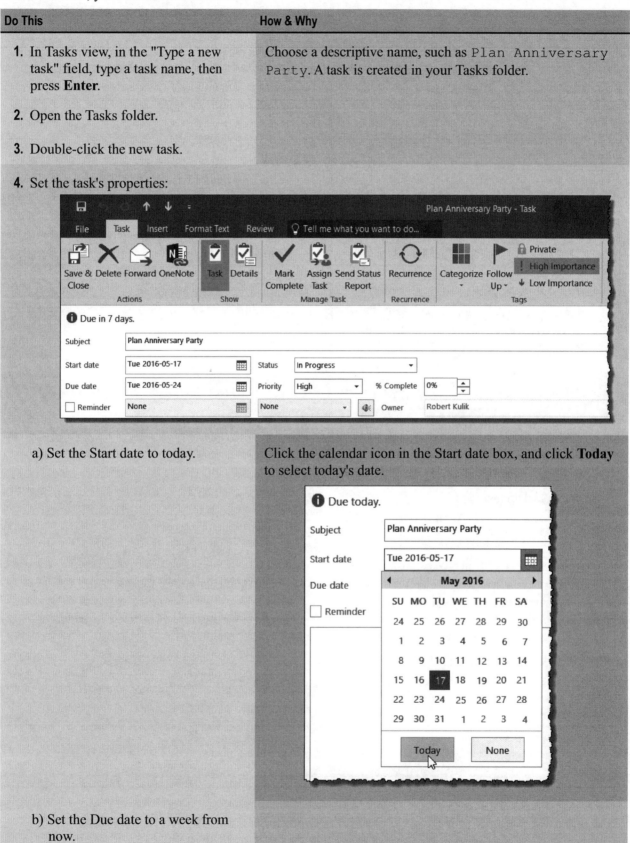

a) Set the Start date to today.	Click the calendar icon in the Start date box, and click **Today** to select today's date.
b) Set the Due date to a week from now.	

Do This	How & Why
c) From the Status list, select **In Progress**.	
d) In the Tags group on the Task tab, click ![! High Importance].	
5. In the Task tab's Show group, click **Details**.	Additional details are displayed. Here you could change the completion date, total hours worked, or other properties.
6. Click **Save & Close**.	

Assessment: Creating tasks

1. You can most easily access your full Tasks list from the:

   - Navigation options
   - Ribbon
   - Calendar
   - Address Book

2. True or false? Not all task views show all tasks.

   - True
   - False

3. You can create a new task from the:

   - Ribbon
   - Address Book
   - To-Do list
   - To-Do-bar

Module B: Managing tasks

When tasks start accumulating in your folder, you can mark them completed, delete them, or move them to other folders. If you find yourself regularly recreating the same task, you might be able to save work by using recurring tasks.

In this module, you'll learn how to:

- Complete tasks
- Delete tasks
- Move and copy tasks between folders
- Print tasks and task lists
- Create recurring tasks

Task completion

Setting a task as 100% complete is as easy as editing any other field when the task is open. When you're simply viewing a field from task view, you can use the following options:

① The *Mark Complete button* sets the selected task as complete, or sets an already completed task as incomplete.

② The Completion check box isn't available in all task views but provides a simple way to mark a task as completed, even without having to select it and move up to the ribbon.

Marking a task as completed changes its appearance, depending on your view. In some views it is crossed out, grayed out, or both. In others, such as the Active or To-Do list views, completed tasks don't appear at all. To view only completed tasks, choose Completed view.

Deleting tasks

Sometimes marking tasks as complete isn't enough, and you'll want them out of your way entirely. The simplest way to remove them is to delete them.

In Outlook's main window, the Home tab's ribbon contains a Delete button. It's also available on the Tasks window's Tasks tab. Using either method, the task is removed to your Deleted Items folder.

1. Select a task you don't need any more.
2. Click the **Delete** button.
   You can use the **Delete** key as well.

Moving tasks

You can move a task from one folder to another by dragging it, or by using the ribbon's Move action. If you want to copy a task to another folder instead of moving it, right-click the task, then drag it to the desired location. You'll then be asked whether to copy or move the task.

For still more complete options, you can use the Move Items window, or the similar Copy Items window.

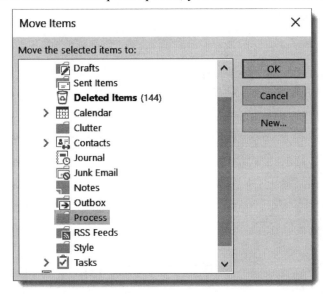

1. In your Tasks list, select a task.
2. On the ribbon, click the **Move** button.
   A list of folders appears.
3. Click **Other Folder**.
   If you'd wanted to copy the task instead of moving it, you could choose **Copy to Folder**.

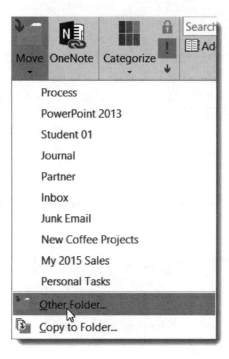

The Move Items window appears.

4. Click another task folder.

    If you don't have another task folder created, you can click **New** to create one.

5. Click **OK**.

    The task is moved to the new folder.

Printing tasks

If you want to quickly print a single task to a default printer, right-click it, and click **Quick Print**. Otherwise, you can use Backstage view for more options.

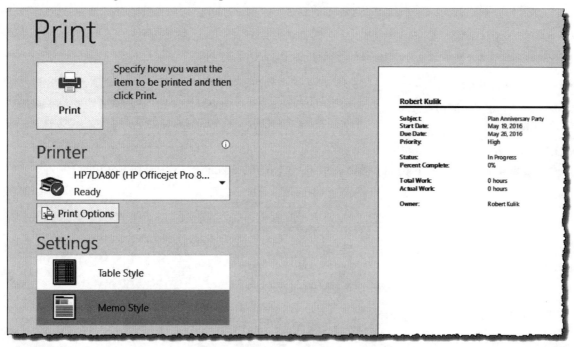

1. If you want to print individual tasks, select one or more. If you want to print a list of tasks, select the folder and view you want to print.

2. Press **Ctrl+P**, or click the File tab's **Print** button.

   Note that on the right side of the printing controls is a preview pane. This shows how the currently selected options will look when printed.

3. If necessary, select the printer you want to use. You can instead click **Print Options** to open the Print window, with more advanced layout settings and printer options.

4. From the Settings list, select the format you want to print. **Memo Style** will print individual tasks you have selected. **Table Style** will print the current task folder view. Use the preview pane to determine which option best suits your needs.

5. Click **Print**.

Task options

To open Outlook Options, click the **File** tab, and click **Options**. Then in the left pane, click Tasks.

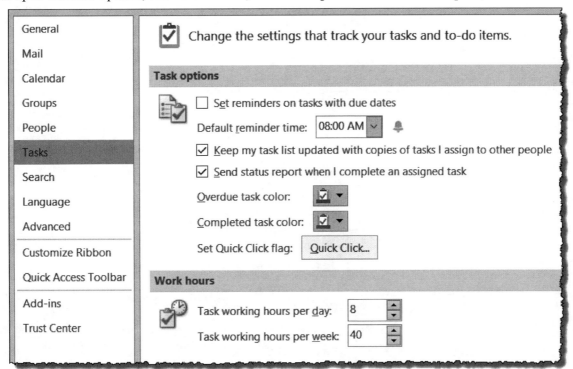

Options you can set include reminders, task display colors, and how Outlook handles assigned tasks. If you track hours used by tasks, you can also set how many working hours you use per day and per week.

Exercise: Managing tasks

In this exercise, you'll practice task management activities.

Do This	How & Why
1. Create three tasks.	Name them `Update price list,` `Buy anniversary gift,` and `Organize supply closet.` You can use the Tasks list in Tasks view to create them.
2. Create a new tasks folder.	
a) Right-click the Tasks folder, and click **New Folder**.	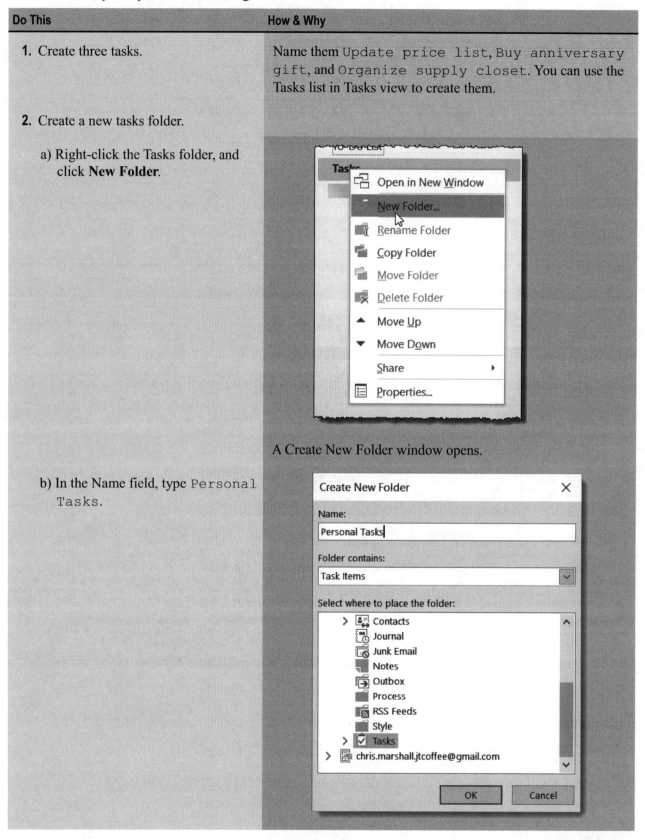
	A Create New Folder window opens.
b) In the Name field, type `Personal Tasks.`	

Do This	How & Why
c) Click **OK**.	A Personal tasks folder in the Navigation Pane. 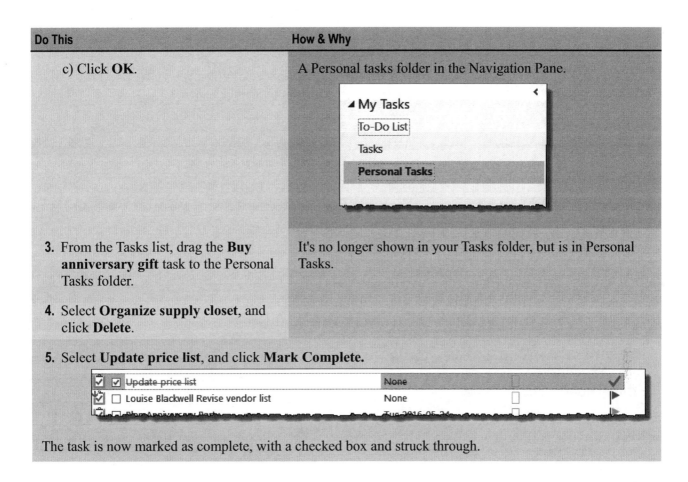
3. From the Tasks list, drag the **Buy anniversary gift** task to the Personal Tasks folder.	It's no longer shown in your Tasks folder, but is in Personal Tasks.
4. Select **Organize supply closet**, and click **Delete**.	
5. Select **Update price list**, and click **Mark Complete**.	

	✓ Update price list	None		✓
✓	☐ Louise Blackwell Revise vendor list	None	☐	▶
	☐ Plan Anniversary Party	Tue 2016-05-24	☐	▶

The task is now marked as complete, with a checked box and struck through.

Recurring tasks

A recurring task automatically repeats at regular intervals. For example, if you wished to create a task to track your progress on a monthly report, you could make the task recur instead of creating a new one every month. Outlook provides a wide variety of options for scheduling recurring tasks.

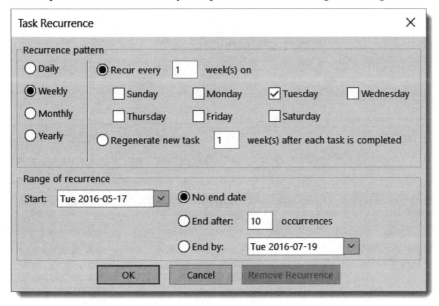

First, you need to specify a *recurrence pattern*, or how often the task repeats. The basic pattern may be daily, weekly, monthly, or yearly; each of these options has further specific options. For example, a monthly task might recur on the 15th of the month, or on the second Tuesday of every month.

Second, it has a *range of recurrence*, which specifies how many times the task repeats. You can set a task to recur indefinitely, a set number of times, or until a specific future date.

When you mark a recurring task as complete, its next recurrence is created. When you delete a recurring task, you're asked whether all recurrences of the task or just the current one should be deleted.

Creating recurring tasks

You can make a task recurring when you create it, or by editing it later.

1. Open a new or existing task in its own window.
2. Click **Recurrence**.
    On the ribbon's Task tab.

3. Choose a basic recurrence pattern: Daily, Weekly, Monthly, or Yearly.
4. Set the specific options for your chosen pattern.
5. Set the recurrence range.
6. Click **OK**.

Setting recurrence doesn't automatically save the task. In the Tasks window, you must still click **Save & Close**.

Exercise: Creating a recurring task

In this exercise, you'll create a new recurring task.

Do This	How & Why
1. Create a new task named **Weekly Sales Report**.	
2. On the ribbon's Task tab, click **Recurrence**.	The Task Recurrence window opens.
3. Select each recurrence pattern in turn to view its options.	You can choose Daily, Weekly, Monthly, or Yearly.
4. Choose **Weekly**, and verify that **Today** is checked.	
5. Under "Range of recurrence," observe the options.	By default, the task is set to recur indefinitely. You can also set a number of occurrences, or a fixed end date.
6. Click **OK**.	The Task Recurrence window closes, but the task is still not saved.
7. Click **Save & Close**.	

Assessment: Managing tasks

1. True or false? You can mark a task complete by checking it off in the folder contents list.

   - True
   - False

2. True or false? Deleted tasks are permanently removed from Outlook.

   - True
   - False

3. Which isn't an allowable interval for a recurring task?

   - Hourly
   - Daily
   - Weekly
   - Monthly

Module C: Assigning tasks

Tasks don't have to be limited to reminders to yourself. If you need someone else to complete a task for you, you can *assign* it to them. You might want to assign a task if something keeps you from completing it yourself, or if you're delegating parts of a project to coworkers.

In this module, you'll learn how to:

- Assign a task
- Accept or reject a task assignment
- Send a status report for an assigned task

About assigned tasks

To assign a task, you send a *task request* to someone else in an email message. The recipient has the option to accept or decline the task request. If the task is accepted, it's added to the recipient's task list.

It's still important to keep track of assigned tasks, however. When you assign a task, you have the option of keeping your own copy of the task. Additionally, when you are assigned a task, you can send status reports to the sender.

Assigning tasks

When you assign a task, you'll need to enter the recipient's email address. Additionally, you can choose whether to keep an updated copy of the task, and whether to request a status report when the task is completed. Finally, you can include additional information in, and even attachments to, the task, just as with an ordinary email.

 MOS Outlook Exam Objective(s): 2.2.8

Once you send a task assignment, it's removed from your task list, and ownership of the task passes on to the recipient.

Task assignment options

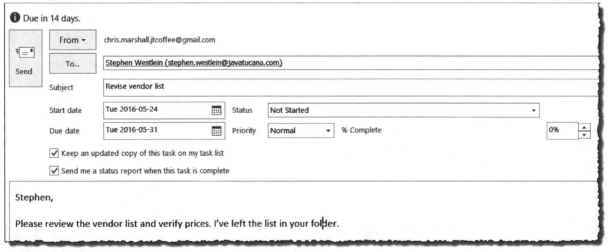

1. Open the task.
2. In the Task tab's Manage Task group, click **Assign Task**.

The body of the Tasks window now shows a new message window, including options specific to assigned tasks.

3. In the To Field, enter the recipient's address.

4. Choose options for the assigned task.

In addition to the usual task properties, you can decide whether to keep an updated copy of the task in your own list, and whether you want a status report when the task is complete.

5. Type into the message body any information the recipient might need.

You can use the Insert and Format Text tabs to add content, just as with any other message.

6. Click **Send**.

Accepting or declining assigned tasks

When you're assigned a task, Accept and Decline buttons appear at the top of the Reading pane. If you open the message, they also appear in the Task tab's Respond group. Once you click either button, you're prompted to send a message informing the original sender that you accept or decline the task. If you accept the task, it's added to your task list.

 MOS Outlook Exam Objective(s): 2.2.4, 3.3.5

The Accept and Decline buttons.

1. Select the task assignment message you've received from the sender.

You don't need to open it in a separate message window, though you can.

2. At the top of the message preview pane, click **Accept** or **Decline**.

3. Choose either **Send the response now**, or **Edit the message before Sending**.

4. Click **OK**.

If you chose to edit the message, a message window opens.

5. If you're editing the message, type your response, and click **Send**.

Sending status reports

Although you'll commonly want to send status reports for tasks you've been assigned, you can send a status report to anyone for any task. If it isn't an assigned task, you'll just have to edit the message's To field manually.

A Task Status Report message body.

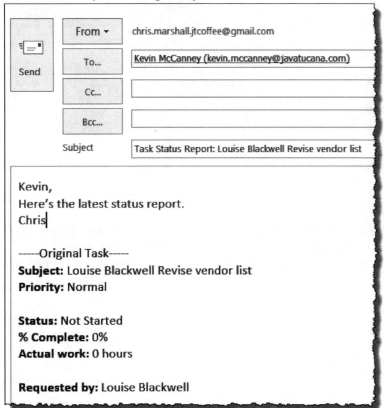

1. Open the task.
2. If necessary, update the task with its current status.

   For example, you should make sure the task's Status and % Complete fields are up to date.
3. On the Task tab, in the Manage Task group, click **Send Status Report**.

   A message window opens.
4. If necessary, add recipients to the message.

   If you're replying to an assigned task, the sender's address is already in the To field, but you can send reports to anyone you wish.
5. Edit the message body to add any other information you want.
6. Click **Send**.

Exercise: Assigning and accepting a task

To complete this exercise, you'll need a partner. You'll assign a task to your partner, and accept the task your partner assigns to you.

Do This	How & Why
1. Create a task.	Name it XX Revise vendor list, substituting "XX" with your name.
2. Assign the task to your partner.	
a) With the task open, click **Assign Task**.	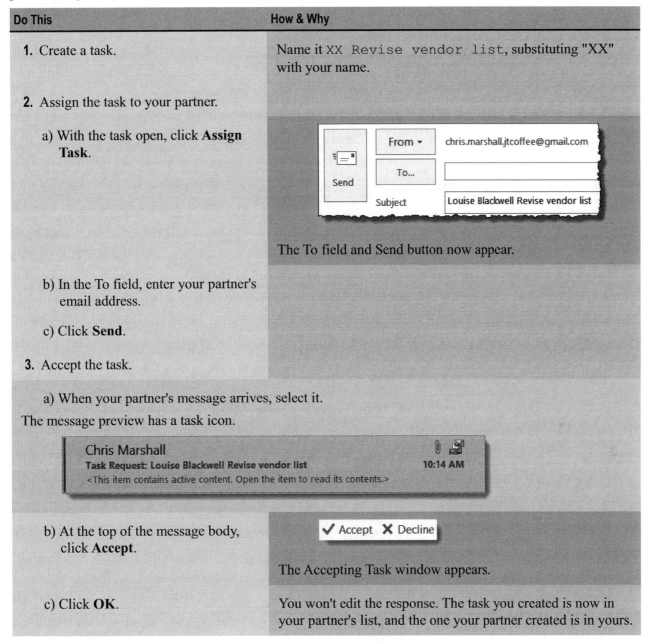 The To field and Send button now appear.
b) In the To field, enter your partner's email address.	
c) Click **Send**.	
3. Accept the task.	
a) When your partner's message arrives, select it. The message preview has a task icon.	
b) At the top of the message body, click **Accept**.	The Accepting Task window appears.
c) Click **OK**.	You won't edit the response. The task you created is now in your partner's list, and the one your partner created is in yours.

Assessment: Assigning tasks

1. Ownership of an assigned task

    - Goes to the recipient.

    - Stays with the sender.

    - Is shared by both.

2. True or false? The Send Status Report button becomes available after you assign a task.

    - True

    - False

3. True or false? You're prompted to send a response whether you accept or decline a task.

    - True

    - False

Summary: Tasks

You should now know how to:

- View, create, and edit tasks
- Complete, delete, and move tasks
- Make recurring tasks
- Work with assigned tasks

Synthesis: Tasks

You'll need a partner to complete this exercise.

In this exercise, you'll use tasks to track a store remodeling project.

1. With your partner, create tasks corresponding to different parts of the project. At least one of these should be a recurring task.
   Some possible tasks include finding contractors, planning the new building layout, pricing materials, and the work itself. Recurring tasks could include progress reports or site reviews.

2. Create a task folder for the remodeling project, and move all related tasks into the new folder.

3. Assign at least one task to your partner. When you're assigned any tasks, complete them and report them to your partner.

Chapter 5: Scheduling

In this chapter, you'll learn how to:

- Create and manage appointments
- Schedule meetings with other people
- Manage and customize your calendar

Module A: Appointments

The most basic tool for managing your schedule in Outlook is the appointment. An *appointment* is a block of time reserved on your calendar for some specific purpose. Outlook can both make sure you don't create conflicting appointments and remind you when an appointment is upcoming. Appointments are visible in Calendar view.

In this module, you'll learn how to:

- Add appointments and events
- Set appointment details
- Forward appointments
- Print appointments
- Create recurring appointments

About appointments

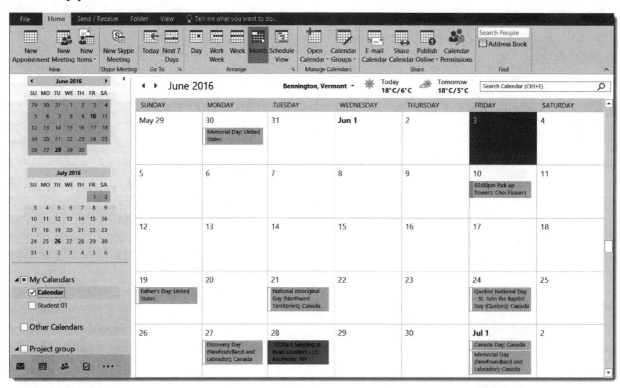

In Outlook, appointments are distinct from tasks and meetings. Unlike a task, which has a due date but no specific duration, an appointment marks time in your schedule when you're otherwise unavailable. Unlike a meeting, which requires you to coordinate your schedule with other Outlook users you're in touch with, you don't need to invite anyone to schedule an appointment.

This isn't to say appointments can't involve other people; for example, if you're having lunch with a friend from out of town, you likely will schedule it as an appointment rather than a meeting, as you and your friend probably don't coordinate your schedules with Outlook.

Creating appointments

MOS Outlook Exam Objective(s): 3.2.1, 3.2.4

You can create appointments by opening a new Appointment window, entering the necessary details, and then clicking **Save & Close**.

You can open the window in multiple ways.

- From anywhere in Outlook, press **Crtl+Shift+A**, or click **New Items > Appointment**.

- In Calendar view, or in the To-Do bar's calendar peek, click **New Appointment**.

- In your calendar, double-click a particular time, or right-click it and click **New Appointment**.

- To modify an existing appointment, double-click it.

- To create an appointment from an email message, drag the message to your calendar. The message subject becomes the appointment subject, and the message body is attached to the appointment.

Once you've created an appointment, you'll still need to set its details and save it.

Appointment details

You can view most of the details of an appointment in your calendar, but all of them can be viewed or modified by opening the appointment.

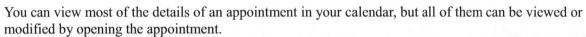
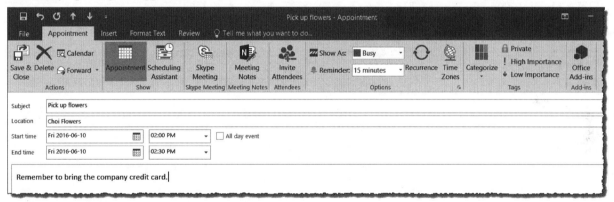

As with other Outlook items, an appointment has a subject, which appears as its name on the calendar. It has a body field in which you can write notes or insert content. Unlike a message or task, an appointment also has a *start time* and an *end time* to define its duration. It also has an optional location, if you need to specify where it will take place.

Scheduling appointments

A newly created appointment is a half hour in duration, by default, beginning at the time selected on your calendar, or at the current time, if you don't have a time selected. It's easiest to schedule appointments in half-hour increments, but you can set any duration you like. You can even create an appointment that spans days.

MOS Outlook Exam Objective(s): 3.2.5

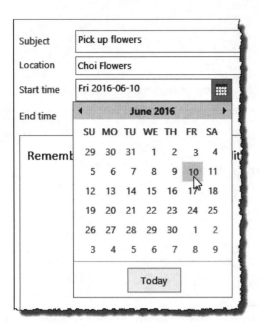

Outlook will warn you when you try to create an appointment that conflicts with or is immediately adjacent to another one. It won't prevent you from creating either—the information is only provided as a warning.

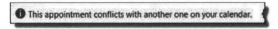

1. In the Appointment window, next to Start time, select the arrow of the date field.

2. From the date picker, select the day for the appointment.

   You can also type a date into the field itself, even using phrases such as "one week from Wednesday" or "New Year's Eve."

3. From the time list, select a time of day, or enter your own.

4. Repeat the previous steps to set the appointment's end date and time. By default, the ending date is the same as the starting date.

   Outlook doesn't allow you to set an ending time or date before the appointment's start.

Events

An *event* is a special type of appointment meant to mark important days, rather than specify a time when you need to do something. For example, you might use an event to mark your birthday or a seminar week, during which you'll be scheduling individual meetings and appointments. You can change any appointment to an event by using the **All day event** check box in its time controls, or you can create an appointment as an event by right-clicking on your calendar and clicking **New All Day Event**.

Because events represent full days, when you mark an appointment as an event, the time controls are disabled. Additionally, event days are marked as free on your calendar, so you won't be given any warning when scheduling an appointment during an event.

Exercise: Creating an appointment

In this exercise, you'll create an appointment to pick up some flowers for a company event.

Do This	How & Why
1. In the Navigation options, click **Calendar**.	Outlook switches to Calendar view.
2. On the Home tab, click **New Appointment**.	An Appointment window opens.
3. Enter the appointment details:	
a) In the Subject field, type `Pick up flowers`.	
b) In the Location field, type `Choi Flowers`.	
c) In the body field, type `Remember to bring the company credit card`.	
d) Set the start date to two days from now.	Notice that the end date is changed to match the start date.
e) Set the start time to **10:00 AM**.	The end time is set to a half hour later. This should be enough time.
4. Review the appointment details.	The scheduled appointment should look like this:

Subject	Pick up flowers				
Location	Choi Flowers				
Start time	Fri 2016-06-10	📅	10:00 AM	▼	☐ All day event
End time	Fri 2016-06-10	📅	10:30 AM	▼	

Remember to bring the company credit card.

Do This	How & Why
5. Click **Save & Close**.	The appointment window closes.

Do This	How & Why
6. In the Navigation pane, click the day two days from now.	The appointment now appears in your calendar, displayed in Day view. 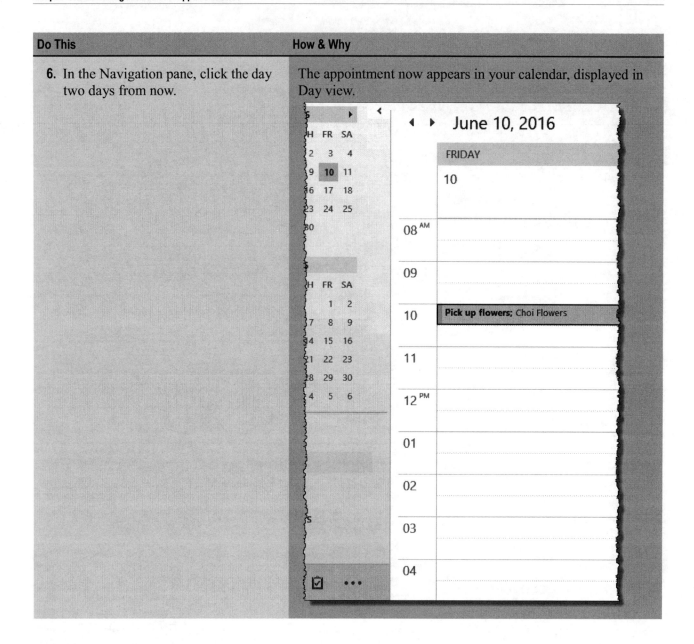

Appointment options

On the Appointment tab, the Options group contains commands for setting additional appointment options.

 MOS Outlook Exam Objective(s): 3.1.2, 3.1.3, 3.2.2, 3.2.7

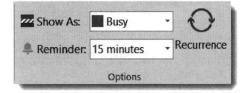

- *Show As* marks how the time of the appointment appears on your calendar: Free, Working Elsewhere, Tentative, Busy, or Out of Office. It's especially useful when you share your calendar with others. By default, an appointment is set to Busy, and an event to Free.

- *Reminder* marks when you'll receive a pop-up window and audio signal reminding you of your appointment. By default, an appointment reminds you 15 minutes before it starts and an event 18 hours before it.

- The *Recurrence* button opens the Appointment Recurrence window. As its name implies, there you can set options for an event's recurrence.

- When scheduling an appointment, you may need to coordinate your schedule across multiple time zones. On the View tab, in the Arrangement group, click **Time Scale > Change Time Zone** to open the Calendar pane of the Outlook Options window, which contains options for adding a second time zone or changing your current one.

Reminders

When you create an appointment, it automatically sets a reminder for fifteen minutes before the appointment or eighteen hours before an all-day event. When the reminder's time arrives, the Reminder(s) window opens and an audio notification plays.

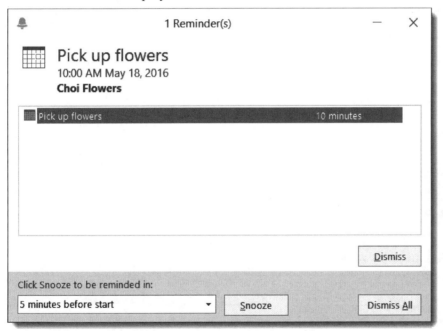

You can click **Open Item** to view the item's details, **Snooze** to be reminded later, or **Dismiss** to close the Reminder(s) window. To view your reminders at any time, in the View tab's Window group, click **Reminder(s) Window**.

Setting reminders

Only appointments, events, and meetings have reminders by default, but you can set reminders for any item by making it a To-Do item. Because To-Do items don't reserve specific times on your calendar, their reminders are set for a specific time.

 MOS Outlook Exam Objective(s): 3.3.3

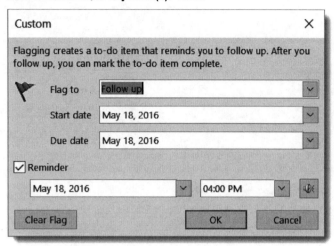

- To set or remove a reminder for a Calendar item, select or open it, and in the Options group, use the Reminder field.

- To set a reminder for a contact or message, in the Tags group, click **Follow Up > Add Reminder**.

- To set a reminder for a task, if it is open, you can click **Follow Up > Add Reminder**.

Creating recurring appointments

 MOS Outlook Exam Objective(s): 3.3.6

Appointments can also recur: the same appointment repeats at the same time every set interval. Although every recurrence of an appointment has the same start time, end time, and duration, you can set the recurrence pattern to daily, weekly, monthly, or yearly intervals. Each of the four options has its own, more specific options. For example, a weekly event can occur more frequently than one day of the week, or could only occur on alternate weeks.

Additionally, you can create an appointment that recurs indefinitely or for a set period of time.

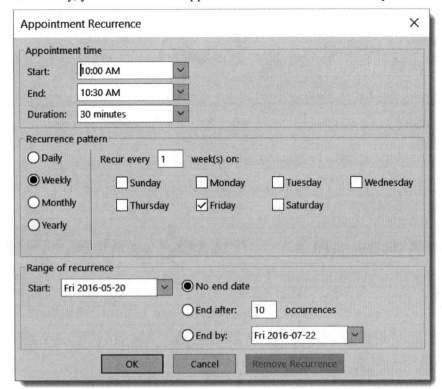

When you open a recurring appointment on your Calendar, Outlook will ask if you want to view that specific recurrence, or the recurring series itself. This way, you can change details for an individual appointment without changing the whole series.

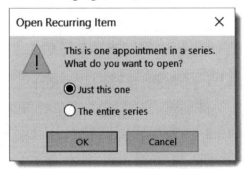

To create a recurring appointment:

1. Create or open an appointment.
2. On the Appointment tab, in the Options group, click **Recurrence**.
3. In the Appointment time section of the Appointment Recurrence window, set the start time, end time, and duration.
4. In the Recurrence pattern section, set the recurrence details.
5. In the Range of recurrence section, set the series start date and end date.
6. Click **OK**.

Once you've closed the Appointment Recurrence window, you'll still need to save the appointment itself. Click **Save & Close**.

Exercise: Creating a recurring appointment

In this exercise, you'll create a recurring appointment for a series of professional association dinners and set appropriate options.

Do This	How & Why
1. Create a new appointment named `Association Dinner`.	Click **New Appointment**, and enter the subject.
2. Enter the location as `Meeting hall`.	
3. Set the appointment for the fourth Tuesday of this month, from 6:00 PM to 8:00 PM.	Use the Start time and End time fields.
4. Set a reminder for the appointment: a) In the Appointment tab's Options group, open the Reminder list. b) Click **1 day**.	

15 minutes

None
0 minutes
5 minutes
10 minutes
15 minutes
30 minutes
1 hour
2 hours
3 hours
4 hours
5 hours
6 hours
7 hours
8 hours
9 hours
10 hours
11 hours
0.5 days
18 hours
1 day
2 days

You'll now be reminded a day before the dinner occurs.

Do This	How & Why
5. Set recurrence options: a) Click **Recurrence**.	The dinner is on the fourth Tuesday of every month. The Appointment Recurrence window opens. Note that the appointment time and start date both match the times you just set.

Do This	How & Why
b) Under Recurrence Pattern, click **Monthly**.	The options on the right side of the section change to those appropriate for monthly events.
c) Select the **fourth Tuesday** of every **1** month.	

d) Under Range of Recurrence, choose **End after6** occurrences.

First click **End After**, then enter 6 into the box.

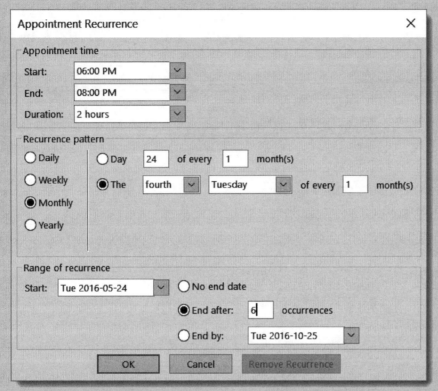

e) Click **OK**.

The recurrence time now appears in the Appointment window, below the meeting location.

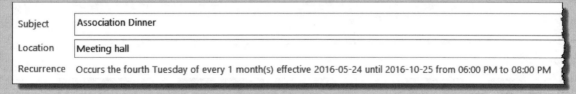

6. Click **Save & Close**.	The Appointment window closes. The appointment appears on the calendar.

Sharing appointments

Unlike messages or meetings, appointments are primarily for your own information rather than for communicating with others. Still, you can easily output an appointment from Outlook, either by printing it, or by forwarding it as a message.

Printing appointments

To quickly print the details of an appointment to a default printer, right-click it on your calendar, and click **Quick Print**. For more control, you can instead print in Backstage view.

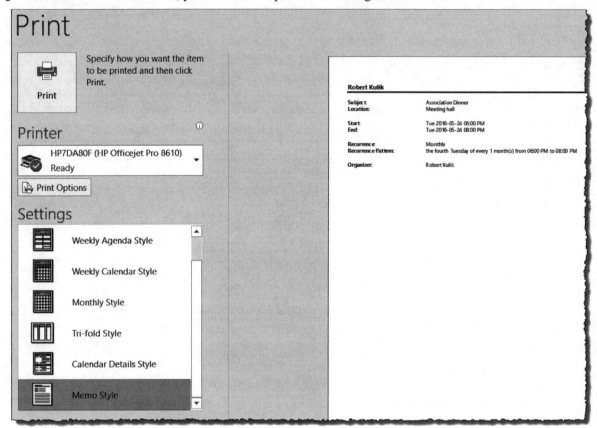

1. On the File tab of the ribbon, click **Print**.

2. From the Printer list, choose the printer you want to use.

3. If you need to access more detailed printer or layout options, click **Print Options**.

4. Click the **Print** button.

Forwarding appointments

If you want to share appointment details with someone, you can forward the appointment as an Outlook item, an iCalendar attachment, or—if Outlook is configured to allow it—a text message. Don't confuse forwarding an appointment with scheduling a meeting: meetings provide additional features for coordinating your calendar with others.

To forward an appointment, with the appointment selected, in the Appointment tab's Actions group, click **Forward**. Additional options are displayed, which are contextual. For non-recurring appointments, these are **Forward** and **Forward as iCalendar**. For recurring appointments, they are **Forward Series**, which allows you to forward all recurrences of that appointment, and **Forward as iCalendar**, which further contains choices for **Forward Occurrence** (for the single occurrence selected in the calendar) and **Forward Series** (for all occurrences).

 MOS Outlook Exam Objective(s): 3.3.2

iCalendar (not to be confused with Apple's iCal application) is a file format used for exchanging calendar data. It does not support all of the features of an Outlook item, but it's compatible with a wide variety of scheduling applications.

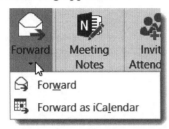

1. Open the appointment, or select it in your calendar.
2. On the Appointment tab, click **Forward** to forward the appointment as an Outlook item.
   You can instead click **Forward** > **Forward as iCalendar**.

    Note: If the appointment is a series, a **Forward Series** option becomes available.

3. In the new Message window, specify a recipient, and click **Send**.

Exercise: Forwarding an appointment

For this exercise, you'll need a partner. You'll forward an appointment to your partner.

Do This	How & Why
1. Open the **Pick up Flowers** appointment.	Double-click it on your calendar.
2. On the File tab, click **Print**.	You can choose print options and view a print preview of the appointment's details. Because this appointment is simple, you don't need to print it.
3. Forward the appointment to your partner:	
a) On the Appointment tab, click the arrow next to **Forward**.	You can forward the message as an Outlook item, an iCalendar attachment, or a text message.
b) Click **Forward**.	You know your partner uses Outlook. A new Message window opens.
c) In the To field, enter your partner's address.	
d) Click **Send**.	
e) Close the Appointment window.	

Do This	How & Why
4. When your partner's message arrives, examine its header.	You'll have to switch to Mail view. 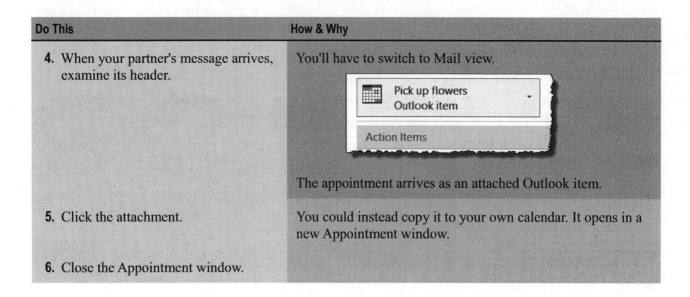 The appointment arrives as an attached Outlook item.
5. Click the attachment.	You could instead copy it to your own calendar. It opens in a new Appointment window.
6. Close the Appointment window.	

Assessment: Appointments

1. Unlike tasks, appointments have specific:

   • Participants

   • Recurrence

   • Dates

   • Reserved times

2. True or false? You can easily convert an appointment to an event, or vice-versa.

   • True

   • False

3. True or false? Appointments, meetings, and tasks automatically have reminders set.

   • True

   • False

4. Which of the following is *not* a valid recurrence range?

   • End after 10 occurrences

   • End after 10 hours total duration

   • End by 04/12/2016

   • No end date

5. True or false? You can forward an appointment, but this is the same as making it a meeting.

   • True

   • False

Module B: Meetings

In Outlook terminology, a *meeting* is a specialized type of appointment. It reserves time on your calendar in the same way, and has most of the same content and options. In fact, from the ribbon, you can even toggle an item from appointment to meeting and back. The difference is that a meeting is coordinated with other people from within Outlook, so that they can add it to their own calendars. Although you can forward an appointment to someone else, with a similar result, meetings provide a much more integrated way of scheduling activities with other Outlook users.

In this module, you'll learn:

- How to request a meeting
- About meeting reply options
- How to modify a meeting request
- How to contact meeting attendees

About meetings

When you create a meeting, you choose attendees from your contacts or by entering email addresses. Outlook then sends a *meeting request* message to the potential attendees. Each attendee has the option to accept or deny the request: accepted requests are added to the attendee's calendar; either way, you receive a message informing you of the decision.

When you create or open a meeting in Outlook, it will look similar to an appointment. The only real differences are those related to attendees: the To field, Send button, and additional options in the Attendees group of the ribbon.

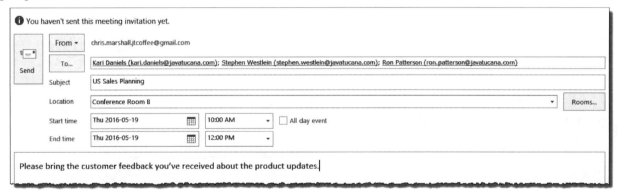

Creating meetings

To create a meeting, first you need to open a new Meeting window, so you can enter its details. As with an appointment, there arc a number of ways you can do so.

 MOS Outlook Exam Objective(s): 3.2.6

- From anywhere in Outlook, press **Crtl+Shift+Q**, or click **New Items > Meeting**.
- In Calendar view, click **New Meeting**.
- In your calendar, right-click a particular time, and click **New Meeting Request**.
- In any Appointment window, on the Appointment tab, click **Invite Attendees** to turn it into a meeting.
- When viewing a contact, click **Meeting** in the Contact tab's Communicate group to request a meeting with that contact.

- When viewing a Contact Card pop-up in a message header, click **Options > Schedule a Meeting** to request a meeting with the sender.

Unlike for an appointment, once you open a meeting, you can't simply save it. You need to add attendees and send them the meeting request.

Adding attendees

 MOS Outlook Exam Objective(s): 3.2.8, 3.3.4

Although most meeting details are like those of an appointment, you need to add attendees before you can send the request. You can do this from the Select Attendees and Resources window.

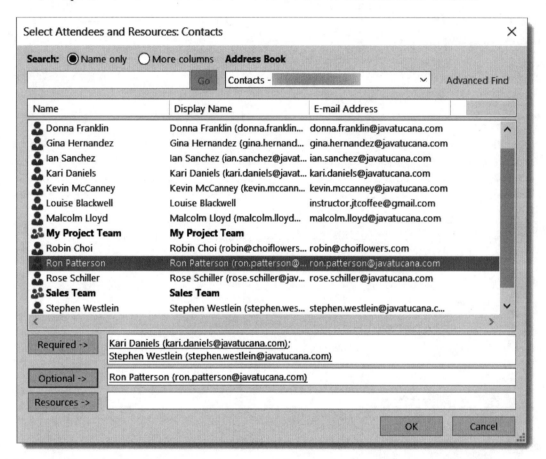

If it looks like the Select Names window you might see when sending an email, that's because it serves much the same function. The important difference is in the fields at the bottom. Instead of To, CC, and BCC, meetings have Required, Optional, and Resources fields.

The *Required* and *Optional* fields are respectively meant for people who are important to the meeting and those who aren't but might wish to attend. As with To and CC, these are distinctions made for courtesy and clarity: a Required attendee can still opt to decline the invitation, and the meeting will still, as far as Outlook is concerned, go on as scheduled for everyone else.

The *Resources* field is a little different. If you're using a Microsoft Exchange email server, your administrator can create resource accounts to represent company resources used in meetings, such as a conference room or a projector. Adding resources to a meeting reserves them for that time period.

1. In the Meeting window, click **To**, or click **Address Book** on the Meeting tab.
2. Select one or more contacts from your Address Book.

3. Click the button corresponding to what the selected contacts should be: **Required**, **Optional**, or **Resources**.

4. When you're done adding attendees or resources, click **OK**.

Required and Optional attendees are added to the To field of the meeting request. Resources are added to the Location field.

Sending meeting requests

After you choose attendees for a meeting request, you'll still need to set additional details. Unlike an appointment, which serves largely to help jog your memory, a meeting request is a way to get information to others. This means you should make sure the meeting request gives the attendees what they need to arrive at the meeting on time and prepared.

 MOS Outlook Exam Objective(s): 3.2.9, 3.3.7

Most meeting options are just like those of appointments, including start and end times, reminders, and recurrence. One exception is Response Options, located on Meeting tab in the Attendees group. These options allow you to decide whether to request responses from attendees, and whether to allow attendees to propose a different time for the meeting. By default, both are allowed.

If your Outlook account is connected to a Microsoft Exchange server, you can even check for room availability. In the Meeting window, click **Rooms**, and select an available room. The room information will then be included in the sent meeting invitation. Alternatively, you can use the Room Finder pane, which is displayed by default. (To display it, on the Meeting tab, click **Room Finder**.) Available rooms are displayed under "Choose an available room."

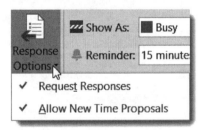

1. Make sure the meeting has a subject and location.

   Even if you don't use Resources for meeting locations, you can still type in whatever you like.

2. Set the meeting start and end time.

   You can turn a meeting into an event just as with an appointment: in this case, it's called an *Invited Event*.

3. Add any information or attachments the attendees might need.

   Remember that the details field of the meeting will appear in the message body when they receive the request.

4. Set any additional options, such as reminders or recurrence.

5. If you don't want meeting responses or new time proposals, click **Response Options**, and clear the appropriate option.

6. Click **Send**.

Exercise: Creating a meeting

You'll need a partner added as a contact. You'll create a meeting request and send it to your partner.

Do This	How & Why
1. On the Calendar, click **New Meeting**.	A blank Meeting window opens.
2. Add your partner as an attendee.	You could simply type your partner's address in the To field, but you'll use the Address book.
a) Click **To**.	The Select Attendees and Resources window opens.
b) Select your partner's address, and click **Required**.	
c) Click **OK**.	The window closes, and your partner now appears in the To field of the meeting window.
3. Set the meeting to begin sometime next week, with a duration of one hour.	Use the Start time and End time fields. Check with your partner to make sure you're using different times.
4. Enter the meeting details:	Use your name here.
a) Subject: `<Name>'s New flyer discussion`.	
a) Location: `Conference Room B`.	
b) Body: `I'll be opening with an overview of the old design and the elements of it we're looking to change, then I'll open the floor to suggestions. You might want to take a look at that on the company website beforehand.`	
5. In the Attendees group, click **Response Options**.	You'll keep both of these options.

Do This	How & Why

6. Close the list and review the meeting request.

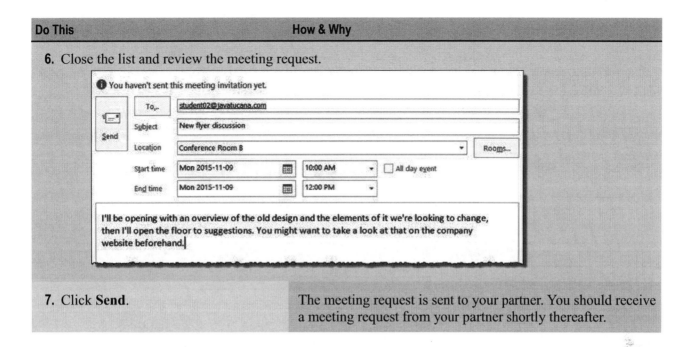

7. Click **Send**.

The meeting request is sent to your partner. You should receive a meeting request from your partner shortly thereafter.

Meeting responses

When someone sends you a meeting request, it arrives in your inbox as a message. You can tell when an incoming message is a meeting, as the normal envelope icon is replaced by a meeting icon.

The message itself shows the meeting information, along with where it would appear on your calendar. Additionally, you will see *response options* allowing you to accept the meeting, tentatively accept, decline, propose a time, or open your calendar in a new window. When you preview the request in the Reading pane, the response options appear as a toolbar at the top of the message. If you open the message, they appear in the ribbon's Respond group.

A meeting request in the Reading pane

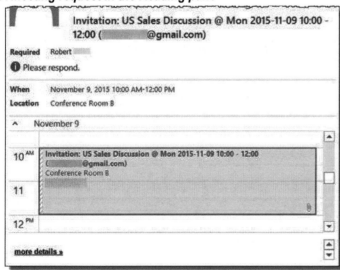

Meeting request respond options in the Reading pane.

✓ Accept ▾   ? Tentative ▾   ✗ Decline ▾   🕰 Propose New Time ▾   🗓 Calendar...

Accepting or declining meeting requests

When you receive a meeting request, you need to decide what to do with it. The simplest options are Accept, which adds it to your calendar; Decline, which does not; or Tentative, which adds it to your calendar but marks the time as Tentative rather than Busy.

When you click any of those three buttons you're presented with three options. Edit the Response before Sending, Send the Response Now, and Do Not Send a Response.

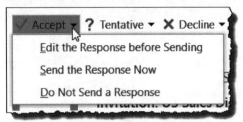

1. Open or preview the meeting request.

2. Click **Accept**, **Tentative**, or **Decline**.

   a) If you want to add something to your reply, choose **Edit the Response before Sending**.
   A new message window will open, which you can edit before clicking **Send**.

   b) If you just want to send your response, click **Send the Response Now**.

   c) If you don't want to notify the sender of your decision, click **Do Not Send a Response**.
   Without receiving responses, the sender might not know whom to expect at the meeting.

If you accepted the meeting, it will be marked as Busy on your calendar. If you tentatively accepted, it will be marked as Tentative. If you sent a response, it will arrive in the sender's inbox. When the sender opens the meeting, a list of attendee responses will appear just below the ribbon.

Proposing new times

If a meeting request doesn't fit your schedule, you don't have to decline it outright. Instead, you can respond by proposing a different time for the meeting. To propose a new time for the meeting, above the meeting request message, click **Propose New Time > Tentative and Propose New Time** (if there's a possibility you can still attend at the scheduled time) or **Propose New Time > Decline and Propose New Time**. Either option opens the Propose New Time window.

 MOS Outlook Exam Objective(s): 3.2.5

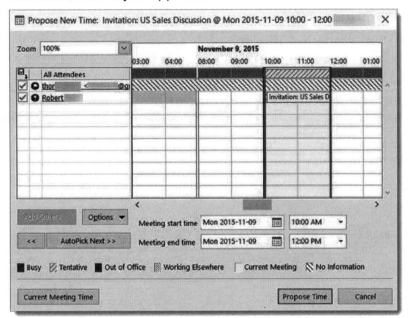

In addition to time controls, the window shows your schedule and that of every other participant whose calendar is shared with yours. You can manually choose a new meeting time or have Outlook choose the next available space.

Your proposal is just that—a proposal. It's up to the meeting organizer whether to accept it, to go on with the meeting as planned, or simply to cancel it altogether.

1. Select or open the meeting request.

2. Click **Propose New Time > Tentative and Propose New Time**, or **Propose New Time > Decline and Propose New Time**.

   The Propose New Time window opens.

3. Select a new time for the meeting.

   a) To find a time when all participants are free, click either of the **AutoPick Next** buttons. This will only work effectively if the other participants have shared their calendar details with you.

   b) Otherwise, manually select new start and end times for the meeting.

4. Click **Propose Time**.

   A New Time Proposed message window opens.

5. Click **Send**.

Accepting new times

When someone proposes a new time for a meeting you've requested, you can accept it to change the meeting time. If more than one recipient proposes a new time, you can view them all at once and select that one that fits best.

1. Open a **New Time Proposed** message.

2. In the Respond group, click **Accept**.

> You can also click **View All Proposals**. This opens a variant of the Propose New Time window, showing each attendee proposal and letting you choose a new time.

> The Meeting window opens again, updated with the new time.

3. Change any other details you want, and click **Send Update**.

Once the updated meeting is sent, all attendees will have to respond to it all over again. Especially with large groups, negotiating a meeting time via Outlook tools alone can be a lengthy process.

Exercise: Responding to a meeting request

For this exercise, you'll need to have an unanswered meeting request from your partner. You'll respond to a meeting request from your partner.

Do This	How & Why
1. View the **New Flyer Discussion** message from your partner.	Meeting reply options appear at the top of the Reading pane.
2. Click **Propose New Time > Tentative and Propose New Time**.	The Propose New Time window opens.
3. Choose a time an hour later than the original meeting, and click **Propose Time**.	A Meeting Response window opens.
4. In the message body, type I need a little more time to prepare, if that's all right.	
5. Click **Send**.	
6. When your partner's response arrives, open it.	You can accept a meeting request in the Reading pane, but not a new time proposal.
7. In the Respond group of the ribbon, click **Accept Proposal**.	As this is the meeting you organized, it opens as a Meeting item.
8. Click **Send Update**.	To send an updated meeting request.
9. When your partner's updated request arrives, select it.	It has response buttons. Even though you proposed the new time, you still have to accept it.
10. Click **Accept > Send the Response Now**.	Only now is your partner's meeting finalized. You'll also receive your partner's final approval of your meeting.

Updating meetings

Even if there's no problem with attendees, you might want to change a meeting's details. For example, you might add attendees, change the time, or just enter additional details.

1. Double-click the meeting on your calendar to open it.
2. Make any changes you need.
   - To change most elements of the meeting, simply select or type the new options.
   - To add attendees, click **To** or **Address Book**.
3. Click **Send Update**.

If you haven't changed the meeting time, existing attendees won't need to respond again. They'll simply receive a notification with new details. If you have changed the time, they'll be prompted to accept or reject it, as will any newly added attendees.

Canceling meetings

If you've requested a meeting, you can cancel it and notify all attendees. The procedure is the same whether you've received replies or merely sent an invitation.

 MOS Outlook Exam Objective(s): 3.2.3

1. Open the meeting.
2. In the Actions group, click **Cancel Meeting**.
3. Optionally, type further information into the meeting details, such as a reason for cancellation or whether you plan to schedule it again at a later date.
4. Click **Send Cancellation**.

The canceled meeting remains on the attendees' calendars until they delete it, but is marked as canceled.

Deleting meetings

Only a meeting's organizer can cancel it, but if you've accepted a meeting request and find yourself unable to attend, you can still delete it.

1. Open or select the meeting.
2. In the Meeting tab's Actions group, click **Delete**.
3. Click **Yes** to send a Meeting Declined notification to the meeting organizer, or click **No** to delete it without sending a response.

   If you send a response, you're then asked whether you wish to edit the response before sending.

Contacting attendees

Even if you don't need to change the meeting details, you might want to contact its attendees. Doing so is simple, though the steps to do so vary, depending whether you're the organizer or an attendee.

* If you're the meeting's organizer, in the Meeting tab's Attendees group, click **Contact Attendees**. You can send a new email to the attendees, reply to the meeting invitation via email or IM, or telephone some or all attendees.

* If you're an attendee, in the Respond group, click **Respond**, and then choose **Reply, Reply All,** or **Forward**, as you would with any other message.

Exercise: Updating a meeting

To complete this exercise, you'll need to have the New Flyer Discussion meeting you created in a previous exercise. You'll send updates to a meeting.

Do This	How & Why
1. Open the meeting you created.	<Name's> New Flyer Discussion.
2. Send an update to the meeting:	
a) In the meeting body, type `Please bring your customer feedback.`	
b) Click **Send Update**.	The meeting update is sent.
3. View the meeting update you've received from your partner.	
a) Select the message in your inbox.	✂ No Response Required
	Because times weren't changed, the meeting doesn't require a response.
b) Open the meeting in your calendar.	The updated text is automatically added.
c) Close the Meeting window.	
4. Cancel the meeting you created.	
a) Open the meeting.	
b) In the Actions group, click **Cancel Meeting**.	A notice appears that the cancellation has not been sent, and the Send Update button changes to Send Cancellation.
c) In the meeting body, type `Something's come up. I'll schedule a new time next week.`	
d) Click **Send Cancellation**.	

Do This	How & Why
5. View the cancellation message from your partner.	You can view it in your Inbox, or open it in your Calendar. The meeting's name is prefixed with "Canceled." and the Remove from Calendar button appears. ✕ Remove from Calendar
6. Click **Remove from Calendar**.	In the Reading pane or on the Meeting tab.

Assessment: Meetings

1. Unlike appointments, meetings have:

   - Other participants
   - Recurrence settings
   - Starting Dates
   - Reserved times

2. To turn an appointment into a meeting, you can:

   - Check the Meeting box next to the start time.
   - Invite attendees
   - Drag it to the Meetings folder.
   - Forward it to the attendees.

3. True or false? When you propose a new meeting time, you automatically share your free times with the meeting organizer.

   - True
   - False

4. True or false? You can use the Contact Attendees commands whether you're the organizer or an attendee of a meeting.

   - True
   - False

Module C: Using the calendar

You can view your upcoming appointments and meetings in a list just as you would any other folder, but it's usually a lot easier to get an idea of how your schedule fits together when you see them in calendar format. Unlike on a paper calendar, Outlook's Calendar view lets you easily change formats or customize layouts to suit your current needs.

In this module, you'll learn:

- About calendar views
- How to navigate the calendar
- How to change calendar options
- How to print the calendar

Calendar views

When you view a Calendar folder, the Reading pane and To-Do bar are hidden, and the folder contents pane shows your calendar along with any appointments, meetings, or events marked on it. You can choose what range of your calendar is shown using the Home tab's Arrange group, or the View tab's Arrangement group.

The Calendar in Week view

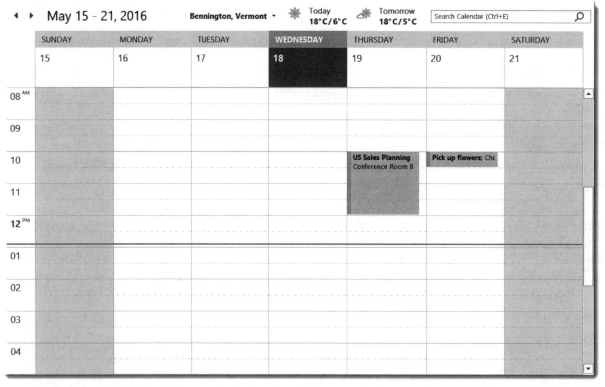

Day, Work Week, and Week views are all similar: the upper part of the pane displays your schedule by day in half-hour increments, like a traditional scheduling book, while the lower pane shows tasks due on that day. As the name suggests, *Day* shows one day at a time, *Work Week* shows your work days for the week, and Week shows the entire week. In any of these views, working hours are shown in white, and non-working hours are highlighted in blue by default. The whole day probably won't fit in the vertical space shown, so you can move through the day using the scrollbar on the right side.

Schedule View is similar to Day view, but it displays the timeline in a horizontal fashion. It's especially useful when you want to compare calendars others have shared with you.

Month view is a bit different. It doesn't show tasks, just the entire calendar month, like a traditional wall calendar. Additionally, while in Month view, on the View tab, in the Current View group, click **Change View** to choose among different levels of detail: **Calendar** (the default view), **Preview**, **List**, and **Active**. Additional options are also provided for customizing your calendars' views.

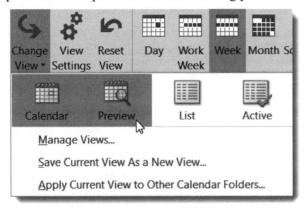

When you select an item in your calendar, the Appointment or Meeting tabs appear on the ribbon, allowing you to edit the item without opening it.

Navigating calendar views

Whatever view you're using, there are several ways to navigate through the calendar. Some will also switch your view settings, unless you're in Schedule View, but you can always switch back.

- Click the **Forward** and **Back** buttons at the upper left of the calendar to page through it by day, week, or month, depending on your view.

- In the Folder pane, you can click any day in the Date Navigator to move the calendar there, with that day selected.

- You can also click the left arrow in the Date Navigator to move to the previous month while remaining in the same view.

- In Month view you can click to the left of each row to zoom in on that week.

- If you're viewing an empty portion of your calendar, on either side of the calendar window, click the **Previous Appointment** or **Next Appointment** buttons to navigate to the nearest page with something scheduled.

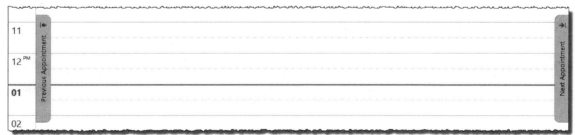

- You can also navigate using the Home tab's Go To group. Click **Today** to view today in Day view; or click **Next 7 Days** to view the upcoming week, displayed much the same as Week view, but which is displayed as Day view in the Arrange group.

- For the most detailed control, press **Ctrl+G**, or click the Go To group's **Launcher** button to open the Go to Date window. You can then choose the date and view to which you want to move.

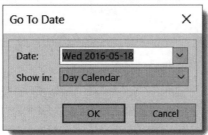

Printing calendars

You can print your calendar in a variety of different formats using the Backstage controls.

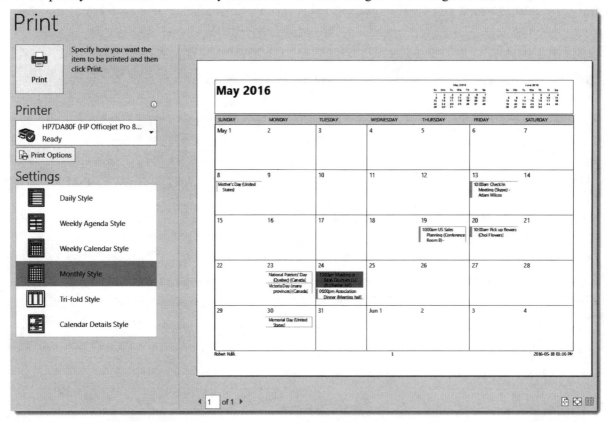

1. Select the calendar view corresponding to the range you want to print.

   You can print a daily or even monthly calendar from Day view, for example, but if you print daily sheets from month view, you'll end up with one page for each day of the month.

2. On the File tab, click **Print**.

3. If necessary, select the printer you wish to use, or click **Print Options** for more detailed printer and layout settings.

4. Click the print setting you want to use. When you select one, a preview will appear to the right.

   a) **Daily Style**, **Weekly Calendar Style**, and **Monthly Style** options all correspond to their respective views.

   b) **Weekly Agenda Style** displays your weekly calendar in a format more similar to a monthly view.

   c) **Tri-fold Style** has three columns: on the left is a daily view, in the middle your daily task list, and on the right a weekly view similar to Weekly Agenda Style.

   d) **Calendar Details Style** only prints the days on which you have appointments, but prints full appointment details for each.

5. Click **Print**.

Exercise: Navigating the calendar

In this exercise, you'll explore calendar views.

Do This	How & Why
1. If necessary, switch to the Calendar.	
2. Click **Day**.	The calendar shows a single day.
3. Scroll up and down in the calendar.	By default, the hours from 8am to 5pm are white, showing that they're normal working hours. The time before and after the work day is highlighted in blue. This doesn't keep you from scheduling anything for those times; it's just a way to highlight the work day.
4. Observe each view in turn:	
a) Click **Work Week**.	The calendar shows this Monday through Friday work week.
b) Click **Week**.	The displayed week expands to include Sunday on the left and Saturday on the right. Weekends are also highlighted as non-working hours.
c) Click **Month**.	This month is displayed in your calendar.
d) Click **Schedule View**.	Your calendar appears in a horizontal day format. At the bottom, there's a button to add and compare other calendars.
5. At the top of the calendar, click Forward.	The calendar moves to the next day.
6. Click any day in the Date Navigator.	To display that day, while remaining in Schedule View.
7. Switch to Month view.	
8. In the Go To group, click **Next 7 Days**.	The calendar now shows the next week, starting today.

Do This	How & Why
9. Press **Ctrl+G**.	You can instead click on the Go To group's Launcher button. The Go to Date window opens.
10. Navigate to a year from today. a) In the Date field, type or select the date one year from now. b) From the "Show in" list, click **Week Calendar**. c) Click **OK**.	
11. Return to today's date.	Use the method and view of your choice.

Calendar customization

Not everyone keeps the same work schedule: your shift, your observed holidays, or other things might be different from those of Outlook's default settings. This doesn't have a hard-and-fast effect on most users, as you can schedule appointments for any time of any day. All the same, you might want to customize your calendar's display settings to match your personal schedule. Outlook lets you easily change your work days, work hours, and holidays to do so.

Changing work hours

By default, Outlook defines work hours as 8 AM to 5 PM, Monday through Friday. If your job, or your company, keeps a different calendar, you'll want to change it. You can do so in the Outlook Options window's Calendar section.

 MOS Outlook Exam Objective(s): 3.1.5

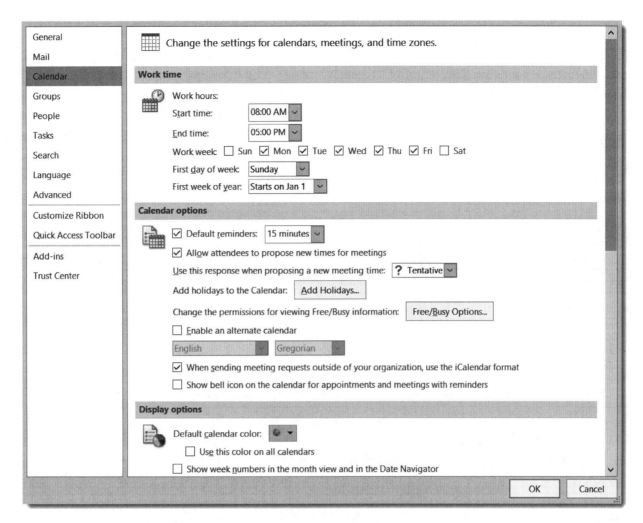

1. In the Home tab's Arrange group, click the Launcher button.

   You can instead click **Outlook Options**, then on the File tab, click **Calendar**.

   The Outlook Options window opens, displaying the Calendar section.

2. In the Work Time section, set the Start time and End time to match your shift.

3. Next to Work week, check and uncheck the days of the week, as necessary, to match your schedule.

4. Select the first day of your week.

   Note that this affects Week and Month views, so it can be a day off. Outlook's default setting displays the first day of the week as Sunday.

5. If necessary, change the first week of the year.

   Available options are **Starts on Jan 1**, **First 4-day Week**, and **First Full Week**.

6. When you're finished setting options, click **OK**.

Adding holidays

You or your company might keep different holidays than Outlook displays by default. For example, you might want to add holidays for your religion, or for a country with which, or in which, your company does business. Although it's easy to set up an individual holiday as a yearly event, you can choose from a number of standardized sets in the Add Holidays to Calendar window.

1. In the Home tab's Arrange group, click the Launcher button.

   You can instead click **Outlook Options**, then on the File tab, click **Calendar**.

   The Outlook Options window opens, displaying the Calendar section.

2. Under Calendar options, click **Add Holidays**.

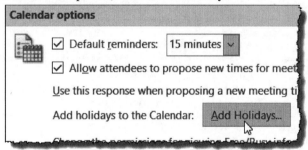

   The Add Holidays to Calendar window opens.

3. Check any locations or other categories you want to add to your holiday list, and clear any that are inappropriate.

4. Click **OK** twice.

Changing calendar colors

By default, Outlook displays its calendar in shades of blue, from the light shading for non-working hours to the very dark blue of a selected block of time. If you have more than one calendar, each has its own color. You can change the color of any calendar to one of your liking.

1. On the View tab, click **Color**.

   You can instead right-click the calendar, and point to **Color**.

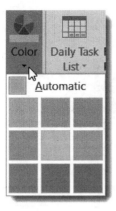

2. Select the color you like.

   The color you choose will apply to all coloration on the calendar, including non-working hours, appointments, day headers, and selected times.

Prioritizing and categorizing calendar items

 MOS Outlook Exam Objective(s): 2.4.4, 3.3.1, 3.3.8

The Calendar Tools' Tags group contains tools for prioritizing and categorizing calendar items.

1. Select the calendar item you wish to prioritize and/or categorize.

   This displays the Calendar Tools Appointment tab or Meeting tab, depending on whether the item is an appointment or a meeting, respectively. However, both these tabs contain a Tags group.

2. Assign a priority to the item.
   Click **High Importance**, **Low Importance**, or **Private**.

3. Assign a category to the item.
   Click **Categorize**, then select the desired option.

4. To create additional categories, click **Categorize > All Categories**.

   The Color Categories window opens. Click **New** to create a new category. You can also rename or delete existing categories. Then click **OK**.

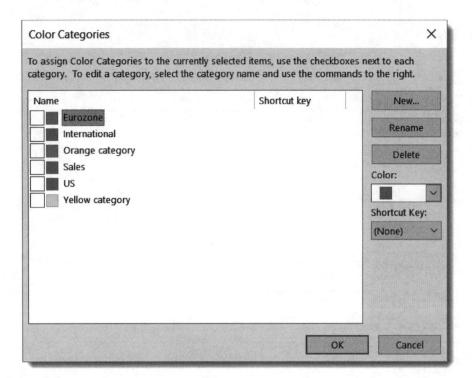

 Note: Once you've created a new category you can then apply it from the list of Categorize options. You can likewise apply categories and prioritization to messages.

Exercise: Customizing your calendar

In this exercise, you'll change your workday settings and calendar color.

Do This	How & Why
1. View your calendar in **Work Week** view.	Outlook displays your working hours as 8:00 AM to 5:00 PM, Monday through Friday. Your usual work week is 9:00 AM to 5:30 PM, Tuesday through Saturday, so you'll need to change it.
2. In the Home tab's Arrange group, click ▣.	The Outlook Options window opens, displaying the Calendar section.
3. Click the list next to Start Time.	You can set the beginning of the work day in half-hour increments.
4. Click **9:00 AM**.	
5. In the End time list, click **5:30 PM**.	
6. In the Work week list, clear **Mon**, and check **Sat**.	
7. Click **OK**.	Your calendar now displays your working hours accurately, and Work Week view now shows Tuesday through Saturday.
8. Right-click anywhere on the calendar, and point to **Color**.	

Do This	How & Why
9. Choose the color you like best.	The whole calendar changes to display shades of your chosen color.

Assessment: Using the calendar

1. Which views display a daily task list?

   - Day
   - Month
   - Schedule View
   - Work Week

2. Which calendar navigation method lets you move to both any time and any view?

   - The Date Navigator
   - The Go To Date window
   - The Next Appointment button
   - Schedule View

3. True or false? You can't use the Calendar Options settings to mark your birthday as a personal holiday.

   - True
   - False

Summary: Scheduling

You should now know how to:

- Plan your schedule by creating appointments, and setting appointment options such as reminders and recurrence options

- Organize meetings with your contacts, respond to meeting invitations, and negotiate mutually compatible times

- Navigate the calendar, change views, and customize its display options

Synthesis: Scheduling

To complete this exercise, you'll need a partner.

In this exercise, you'll schedule tasks related to a store remodeling project with your partner.

1. Communicate with your partner to decide roles for the project. One of you will perform on-site labor, while the other will purchase materials and meet with outside contractors and consultants.

2. Set appointments scheduled during the next month appropriate to your role in the project. They shouldn't fill your whole schedule, but you should spread them out. Don't tell your partner yet when they're scheduled.

3. Schedule meetings with your partner to collaborate on the project. At least one of them should be a weekly status update. Using the meeting response tools, negotiate times convenient for both of you.

Chapter 6: Customization

In this chapter, you'll learn how to:

- Customize the ribbon
- Change Outlook's appearance

Module A: Customizing the ribbon

If you've used applications with traditional menus and toolbars, especially older versions of Outlook, the ribbon might be a bit of an adjustment. Whether you're a new or an old user, however, don't think of it as a "take it or leave it" proposition, but rather as a starting point you can customize to fit your needs.

In this module, you'll learn how to:

- Change how the ribbon is displayed

- Rearrange the ribbon

- Add custom tabs and groups

- Customize the Quick Access toolbar

Ribbon customization

You can change how the ribbon is displayed, rearrange its commands, or add new tabs and groups. You can also add new commands to the Quick Access toolbar.

Hiding or restoring the ribbon

The ribbon is always available at the top of the Outlook window, but if it's taking up too much space, you can minimize it. When the ribbon is minimized, all you can see is its tabs. Clicking a tab temporarily opens the ribbon so you can use its commands.

You can minimize or restore the ribbon in multiple ways, but the effect is the same for all.

- Press **Ctrl+F1**.
- Double-click the active ribbon tab.
- Right-click anywhere on the ribbon, and click **Collapse the Ribbon**.
- Click the **Collapse the Ribbon** button.

Rearranging ribbon commands

The ribbon isn't a fixed tool. You can rearrange the display order of its tabs, or hide tabs entirely. Likewise, you can change the order of groups on a tab, move groups between tabs, or even remove them from the ribbon entirely. To do so, you'll either need to open the Outlook Options window from the File tab; or right-click the ribbon, and choose **Customize the Ribbon**. Either method opens the Customize the Ribbon options. This list shows all tabs in Outlook. Note that there are multiple versions of the Home tab, corresponding to each view type. You can customize each of these views separately.

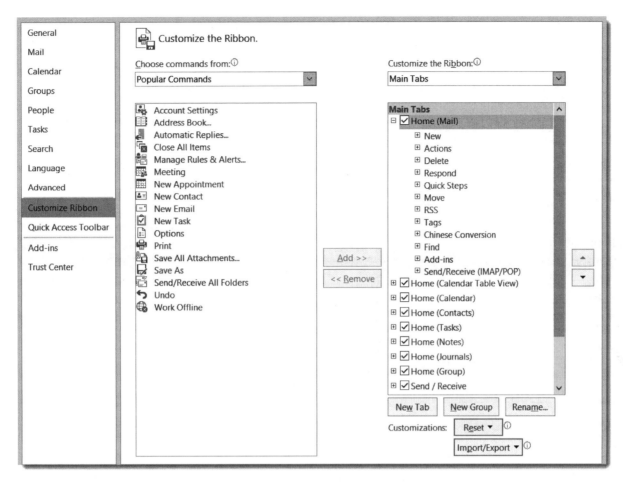

- Use the + and - buttons to expand and collapse the list.

  Note that although you can expand a group to view the commands inside, you can't change the commands themselves.

- To move a tab or group, select it and click ![up] or ![down] . You can use this method to move a group from one tab to another.

- To rename a tab or group, select it and click **Rename**.

- To show or hide a tab, toggle its check box.

- To remove a group, select it, and click **Remove**.

- By default, only the main tabs of the Outlook window are shown. To view Tool tabs, click the **Customize the Ribbon** list, then click **Tool Tabs** or **All Tabs**.

Changes you make to the ribbon aren't committed until you click **OK**. If you make any changes you don't want to keep, click **Cancel**.

Adding tabs and groups

Although you can move groups and tabs around, you can't change or move the commands inside an existing group. Instead, you can create an existing group and place any commands you like inside it. You can also create new tabs, giving you additional freedom to customize the ribbon.

You can add groups to standard tabs or to custom tabs. Once they're created, you can move both standard and custom groups between standard and custom tabs.

1. In the Outlook Options window, open the Customize Ribbon section.

You can either right-click the ribbon and click **Customize the Ribbon**, or open Outlook Options, and click **Customize Ribbon**.

2. Click **New Tab**.

When you create a custom tab, it automatically contains one custom group. You can use the New Group button to add more.

Custom tabs and groups are called "New Tab" and "New Group" by default, but you can rename them whatever you like. A new group is empty by default, so you'll have to add commands next.

Adding commands to the ribbon

Once you've made a custom group, you'll want to add commands to it. You can add any command to the Outlook ribbon, but because there are so many to choose from, the "Choose commands from" list has several categories to help narrow your choices. You can even look for commands not already in the ribbon.

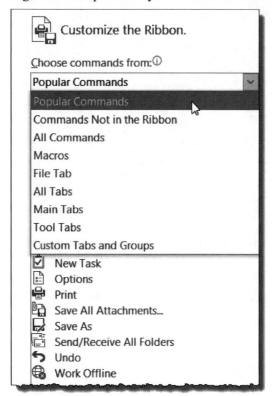

1. In the list of current ribbon contents, select the custom group to which you wish to add commands.

2. In the "Choose Commands from" list, click the category you want.

3. Click any command in the list to select it.

4. Click **Add.**

5. To rename a command you've added, or to change its icon, select it and click **Rename**.

6. If you want to remove a command you've already added, select it and click **Remove**.

7. When you're finished adding commands, click **OK**.

Customizing the Quick Access toolbar

By default, the Quick Access toolbar shows only the Send/Receive and Undo commands, but you can add whatever commands you like. You can also choose whether to display the toolbar above or below the ribbon. To quickly add or remove commands, use the **Customize Quick Access Toolbar Commands** button, and check or clear the available commands. Adding more commands is similar to adding commands to the ribbon.

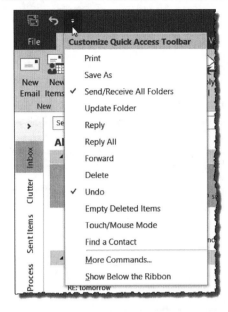

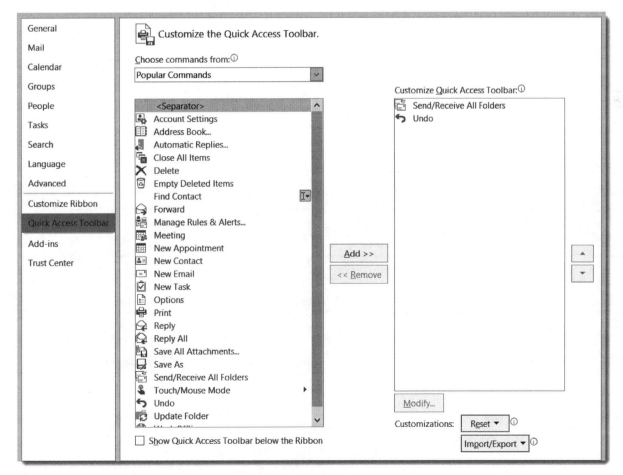

1. Click [⌄] > **More Commands**; or, in the Outlook Options window, click **Quick Access Toolbar**.

2. From the left list, choose a command.

   You might need to use the "Choose commands from" list to find the one you want.

3. Click **Add**.

4. Click **OK** to save your changes.

Resetting customizations

You might want to undo a ribbon customization you've made. It's easy enough to restore hidden tabs or remove custom commands, but for other changes, it's easiest to merely reset a tab or the entire ribbon. The Reset commands are available in the Ribbon Customization options.

Similarly, if you want to reset the Quick Access toolbar to its default state, you can do so from the Quick Access Toolbar section of the Outlook Options window.

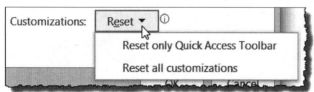

- To reset a single tab to its defaults, in Ribbon options, select it, and click **Reset > Reset only selected Ribbon tab**.

- To reset the Quick Access toolbar, open its customization options, then click **Reset > Reset only Quick Access Toolbar**.

- To reset all customization to both the ribbon and Quick Access toolbar, open the options for either. Then click **Reset > Reset all customizations**. Finally, click **Yes** to verify the change.

Exercise: Customizing the ribbon

In this exercise, you'll customize the ribbon and Quick Access toolbar.

Do This	How & Why
1. Double-click the **Home** tab.	The Ribbon minimizes, with only the tabs themselves left visible.
2. Click **View**.	The View tab of the ribbon is temporarily visible.
3. Right-click any ribbon tab and click **Minimize the Ribbon**.	The ribbon is expanded again.
4. On the Quick Access toolbar, click [⌄].	The customization options button. A list of common commands appears.
5. Click **Delete**.	The Delete icon is added to the toolbar.

Do This	How & Why
6. Right-click anywhere on the ribbon, and click **Customize the Ribbon**.	The Outlook Options window opens, with Customize Ribbon selected. First, you'll remove some commands you don't expect to use much.
7. In the list of Main Tabs, next to Folder, clear the check box.	You might need to scroll to see it.
8. On the Home (Mail) tab, click **RSS**.	The group is selected.
9. Click **Remove**.	Next you'll add some commands.
10. Expand the New group.	The contents of existing groups can't be changed, so to add commands, you'll need to add a custom group.
11. In a custom tab, create a custom New Items group.	
a) Click **New Tab**.	A custom tab appears, with a custom group already inside it.

Do This	How & Why
b) Select **New Group (Custom)**, and click **Rename**.	The Rename window appears.

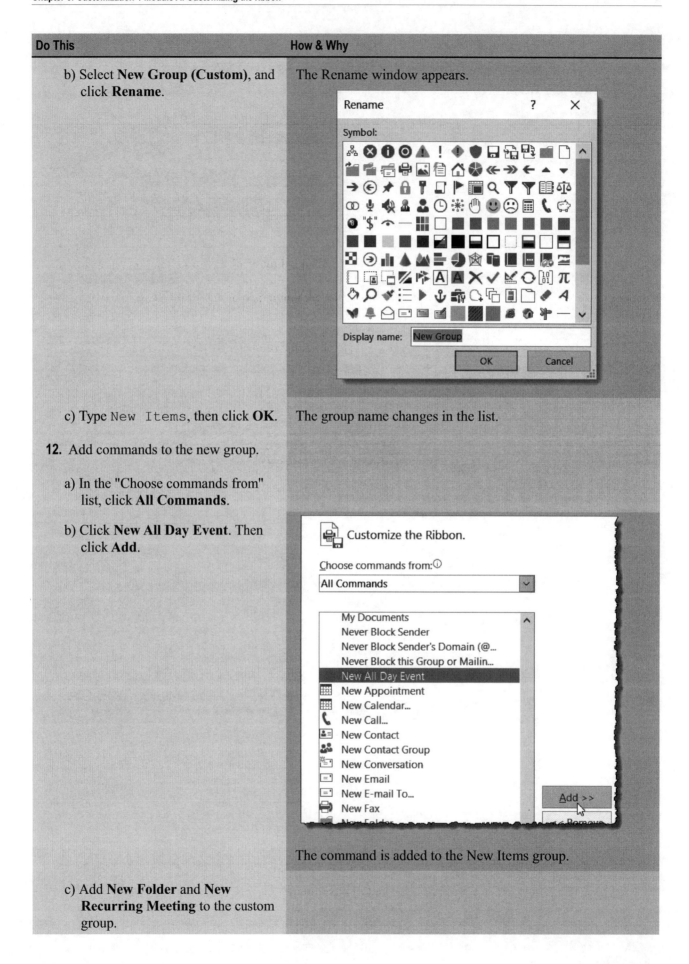

Do This	How & Why
c) Type `New Items`, then click **OK**.	The group name changes in the list.
12. Add commands to the new group.	
a) In the "Choose commands from" list, click **All Commands**.	
b) Click **New All Day Event**. Then click **Add**.	

Do This	How & Why
	The command is added to the New Items group.
c) Add **New Folder** and **New Recurring Meeting** to the custom group.	

Do This	How & Why
13. Select **New Tab (Custom)**, then click ▲ (repeatedly, if necessary) until it appears at the top of the list.	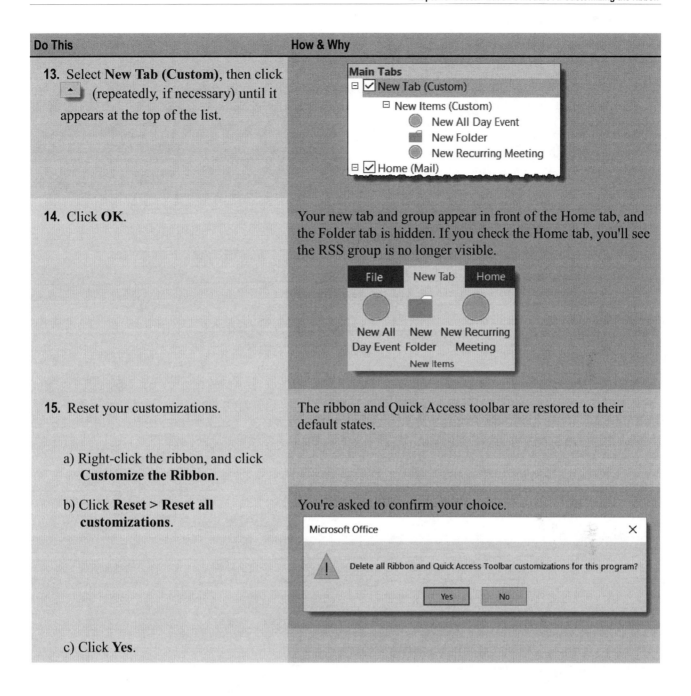
14. Click **OK**.	Your new tab and group appear in front of the Home tab, and the Folder tab is hidden. If you check the Home tab, you'll see the RSS group is no longer visible.
15. Reset your customizations.	The ribbon and Quick Access toolbar are restored to their default states.
a) Right-click the ribbon, and click **Customize the Ribbon**.	
b) Click **Reset > Reset all customizations**.	You're asked to confirm your choice.
c) Click **Yes**.	

Assessment: Customizing the Ribbon

1. True or false? You can still access ribbon commands easily while it's minimized.

   - True
   - False

2. You can customize the ribbon by:

   - Adding commands to an existing group.
   - Adding groups to an existing tab.
   - Removing an existing tab.
   - Removing groups from an existing tab.

3. True or false? To reset all customizations, you must use both the Customize Ribbon and Quick Access Toolbar options.

   - True
   - False

Module B: Customizing Outlook

Because Outlook is an organizer and workspace, rather than an editing tool, you might find it helpful to arrange the application layout to better suit your needs. You can change how panes are displayed, and move or hide features you don't use to make easier access for the ones you rely on.

In this module, you'll learn how to:

- Customize the Outlook interface
- Set language options
- Change Outlook program options

Interface customization

Views and arrangements are a starting point for customization, but the View tab allows you to make more detailed adjustments to both. You can also change the display and contents of the Folder pane, Reading pane, and To-Do bar. As with the rest of the ribbon, the specific options available depend on what part of Outlook you're currently using.

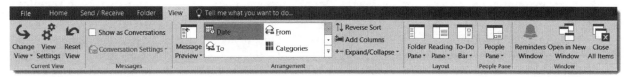

Customizing pane layouts

You can maximize or minimize most of Outlook's panes using the buttons displayed on them, but you can access further customization in the Layout and People Pane groups of the View tab. Each pane has its own specific display options, but you can choose to display or hide everything but the item list itself. Some customizations apply only to the current view, while others will persist through different views.

- Click **Folder Pane** to minimize, expand, or disable the pane. In Mail view you can also choose whether to display your Favorites folders. The Folder pane display changes persist through different views. However, with the Folder pane off, in some cases you might need to use keyboard shortcuts to navigate folders.

    Clicking **Folder Pane > Options** opens the Folder Pane Options window, where you can customize both the display and the order of options. Another way to access these options is by clicking ··· ("overflow") in the Navigation options.

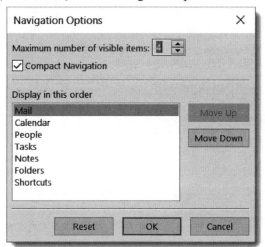

- Click **Reading Pane** to display to the right of the item list or below it. You can also turn it off. Reading pane display settings depend on view: by default, it's shown only in Mail folders and the To-Do List.

    Clicking **Reading Pane > Options** opens the Reading Pane window. There you can change reading options, including whether viewing items in the Reading pane marks them as read.

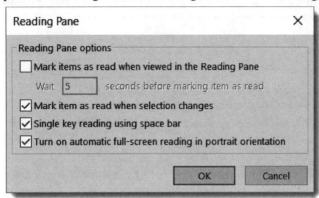

- Click **To-Do Bar** to display Calendar, People (contacts), and/or Tasks peeks, or to disable the bar completely.

- You can also minimize, expand, or disable the **People pane** by clicking it. You can also view **Account Settings**, which display the social network accounts you've integrated with Outlook.

    Although People pane settings persist across views, it displays only when the Reading pane is visible in Mail view, and only on items involving other people. For example, it will appear in a meeting but not an appointment.

- The **Daily Task List** option becomes available only in Calendar view, and is automatically disabled in Month or Schedule views. As with the others, you can choose how to display it, and also how to arrange the tasks it shows.

Viewing conversations

 MOS Outlook Exam Objective(s): 2.4.9

By default, Outlook displays replies and forwarded messages as part of a single conversation. Only the most recent message in the folder is shown as an item. When you select a message, in the main part of the Reading pane, to the right of the Item list, the entire message thread is displayed. At the top of the message thread, options for acting on the message are displayed.

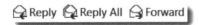

- To expand a conversation, click its expand arrow. You'll then see all messages in the conversation, and can preview or open any of them.

- To turn conversation view off or on, click **Show As Conversations** on the View tab, or right-click the message list header and click **Show As Conversations**. Either way, you'll be prompted whether to change settings for the current folder or for all folders.

- To change how conversations are displayed, in the View tab's Conversations group, click **Conversation Settings**.

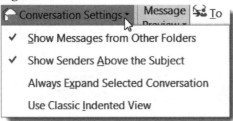

Customizing Outlook Today

If you commonly use Outlook Today, you can customize it to better suit your needs. To do so, in the bottom-right corner of the window, click **Customize Outlook Today**.

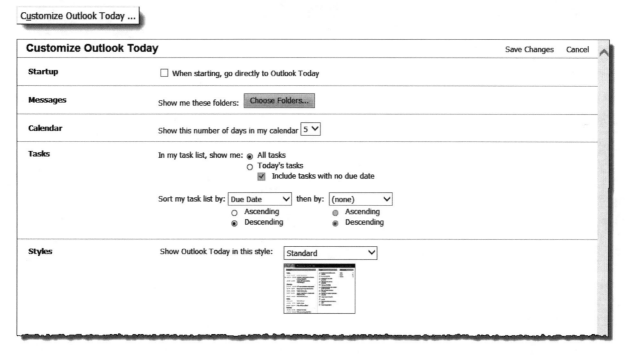

- In Startup, use the check box to go directly to Outlook Today when you start Outlook.
- Click **Choose Folders** to select what folders display in your Messages list.
- In Calendar, select how many days of appointments you want to appear in your Calendar list.
- Use the Tasks section to filter and sort the tasks you want Outlook Today to display.
- Select options from the Styles list to change Outlook Today's appearance.

After you've made all changes, you still need to click **Save Changes** to apply them.

Exercise: Changing your mailbox view

In this exercise, you'll change the appearance of your mailbox.

MOS Outlook Exam Objective(s): MOS 77-884 1.3.2

Do This	How & Why
1. Select your Inbox folder.	
2. Change your pane settings as follows:	All settings are on the View tab.
a) Click **Folder Pane > Minimized**.	
b) Click **Reading Pane > Bottom**.	The Reading pane moves below the item list pane.
c) Click **To-Do Bar > Calendar**, and then click **To-Do Bar > Tasks**.	The To-Do bar opens on the right, displaying the Calendar and Tasks peeks.
3. In the Messages group, click the **Show as Conversations** check box.	A window appears, asking if you want to apply the change to this folder or to all folders.

4. Click **This folder**.

Your mailbox should look something like this:

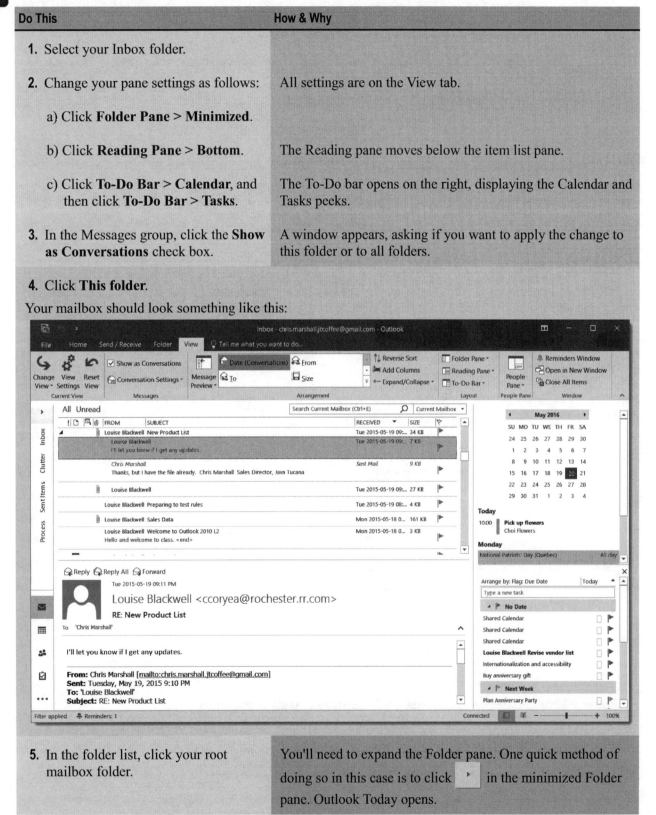

5. In the folder list, click your root mailbox folder.	You'll need to expand the Folder pane. One quick method of doing so in this case is to click ⟩ in the minimized Folder pane. Outlook Today opens.

Do This	How & Why
6. Apply the Winter style to Outlook Today:	
a) Click **Customize Outlook Today**.	To open the customization screen.
b) In the Styles list, click **Winter**.	
c) Click **Save Changes**.	Outlook Today now appears in two-column format with a wintery color theme.
d) Return to your Inbox.	

Changing view settings

If the existing views don't suit your needs, you can customize an existing one. The Advanced View Settings window lets you change displayed columns, grouping, sorting, filtering, formatting, and other settings.

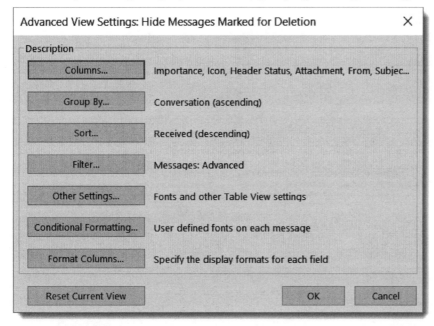

1. Select the view you want to use as a starting point for customization.
2. In the View tab's Current View group, click **View Settings**.

The Advanced View Settings window opens.

3. Use the buttons on the left to change view settings. Each opens its own window with a set of options.
4. When you've finished making changes, click **OK**.

If you want to return to the original view, you can open the window again, and click **Reset Current View**.

Customizing columns

In list type views, you can change what columns are displayed and their order. To do so, on the View tab's Arrange group, click **Add Columns**.

This opens the Show Columns window, which shows currently displayed columns on the right and available columns on the left.

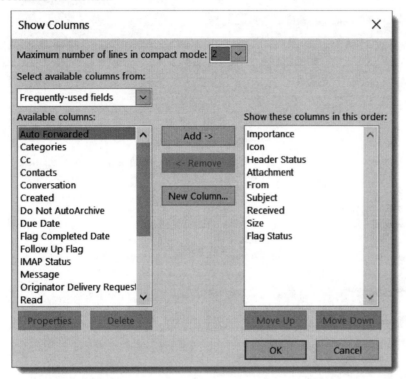

You can then customize the list.

- To change a column's display order, select it in the right list, and click **Move Up** or **Move Down**.
- To remove a column, select it, and click **Remove**.
    You can select multiple fields by pressing and holding **Ctrl**.
- To add a column, in the "Select available columns from" list, select a category. Then, on the left, select a field, and click **Add**.
- To create a new column, click **New Column**. You'll then be prompted to choose a name, type, and format.
- When you've finished making changes, click **OK**.

Managing views

 MOS Outlook Exam Objective(s): 1.1.4

When you customize existing views or create your own, you might want to save the changes you've made, or undo them. You can do so using the View tab's Current View group.

- Click **Change View > Save Current View As a New View** to save your current view settings.

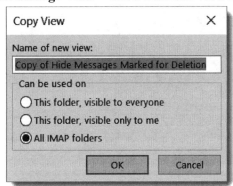

- Click **Change View > Apply Current View to Other Mail Folders** to apply a view to any folders of the current type.

    The exact command name depends on the type of folder you're viewing: mail, contacts, tasks, and so on.

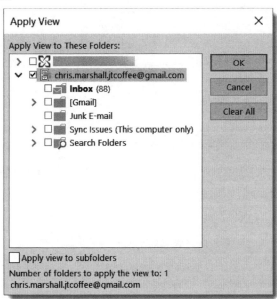

- Click **Reset View** to return your current view to its default settings.
- Click **Change View** > **Manage Views** to view more options.

The Manage All Views window provides detailed tools for creating, modifying, and renaming views.

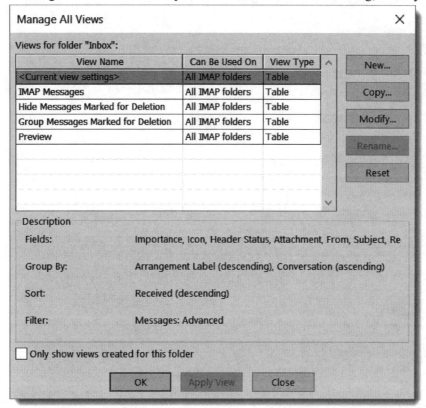

Exercise: Customizing your inbox list

In this exercise, you'll customize the columns displayed in your inbox and save it as a new view.

Do This	How & Why
1. Select your Inbox folder.	First, you're going to display the sensitivity level of messages in your inbox, so you know when the sender has marked them as personal.
2. On the View tab, click **Add Columns**.	Look in the Arrangement group. The Show Columns window appears.
3. Place the Sensitivity column just after Importance: a) In the Available Columns list, click **Sensitivity**.	
b) Click **Add**.	Sensitivity is added to the bottom of the right list.

Do This	How & Why
c) Click **Move Up** repeatedly, until Sensitivity is listed just below Importance.	
d) Click **OK**.	The Sensitivity field now appears in your message list. 
4. Save your current view as `Importance View`.	
a) Click **Change View > Save Current View As a New View**.	The Copy View window opens.
b) Type `Importance View`.	By default, this view will apply to "All Mail and Post folders" (or "All IMAP folders"). You'll accept this option.
c) Click **OK**.	The window closes, saving your changes.
5. Click **Change View**.	Importance View is now displayed in the view options. 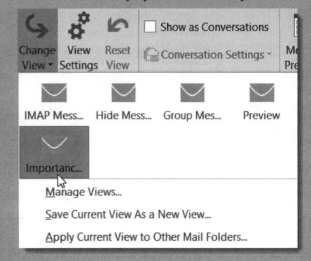

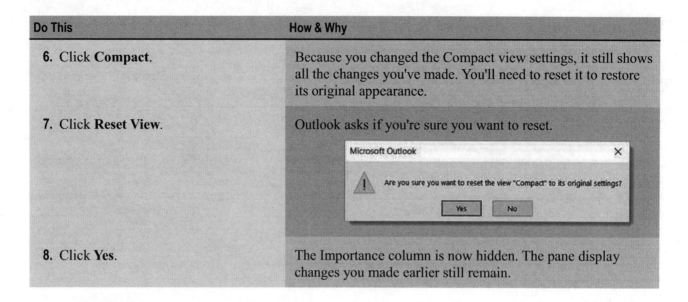

Do This	How & Why
6. Click **Compact**.	Because you changed the Compact view settings, it still shows all the changes you've made. You'll need to reset it to restore its original appearance.
7. Click **Reset View**.	Outlook asks if you're sure you want to reset.
8. Click **Yes**.	The Importance column is now hidden. The pane display changes you made earlier still remain.

Outlook Options

The Outlook Options window contains a wide variety of other settings you can use to configure Outlook's appearance and behavior. Although some of them are also available in the ribbon or other parts of Outlook, not all of them are. If you can't figure out how to change a setting, try looking in Outlook Options, which you can access on the File tab by clicking **Options**.

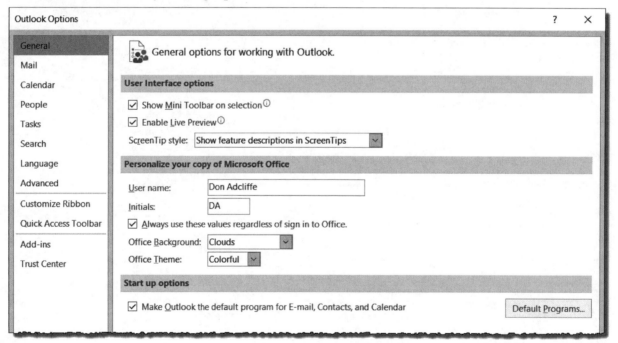

The left pane of the window displays a list of sections, while the right displays a list of options from the current section.

General   Settings related to general user interface and start up options. You can also set your user name and initials here.

Mail   Settings related to creating and receiving messages. This section contains options such as default message formats and settings, editor options, and how you're notified when new mail arrives.

Calendar   Settings related to calendars and scheduling. This section contains options for calendar display, work hours, and time zones.

General	Settings related to general user interface and start up options. You can also set your user name and initials here.
People	Settings related to how contacts are displayed.
Tasks	Settings related to tasks, such as appearance, reminder settings, and working hours used for tasks.
Search	Settings for Instant Search, including where Outlook searches, how it compiles its search index, and how search results are displayed.
Language	Language settings, for both the Outlook interface and the editor.
Advanced	Includes send and receive options, dialup collections, reminders, international options, and others.
Customize Ribbon	Settings for ribbon customization.
Quick Access Toolbar	Settings for customizing the Quick Access toolbar.
Add-Ins	Tools to list and display the Office Add-Ins used by Outlook.
Trust Center	Contains links to Microsoft's privacy and security documentation, and the Trust Center window, which lets you change Outlook's security settings.

Exercise: Exploring Outlook Options

In this activity, you'll view the various sections of the Outlook Options window.

Do This	How & Why
1. On the File tab, click Options.	The Outlook Options window opens, with the General section selected.
2. Click each item down the left pane of the window.	Look briefly over each section. Try to spot which settings control Outlook features you've already used, and which are unfamiliar.
3. When you reach the Trust Center section, click **Trust Center Settings**.	You probably won't need to change Outlook's security settings, but it's an example of the additional windows and tools you can find in Outlook Options. The Trust Center window opens.
4. Click **OK** twice.	To close the Trust Center and Outlook Options windows.

Assessment: Customizing Outlook

1. What options setting *isn't* on the View tab?

    - Conversation Settings
    - Navigation Pane
    - Outlook Today
    - People Pane

2. True or false? When viewing a conversation, you can even preview or open items not in the current folder.

    - True
    - False

3. What settings can you access from the Advanced View Options window?

    - Add-Ins
    - Columns
    - Conversations
    - Group by

4. You can most easily open Outlook Options from the:

    - File tab
    - Home tab
    - Outlook Today screen
    - View tab

Summary: Customization

In this chapter, you learned how to:

- Hide, rearrange, and add commands to the ribbon and Quick Access toolbar
- Customize the Outlook interface, change view settings, and access program options

Synthesis: Customization

In this exercise, you'll customize Outlook to better suit your needs.

1. Create a new ribbon tab with at least one group. Add a number of commands you might want all in one place.

2. Add at least one command you use frequently to the Quick Access toolbar.

3. Create a new List view for your contacts folder, and modify it to your liking.
   Consider adding or rearranging columns, changing grouping and sorting, or even applying new formatting options.

Chapter 7: Organizing Outlook

You will learn how to:

- Create and manage email accounts
- Organize Outlook items using folders
- Organize Outlook items using categories
- Use advanced searching and filtering options
- Use Quick Steps

Module A: Account management

Especially if you use Outlook on your own computer, you might need to add or configure email accounts.

You will learn:

- About the types of email account supported by Outlook
- How to add an account
- How to change account settings

Email accounts

In order to send and receive messages, Outlook must have an email account configured. This may seem obvious, but especially in the workplace you might have your account set up by an IT technician and never have to worry about it. If you're setting up or managing Outlook yourself, you'll need to set up your account and make any later configuration changes.

You can also configure Outlook to use multiple email accounts, for example, if you use both personal and business accounts on the same computer. Multiple accounts aren't difficult to manage, but they require you to be aware of which account you're using when viewing or sending messages.

Account types

There are three common protocols used for receiving email: Microsoft Exchange, POP3, and IMAP. Outlook supports all three types, but each has different features and configuration options.

POP3, or Post Office Protocol version 3, is an older but still popular format for internet email accounts. It's the simplest of the three: the mail server stores incoming messages until a client such as Outlook retrieves them, and then they're stored locally in Outlook. By default, when you retrieve messages from a POP3 account, they're then deleted from the server. This means that you don't have to worry about storage space limits on the server, as long as you check your messages regularly. Years ago, when most accounts had strict space limits, this was a pretty big advantage. However, the drawback is that it effectively ties POP3 accounts to a single computer: if you're like many users and access the same email account from home, work, and your phone, POP3 accounts can be complicated to use.

IMAP, or Internet Message Access Protocol (currently version 4), is an increasingly popular standard for Internet email accounts. Although you can still download messages to your client for offline browsing, all messages are retained on the mail server until you delete them. This allows you to easily access the same account from multiple devices, and even see what messages you've read or replied to from another device. The obvious drawback is that IMAP accounts require more server resources, but because today even free email accounts often offer gigabytes of storage, this isn't a problem for most users. Additionally, an IMAP account might use its own folder structure, separate from your default Outlook mailbox. This isn't necessarily a drawback, but is something with which you might need to become familiar.

Microsoft Exchange, also called MAPI, or Exchange ActiveSync, is a proprietary protocol used by Microsoft Exchange servers. It's most often used by companies that own their own Exchange servers, or Microsoft web services like Outlook.com or Office 365. Exchange is used for more than just email, also allowing you to synchronize calendars, contacts, and other information between multiple clients. As with IMAP, messages are stored on the server by default, though there are options for online storage.

Although Microsoft Exchange accounts send email as well as receive it, POP3 and IMAP accounts both send mail using *SMTP*, or Simple Mail Transfer Protocol. This matters less for most users, but can be important to know when you set up an account.

Adding accounts

Before adding a new email account to Outlook, you must make sure you have all relevant information. For some accounts, you might need to know only your address and password, and Outlook will be able to automatically configure the rest. For others, you might need specific server and settings information, or you might need to use your browser to configure server settings for your account. Your email provider may offer a specific procedure for Outlook configuration; if so, you should use that instead of the general one.

 MOS Outlook Exam Objective(s): 1.1.6

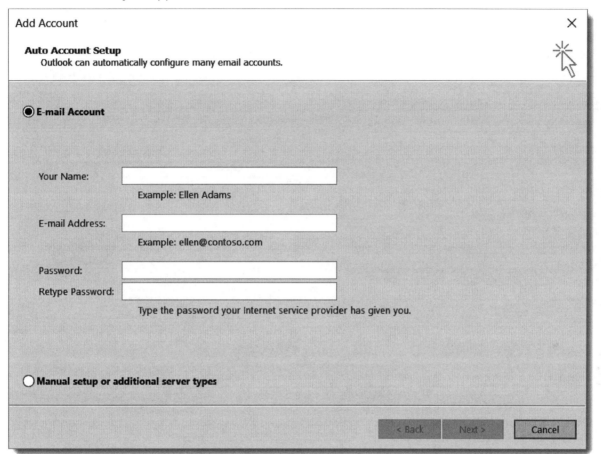

1. In Backstage view, click **Add Account**.

   The **Add Account** window opens.

2. Choose between automatic and manual configuration:

   - If you think automatic setup might work with your account, enter your name, full email address, and password. Then click **Next**. Outlook will attempt to automatically configure your account. Follow the on-screen instructions.

   - If automatic setup for a POP3 or IMAP account fails, or if your account information specifies custom settings, click **Manually configure server settings or additional server types**. Then click **Next**.

   - If automatic setup for a Microsoft Exchange account fails, you'll need to quit Outlook and add it manually from the Control Panel.

Manually configuring POP3 and IMAP accounts

Manually configuring your account requires additional information. At the least, you'll also need to know your incoming POP3 or IMAP server, and your outgoing SMTP server. You may also need to set ports, encryption type, and whether your outgoing server requires authorization. Your email provider should be able to provide all this information.

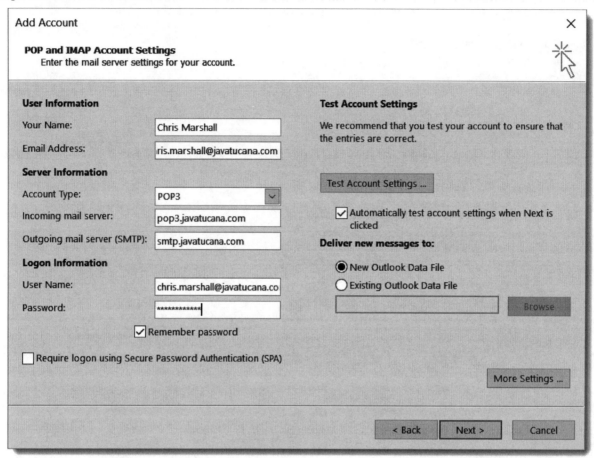

It's the same basic process to manually configure both POP3 and IMAP accounts, though there are some differences between the two.

1. In the **Add Account** window, click **Manual setup or additional server types**, and then click **Next**.
   To open the Choose Service pane.

2. Click **POP or IMAP**, and then click **Next**.
   To open the POP and IMAP Account Settings pane.

3. Enter your account information in the labeled fields:

   - Make sure that the user name matches your provider's instructions exactly. If your user name is supposed to be "student01@javatucana.com," simply entering "student01" won't work.

   - When you set up a POP3 account, you can decide whether to attach the account to an existing Outlook data file or create a new one. IMAP accounts always create a new data file.

   - If you need to change additional settings, click **More Settings**. This opens a new window with several tabs, showing settings specific to your account type.

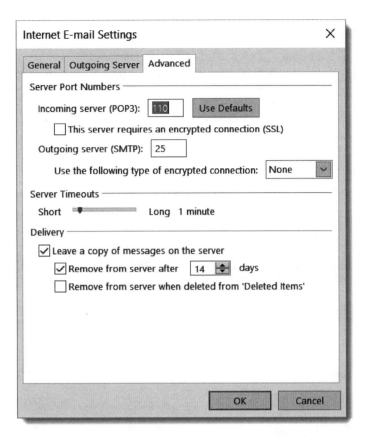

- To test your current settings, click **Test Account Settings**. Outlook will send itself a test message using the account.

4. When your account is configured, click **Next**.

    If you've already tested the account and found it working, first clear the **Test Account Settings by clicking the Next button** check box.

5. Click **Finish** to close the wizard.

Manually configuring Exchange accounts

You can't manually configure a new Microsoft Exchange account while Outlook is running. Instead, in Windows 10, click **Start > All apps > Mail** to open the **Mail** window; then click **Add account** to open the **Choose an account** window. From here, you can access and create Exchange (or Outlook.com) accounts without opening Outlook. For earlier Windows versions, click **E-Mail Accounts** in the Control Panel Mail settings.

1. In Windows 10, click **Start > All apps > Mail**.

    The **Mail** window opens.

2. Click **Add account**.

    The **Choose an account** window opens.

3. Click **Exchange** or **Outlook.com**.

    To configure a Microsoft Exchange or Outlook.com account, respectively.

4. Enter your account settings.

    You'll need the server name and user name. If your administrator's instructed you to do so, you can click **More Settings**.

5. Click **Next**, then **Finish**.

Changing account settings

MOS Outlook Exam Objective(s): 1.1.5

You can change account settings at any time from the **Account Settings** window. Although you can't change one account type to another without removing and remaking it, you can change almost anything else.

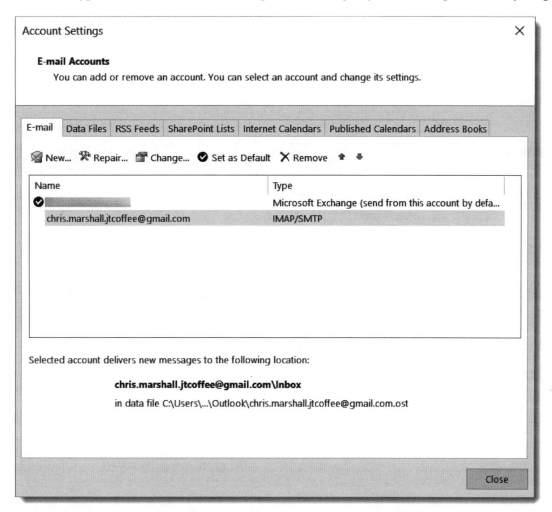

1. In Backstage view, click **Account Settings > Account Settings** to open the **Account Settings** window.
2. On the E-mail tab, select the account you want to change.
   - To make an account the default for sending new messages, click **Set as Default**.
   - To change the inbox folder for a POP3 account, click **Change Folder**.
   - To make any other changes, such as server settings, click **Change**.
   - To delete an account, click **Remove**. You'll be asked to confirm the action.

Exercise: Viewing account settings

These steps assume you have a POP or IMAP account. If you're using an Exchange account, the steps might differ. You'll view your account settings.

Do This	How & Why
1. In Backstage View, click **Account Settings > Account Settings**	To access Backstage View, click the ribbon's **File** tab. The **Account Settings** window opens.
2. On the E-mail tab, observe the account listing.	The name and type of each account is shown. There is a check mark next to the default account.
3. If necessary, click your default account.	To select it.
4. Click **Change**.	The **Change Account** window opens.
5. Observe the account settings.	
a) If it's a POP or IMAP account, compare the E-mail Address and User Name fields.	Depending on your account, they might be identical, or different.
b) Click **More Settings**.	A new window opens with multiple settings tabs. You can view these if you want, but don't change anything.
c) Click **OK**.	The More Settings window closes.
6. Click **Cancel**, then click **Close**.	To return to Outlook.

Assessment: Account management

1. What account type is generally meant to be accessed from just one device? Choose the best response.

    - IMAP

    - Microsoft Exchange

    - POP3

    - SMTP

2. True or false? You might need to close Outlook to add an account.

    - True

    - False

3. True or false? To change most account settings, you'll need to delete and recreate the account.

    - True

    - False

Module B: Using folders

One way you can better organize your Outlook items is by using folders.

You will learn:

- About Outlook folders
- How to create folders
- How to move items between folders

About folders

Outlook items are stored inside *folders*, which in turn are stored inside an Outlook data file. This is somewhat similar to how files are stored in folders on your computer, but it's not exactly the same.

Much as on a hard drive, you can create folders inside a data file, move items between them, move items or folders from one data file to another, and even place folders inside of other folders. Unlike a hard drive, on which any folder can contain any type of file, an Outlook folder can only contain one type of item. For example, the Inbox folder only holds messages, and the Calendar folder only holds calendar items. You can tell the type of item a folder holds by its icon.

By default, the Outlook data file holds a folder for each type of item: Inbox for mail you receive, Calendar for appointments and meetings, Contacts, Tasks, and so on. It also has some more specialized folders, such as Drafts for messages you haven't sent, and Suggested Contacts for people you've sent messages to but not yet designated as contacts. These may be all you need, but if you want to better organize items, you can create your own folders to store your items.

A folder list, showing two new folders nested inside default folders

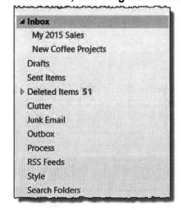

You can create folders, and manage existing ones, using the ribbon's Folder tab. As with other tabs, the Folder tab's commands depend on the area of Outlook you're in and what kind of folder you're already viewing. You can also access many of the same commands in the context menu that's displayed when you right-click a folder or item.

The Folder tab

Creating folders

 MOS Outlook Exam Objective(s): 2.4.3

When you create a folder, you need to choose a name, and specify what kind of folder it is and where you want to place it in the data file. You do so from the **Create New Folder** window.

1. On the ribbon, click **New Folder**; or right-click any folder in the Folder pane, and click **New Folder**. In Calendar view, the command will be named **New Calendar**, but it still has the same effect.

   The **Create New Folder** window opens.

2. In the Name field, type a name for the new folder.

3. From the Folder contains list, select the type of items you want to store.

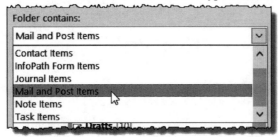

4. Select a destination for the new folder.

   If you don't want to place the new folder inside an existing one, click the data file itself at the top of the list.

5. Click **OK**.

Moving items to a folder

You can move items between folders simply by dragging them to another folder of the same type. Dragging to a folder of a different type doesn't move the original, but instead takes action on it; for example, dragging a contact to a mail folder creates a message addressed to that contact, while dragging a message to your calendar creates a new appointment based on it.

To have more control, you can instead use the Move menu, located on the Home tab or in the context menu you see when right-clicking an item.

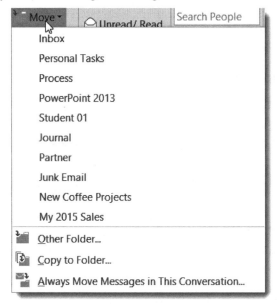

If the folder to which you want to move items isn't in the list, you can click **Other Folder** to open the **Move Items** window. Note that if you try moving an item to a different type of folder, it won't actually move it, but will act as though you dragged it there.

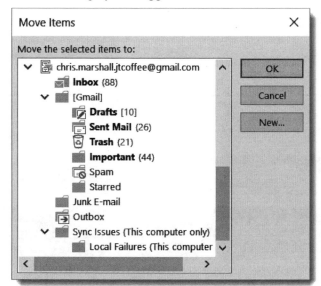

1. Select one or more items in a folder.

    To select multiple items, hold down **Shift** or **Ctrl** before clicking them.

2. On the Home tab, click **Move**.

3. Select a destination.

    - If the folder you want is in the list, click it to move the items.

    - If the folder isn't listed, click **Other Folder** to open the **Move Items** window.

4. In the **Move Items** window, select the destination folder, and click **OK**.

    You can instead click **New** to create a new destination folder.

Copying items to a folder

Copying items to a folder is just like moving them, except that the **Move Items** window is replaced by the nearly identical **Copy Items** window. Remember that simply dragging items to another folder of the same type moves them instead of copying, but you can instead right-click as you drag, which opens a context menu, from which you can choose from many options, including Move and Copy.

1. Select one or more items.

2. On the Folder tab or in the context menu, click **Move > Copy to Folder**.
    To access the context menu, right-click on the selected item(s).

3. In the **Copy Items** window, select the destination folder.

4. Click **OK**.

Managing folders

You can manage folders themselves in the same way that you can items within a folder. You can manipulate them by dragging, or use commands on the Folder tab or context menu.

Note that although you can copy the default folders included with Outlook, you can't move, rename, or delete them.

- To move a folder, drag it, or click **Move Folder**.

- To copy a folder with all its contents, right-click it; then drag it, or click **Copy Folder**.
    If you copy a folder to its current location, it will append a number to the end of its name to differentiate it from the original, such as "My Folder1."

- To rename a folder, click **Rename Folder**, then type the new name. You can instead click it, and after a brief pause, click it again.

- To delete a folder, click **Delete Folder** and then click **Yes** to confirm the deletion; or simply drag it to the Deleted Items folder.

Exercise: Using folders

For this exercise, you'll need to have received the Sales Data message from your instructor. You can instead complete this exercise with any other message. You'll create a folder, move items into it, and then manipulate the folder itself.

Do This	How & Why
1. In your Inbox, create a current year sales folder.	
a) On the Folder tab, click **New Folder**.	You can instead right-click any folder, then click **New Folder**. The **Create New Folder** window opens.
b) In the Name field, type `2016 Sales`.	Or use the current year.
c) From the Folder Contains list, select **Mail and Post Items**.	If necessary.
d) In the folder list, click **Inbox**.	

Do This	How & Why
e) Click **OK**.	The 2016 Sales folder is now inside your Inbox. You might have to expand your Inbox folder to see it.
2. Copy the Sales Data message into the new folder.	If you were to move it, you could just drag it there, but you'll have to use another method.
a) Select the message.	
b) On the Home tab, click **Move** > **Copy to Folder**.	You could instead right-click it, then drag it. The **Copy Items** window opens, containing a list of all your folders.
c) Click **2016 Sales**, then click **OK**.	
3. Click the **2016 Sales** folder.	A copy of the Sales Data message is in the folder.
4. Make a copy of the folder in the same location.	
a) On the Folder tab, click **Copy Folder**.	The **Copy Folder** window appears.
b) Click **Inbox**, then click **OK**.	Because you copied it to the same location as the original, the copy is named "2016 Sales1."
5. Rename the new folder My 2016 Sales.	
a) Click **2016 Sales1**.	Notice that the message inside was also copied.
b) Click **Rename Folder**.	
c) Type `My 2016 Sales`.	
6. Delete the 2016 Sales folder.	
a) Select the folder.	
b) Click **Delete Folder**.	A confirmation window appears.
c) Click **Yes** to confirm the deletion.	The folder is now moved to the Deleted Items folder.

Assessment: Using folders

1. True or false? An Outlook folder is specialized for one type of item.

   - True
   - False

2. What happens when you drag a contact into a calendar folder? Choose the best response.

   - A meeting is scheduled with that contact.
   - The contact is copied to your calendar.
   - The contact is moved to your calendar.
   - You receive an error message.

3. True or false? You should be careful not to delete standard Outlook folders, like Sent Items, by mistake.

   - True
   - False

Module C: Categorizing items

Color categories are another way to organize your Outlook items.

You will learn:

- About categories
- How to assign categories to items
- How to sort or search by category

About categories

You don't need folders to sort and classify your items. You can instead assign *color categories* to items, which visibly mark them and thus allow you to easily sort or find items by category. Each category has a name and color. For example, you can make a blue "Sales" category, and then assign it to all your sales-related messages. You can even assign multiple categories to one item, if applicable.

A message with a category assigned

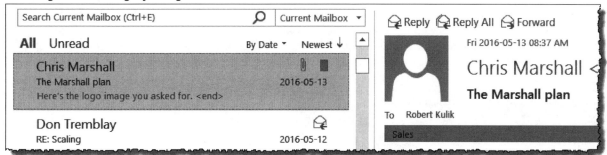

You can assign a category to any type of item, and the same category list is used for all items. So, for example, if you were to make a "Personal" category, you could use it for messages, contacts, and calendar items.

When you assign a category to an item, the item's appearance changes, depending on how you view it.

- Items in list views, such as message or task folders, have a Category column. Depending on the exact view, you might see the category name and color, or just the color.

- Notes and calendar entries change color entirely to match their categories. If more than one category is assigned to an item, it will assume the color of the most recent category assigned.

- Some views, such as a contact's Business Card view, don't show categories at all. However, even in this view, you can still assign or search by categories.

- When you open a categorized item, the category name and color will appear just below the ribbon.

Assigning categories

By default, Outlook has a number of categories already defined. Clicking a category assigns it to the item, and clicking it again removes it. The **Clear All Categories** option removes all categories from that item.

The Categorize menu on the Home tab

The first time you use a particular category, the **Rename Category** window appears. You can use it to change the category's name or color, or to assign it a shortcut key. Renaming a category is optional, but naming it, for example, "Personal" would make it easier to remember than "Red Category."

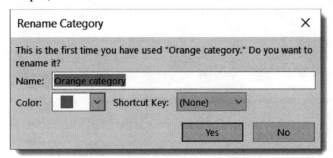

You can access the Categorize menu multiple ways, depending on which you find most convenient.

- On the Home tab, in the Tags group, click **Categorize**.
- Right-click an item, and point to **Categorize**.
- To change an item's category, right-click its current categorization, and click **Categorize** in the context menu.

Setting Quick Click

If you use one category most often, or are setting a lot of items to a single category at once, you can set a *Quick Click* category. Then, you can assign it to an item in any list view by simply clicking in the Category column.

1. Click **Categorize > Set Quick Click**.
2. In the **Set Quick Click** window, choose a category from the list.
3. Click **OK**.

Managing categories

For more detailed management of your categories, you can use the **Color Categories** window. It allows you to assign categories to items, as well as create, modify, or delete categories.

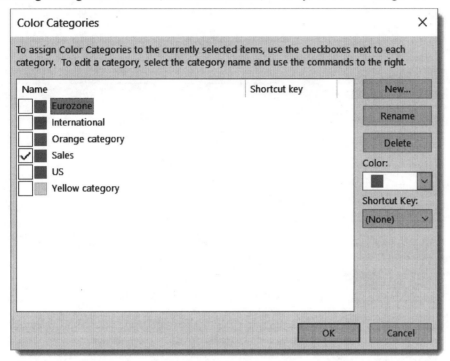

1. Select one or more items.
2. Click **Categorize > All Categories**
3. Make changes in the **Color Categories** window.

   - To assign a category to selected items, check that category.

   - To modify a category, assigned or not, click it. You can then use the **Rename** button or assign it a new color or shortcut key from their respective lists.

   - To delete a category, click it to select it, then click **Delete**.

   - To create a new category, click **New**. You'll have to choose a name and color.

4. After making all changes, click **OK** to save them.

Exercise: Assigning categories

To complete this exercise, you'll need to have the sales team contacts in your Contacts folder, and the Sales Data message from your instructor. You'll define categories and assign them to items.

Do This	How & Why
1. Create a blue "Sales" category, and assign it to the Sales Data message.	
a) In your Inbox, click the Sales Data message from your instructor.	To select the message.
b) Click **Categorize > Blue Category**.	The **Rename Category** window appears.
c) In the Name field, type Sales.	
d) Click **Yes**.	

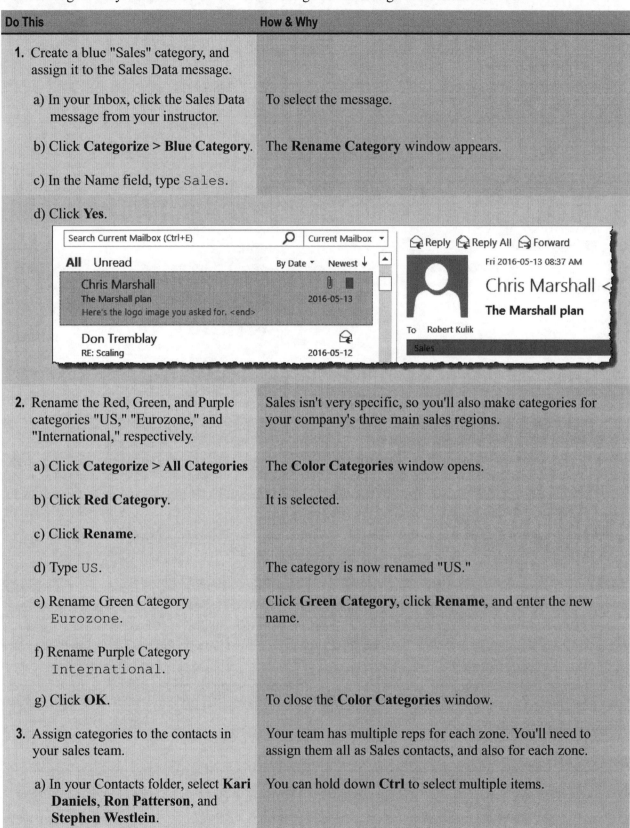

2. Rename the Red, Green, and Purple categories "US," "Eurozone," and "International," respectively.	Sales isn't very specific, so you'll also make categories for your company's three main sales regions.
a) Click **Categorize > All Categories**	The **Color Categories** window opens.
b) Click **Red Category**.	It is selected.
c) Click **Rename**.	
d) Type US.	The category is now renamed "US."
e) Rename Green Category Eurozone.	Click **Green Category**, click **Rename**, and enter the new name.
f) Rename Purple Category International.	
g) Click **OK**.	To close the **Color Categories** window.
3. Assign categories to the contacts in your sales team.	Your team has multiple reps for each zone. You'll need to assign them all as Sales contacts, and also for each zone.
a) In your Contacts folder, select **Kari Daniels**, **Ron Patterson**, and **Stephen Westlein**.	You can hold down **Ctrl** to select multiple items.

Do This	How & Why
b) Click **Categorize > US**	Notice that the categories you created are now in the list, and because you've already set them up, you're not prompted to rename them. The US category is assigned to the three US sales reps. Because you're in Business Card view, the change isn't immediately visible.
c) Assign the Sales category to the three reps.	They should still be selected, so click **Categorize > Sales**.
d) Assign the **Sales** and **Eurozone** categories to Donna Franklin, Gina Hernandez, Ian Sanches, and Rose Schiller.	Select the contacts, then assign both categories to them.
e) Assign the **Sales** and **International** categories to Louise Blackwell, Malcolm Lloyd, and Kevin McCanney.	
4. Switch to List view.	In the Current View gallery, click **Change View > List**. You may need to scroll right to see the Category column.

Using categories

Once you've assigned categories, you can use them to help organize your items. Even without taking any other steps, you can use color to look for items in a category. In most list views, you can also arrange items by category to sort them. You can also search a folder by category, to find items only in that category.

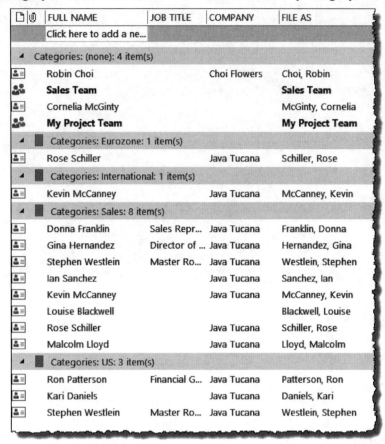

Arranging items by category

You can arrange items by category in most list views. You can't do so with non-list views, such as Calendar or Business Card views. Note that if multiple categories are assigned to an item, the item will appear multiple times in the arranged list, once for each category.

1. Select a list view, if necessary.

2. Click the **CATEGORIES** column header. Or, on the Home tab, in the Arrangement gallery, click **Categories**.

The contacts list is sorted by category.

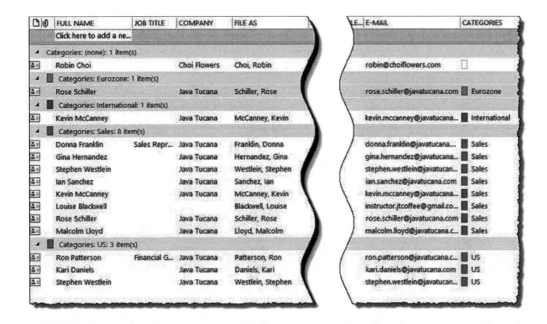

Searching items by category

You don't need to display a list view to search for items by a specific category. Rather, you can do so wherever the Instant Search box is available.

1. In any folder, click in the Instant Search box.

    This activates the ribbon's Search tab.

2. On the Search tab, click **Categorized**, then click whatever category you want to search for.

    You can instead search for items belonging to any category, or for uncategorized items.

If you want to change your search to items of a different category, you'll have to clear the existing search first. Otherwise, the search will display only those items belonging to both categories.

Exercise: Using categories

To perform this exercise, you need to have completed the previous "Assigning categories" exercise. You'll arrange your contacts by category, then search for contacts in a specific category.

Do This	How & Why
1. In People view, select **List** view.	If necessary, in the Current View gallery, click **List**.
2. On the View tab, in the Arrangement gallery, click **Categories**.	Your contacts are now arranged by category.
3. Observe the Sales category.	Each member of the Sales category is also listed in the Eurozone, International, or US categories.
4. Switch to Business Card view.	Use the Home tab's Current View gallery.
5. Click the **View** tab.	The Arrangement gallery is unavailable, so you can't arrange this view by categories. You'll perform a search instead.
6. Click in the Instant Search box.	You can instead press **Ctrl+E**. The ribbon's Search tab is now active.
7. In the Refine group, click **Categorized > International**.	Now only the three International contacts are displayed: Louise Blackwell, Malcolm Lloyd, and Kevin McCanney.
8. Click **Close Search**.	The search closes, and all your contacts are again visible.

Assessment: Categorizing items

1. True or false? Each item type has its own category listing.

   - True
   - False

2. What do you need to do the first time you use a category? Choose the best response.

   - Assign it a shortcut key.
   - Assign it an unused color.
   - Choose other items to which to apply it.
   - Confirm its name and color.

3. True or false? You can search and arrange by category regardless of the current folder view.

   - True
   - False

Module D: Searching and filtering

Once you've used Outlook for a while, you'll likely accumulate so many items that finding the ones you need can be a challenge. Fortunately, Outlook has a number of searching and filtering tools to help you organize your data.

You will learn:

- How to use the Search tab to refine Instant Searches
- About Advanced Find
- How to apply and remove filters
- How to create search folders

The Search tab

When you activate Instant Search by clicking in the field or pressing **Ctrl+E**, the Search tab becomes active on the ribbon. It contains commands that give you more control over search options.

The Search tab, while viewing a mail folder

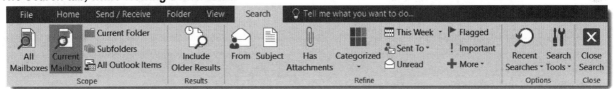

The Search tab contains five groups.

Scope   Commands to specify the folders in which you want to search.

Results   The Include Older Results option, when available, allows you to select previous search strings.

Refine   Commands to search for or within specific properties of items. Other than the Categorized menu, the contents of this group depend on the kind of folder you're viewing.

Options   Commands for repeating past searches, conducting more advanced search operations, or configuring Outlook's search options.

Close   The Close Search command, which ends the current search and closes the Search tab.

Change search scope

Every search has a *scope*, the area the search covers. If you want to change it, you can use commands in the Scope group. Each Navigation view has its own arrangement of options available in the Scope group. For example, Mail view has options relevant to mailboxes and folders, while People view has options relevant to contacts.

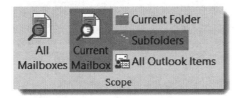

- If you have multiple mailboxes, **Current Mailbox** is the default, but you can return to it if you've changed it and don't like the results.
- If you have multiple mailboxes, click **All Mailboxes** to search in all of them.

- Click **Current Folder** to search within the currently displayed folder.

- Click **Subfolders** to search in the current folder and all its subfolders.

- Click **All Outlook Items** to search all of Outlook. This will make the Refine group show Mail folder fields, even if you're not already in a mail folder.

Refining searches

You can use the commands in the Refine group to search for, or within, certain properties of items. This can be a great help when your initial search turns up too many—or too confusing—results. For example, you might want to narrow a search to those messages with attachments, or you might want to look for meetings with "June" in their title, but not those merely organized by your coworker named June.

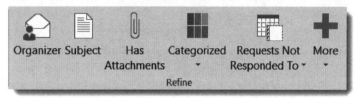

The specific commands available in the Refine group depend on the type of folder you're viewing, but only because different types of items have different properties: you can't search contacts for a due date, as you would tasks, for example. Otherwise, searches work the same way for all folders.

Another important thing to remember is that every Refine command you use simply inserts additional criteria as text, separated by a space, into the Instant Search box, along with what you've already entered. You can type them all out yourself for the same result, once you know the common search syntax. Editing or deleting refinements you've already added is even easier.

The result of using the From, Has Attachments, and Categorize criteria in the Refine group

Searching effectively can be a complex skill, and exactly what you have to do depends on your needs. Knowing just how each refinement works will help you design precise searches in large folders.

- Some commands will simply look for the existence of a flag or property. For example, **Has Attachments** will find items with any kind of attachment, and **Has Business Phone** will display any contact whose Business Phone property isn't blank. An advanced trick is to use the commands that follow for further editing. Also, in Calendar view you see the **Organizer** option; in Mail view, the corresponding options becomes **From**.

- Some commands will require you to add additional keywords. For example, if you click **Subject**, you'll then need to type the subject you're looking for. subject:(keywords) 🔎 The cursor will automatically be placed where you need to type, but depending on the command it might be in the Instant Search field or in a separate field below it.

- If the property by which you want to search isn't visible in the Refine group, click **More**.

- When you type a search item or keyword, the search results will include any word that *begins* with your input. For example, if you search message subjects for "sal" your results would include messages titled "Today's Sales" or "Salmon Fishing," but not "Basalt Tiles."

- Every refinement you add to a search narrows it further; the displayed results will meet all search criteria. If adding another term narrows the search too far, manually delete it from the box, or close the search and start over.

Repeating recent searches

The Recent Searches menu, in the Options group, shows the last 10 searches you've made. There's a different Recent Searches list for each folder type, so if you click it when searching contacts, it won't show past searches you've made in message folders.

Note: If you want to include the results of previous searches, you can use the **Include Older Results** option in the Results group, if available.

1. Activate the Search tab.
2. Click **Recent Searches** to open the menu.
3. Click the past search you want to repeat.

Using Advanced Find

If the Scope and Refine tools aren't enough for you to get the search results you want, you can try the **Advanced Find** window. While more complicated than the Instant Search field, it provides a more powerful interface and allows you to search for almost any combination of search criteria you can think of. Unlike Instant Search, it doesn't begin searching as you type; instead, you first enter all your criteria, then perform the search.

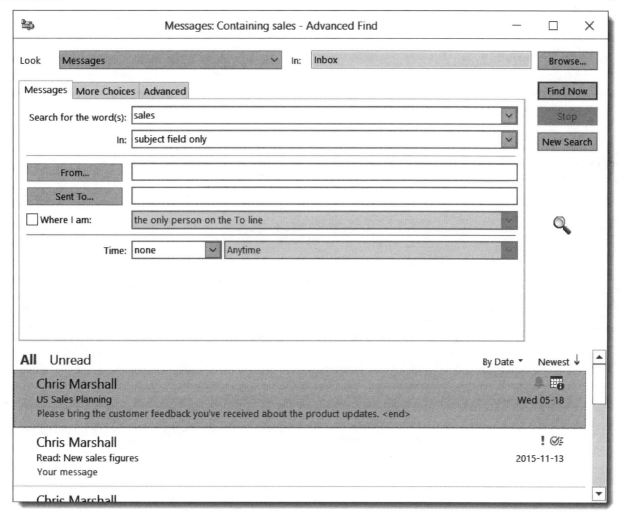

MOS Outlook Exam Objective(s): 1.3.3

1. On the Search tab, click **Search Tools > Advanced Find**.

2. From the Look for list, choose what type of content you're searching for.

You can choose Outlook item types like messages or tasks, or even Outlook or Office file types.

This changes both the default location to search, and the first tab of the window.

3. Refine your search further.

- Click **Browse** to select which folders to search.

- Use the first tab to select search criteria specific to the item type you've chosen.

- Use the More Choices and Advanced tabs to enter additional criteria as needed.

4. Click **Find Now**.

If a complex search on a large data file takes too long, you can click **Stop** at any time.

Accessing Search Options

You can change Outlook's search options in the **Outlook Options** window's Search section.

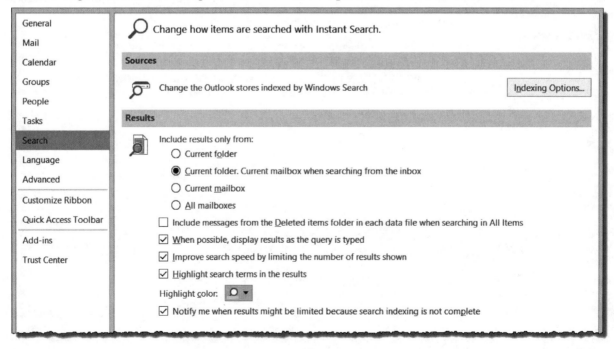

1. On the Search tab, click **Search Tools > Search Options**.

In Backstage view, you can instead click **Options**, then **Search**.

2. Make any changes you need.

3. Click **OK** to save your changes.

Exercise: Customizing a search

For this exercise, you'll need to have a partner, and the Sales Data message sent by your instructor. You should also have completed the Using Folders exercise: you can complete this exercise without doing so, but some steps will produce different results. You'll use scope and refinement options to search your inbox.

Do This	How & Why
1. Send a message to your partner with the subject `Data files`.	You can enter whatever you like in the message body.
2. While viewing your inbox, click in the Instant Search box.	Or press **Ctrl+E**. The Search tab becomes active.
3. Search for all messages with "Data" in the subject.	
a) In the Refine group, click **Subject**.	A "subject:" search appears in the box, with the keywords placeholder selected. subject:(keywords) 🔍
b) Type `dat` to begin the word "data."	You don't need to capitalize or even complete the word. Your results include the Data files message from your partner, and the Sales Data message from your instructor. For both, the search term you typed is highlighted. ✉ Sales Data Louise Blackwell
c) In the Scope group, click **All Mail Items**.	You might need to expand conversations to see all results. More results are added to the search. Now you'll also see the Data files message you sent to your partner, and the other copy of Sales Data you moved to a folder earlier. ▲ Sales Data Class Instructor ✉ Class Instructor ✉ Class Instructor
4. Click **Has Attachments**.	In the Refine group. Now only the Sales Data messages from your instructor are displayed.
5. Click **Close Search**.	The Search tab closes, and you're viewing your full inbox again.

About filters

You might find yourself wanting to use the same search for a while, without worrying about clearing and having to reapply it when you do something else like switch between folders. In this case, you might want to try a filter instead. A *filter* is similar to a search applied to a single folder: it displays items that meet only the filter's criteria. The difference is that a filter lasts until you remove it, so you don't have to worry about clearing it by mistake.

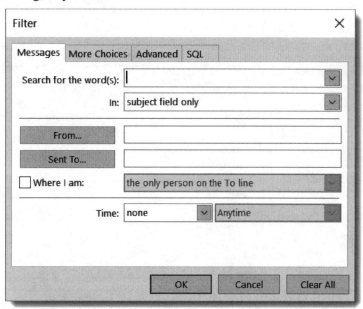

Applying filters

You can apply filters to as many different folders as you like, but every filter you apply affects only one folder. If you want to apply a filter to two mail folders you have to apply it separately to each, even if one is a subfolder of the other.

1. With the folder contents list displayed, click **View Settings**.

    The **Advanced View Settings** window opens.

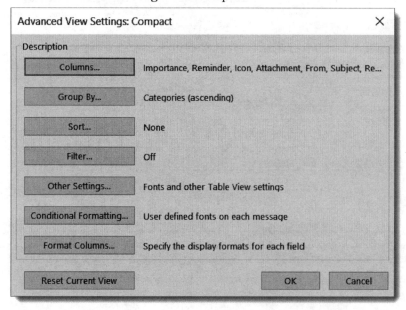

2. Click **Filter**.

The **Filter** window opens. As with the Search tab, the options available will depend on the type of folder selected.

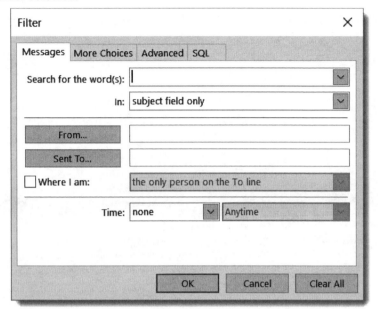

3. Set the filter options.

4. Click **OK**.

Changing or clearing filters

Editing or removing a filter is virtually the same as adding one.

1. Open the **Filter** window.

2. Make any changes you'd like to the filter.

- Click **Clear All** to remove all filter terms if you want to clear the filter or start over.

3. Click **OK**.

Exercise: Filtering a folder

For this exercise, you'll need to have received a welcome message from your instructor. You must also have completed the Using Folders exercise. You'll add a filter to your inbox, then clear it again.

Do This	How & Why
1. From your inbox, in the View tab's Current View group, click **View Settings**.	The **Advanced View Settings** window opens.
2. Click **Filter**.	The **Filter** window opens. Because this is a mail folder, the Messages tab is displayed.
3. Observe the available tabs.	
a) Click **More Choices**.	Here you can filter by category, size, or other message properties.
b) Click **Advanced**.	Here you can define more criteria to add to the filter.
c) Click **SQL**.	Here you can use Structured Query Language commands to define your filter criteria.
d) Click **Messages**.	You'll make a filter based off basic message properties instead.
4. Filter for messages with "welcome" in the subject field.	
a) In the "Search for the word(s)" field, type `welcome`.	
b) Make sure that **subject field only** is selected from the In list.	
c) Click **OK**.	Your Inbox folder now shows only messages with "welcome" in the header.
5. View the **My 2016 Sales** folder.	The Sales data message is visible here, so the filter doesn't apply in this folder.
6. Close, then reopen Outlook.	You're viewing your Inbox again, but the filter is still in place even after quitting Outlook. You'll have to remove it manually.
7. Remove the filter.	
a) Open the **Filter** window.	Right-click a blank space in your inbox, and click **Filter**.
b) Click **Clear All**.	The search criteria you entered is removed.
c) Click **OK**.	All of your messages are visible again.

Search folders

Searches are temporary, and filters tie up a folder for as long as they're in place. If you have a search you want to save and use repeatedly, you might want to define a search folder. A *search folder* is a virtual folder used for search results: Although it appears in your folder list, like any other folder, and although you can rename or delete it as you would an ordinary custom folder, it's actually just a way of saving the results of a search. When you click the search folder, it performs the search and displays results.

 MOS Outlook Exam Objective(s): 1.3.1

A search folder showing messages from "Instructor."

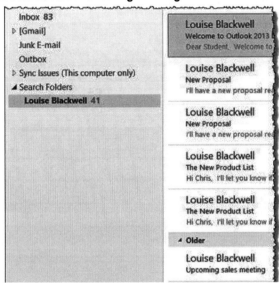

Search folders can display results from multiple folders, and because they store search criteria rather than search results, they're constantly updated. If you created a search folder for "Marketing" last month, you can check it today and see the marketing messages you got yesterday. Search folders do have some limitations: they apply only to mail folders, and they can search inside only one Outlook data file at a time.

Creating search folders

 MOS Outlook Exam Objective(s): 1.3.1

You can create search folders from the **New Search Folder** window, which provides a list of starting points you can customize further to suit your needs.

1. On the Folder tab, click **New Search Folder**.

2. On the list, click the general type of search folder you want to create.

3. Customize your search folder, as necessary.

   - If you have more than one Outlook data file, choose the one in which you want to search.

   - For some search-folder types, you'll need to specify additional options, such as contacts or search terms. If so, click **Choose**, and follow the instructions.

4. Click **OK**.

Customizing search folders

You can customize a search folder once you've created it. You can change its criteria, its name, or the folders in which it searches.

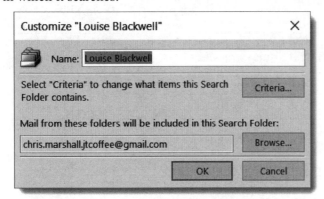

1. Right-click a search folder, and click **Customize This Search Folder**.
2. Change the properties of the folder.
    - Type a new folder name in the Name field.
    - Click **Criteria** to change the search criteria.
    - Click **Browse** to change what folders the search folder includes.
3. Click **OK**.

Creating custom search folders

If none of the existing search folder types do what you need, you can create a custom one. This way you can access nearly all of the search options available in a filter.

1. On the Folder tab, click **New Search Folder**.
2. Click **Create a custom Search Folder**, then click **Choose**.
    In the Custom category of the Select a Search Folder box.
3. Click Choose.
    To add criteria for the custom search folder.
    The **Custom Search Folder** window opens, just as if you were customizing an existing search folder.

4. Add criteria:
    a) Click **Criteria** to open the **Search Folder Criteria** window.

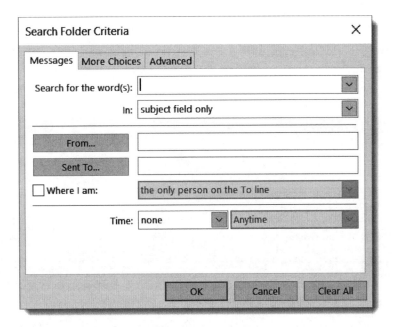

b) On the Messages, More Choices, or Advanced tabs, enter whatever criteria you want.

c) Click **OK**.

5. In the **Custom Search Folder** window, enter a name for the custom search folder

6. Click **OK**.

7. In the **New Search Folder** window, click **OK**.

Exercise: Creating a search folder

To complete this exercise, you'll need a partner who has already sent you at least one message. You'll create a search folder for messages from your partner.

 MOS Outlook Exam Objective(s): 1.3.1

Do This	How & Why
1. On the Folder tab, click **New Search Folder**.	The **New Search Folder** window opens.
2. In the Select a Search Folder list, click **Mail from specific people**.	
3. In the Customize Search Folder section, specify your partner.	
a) Click **Choose**.	The **Select Names: Contacts** window opens.
b) In the From list, enter your partner's address.	
c) Click **OK**.	Your partner is now listed in the Customize Search Folder section.
4. Click **OK**.	The search folder is now created and selected in your folder list. It shows all the messages you've received from your partner.
5. Send a message to your partner.	When your partner's message arrives, it now also appears in the new search folder.

Assessment: Searching and filtering

1. What ribbon group do you use to control the folders covered by a search? Choose the best response.

    *   Filters

    *   Options

    *   Refine

    *   Scope

2. You're making a project of looking up and adding phone numbers to all of your contacts that don't have them already. You'll be switching folders a lot and performing other tasks while you work on it, but you otherwise don't really need to use your contacts folder until it's finished. What tool would help you focus on contacts without phone numbers, with the least trouble? Choose the best response.

    *   Filters

    *   Instant Search

    *   Recent Searches

    *   Search Folders

3. You've just refined a search to show messages received this week. What will you see if you click the Has Attachments refinement? Choose the best response.

    *   All messages with attachments, received at any time.

    *   All messages with attachments, and all messages that were received this week.

    *   All messages with attachments that were received this week.

    *   An error message.

Module E: Quick steps

As you work in Outlook, you'll find you're doing the same things repeatedly. For example, when you receive a customer email, you might need to reply to it, send a copy to your manager, and move it to a "Customers" folder. Although performing the same sequence of steps can be very routine, once you're used to it, in the long run you'll save even more time by defining a *Quick Step* to do so with a single click.

You will learn how to:

- Use Quick Steps
- Edit Quick Steps
- Create Quick Steps

About Quick Steps

When you're viewing a mail folder, the Quick Steps group is on the Home tab.

Outlook always displays five Quick Steps—the default set and/or any folders you've created. In any case, you can always add new ones. The original default Quick Steps include:

Process	Marks the message as read and moves it to a predefined folder.
To Manager	Forwards the message to your manager.
Team E-Mail	Creates a new message to your team.
Done	Marks the message read, marks it as complete on your To-Do List, and moves it to a specified folder.
Reply & Delete	Opens a reply to the message and then deletes the original copy.
Create New	Opens the **Edit Quick Step** window. Use this to create a new Quick Step or edit an existing one.

Once you've created a new Quick Step folder, one or more of the default Quick Steps are replaced in the gallery. To manage Quick Steps, click ▣ (Launcher) in the Quick Steps group.

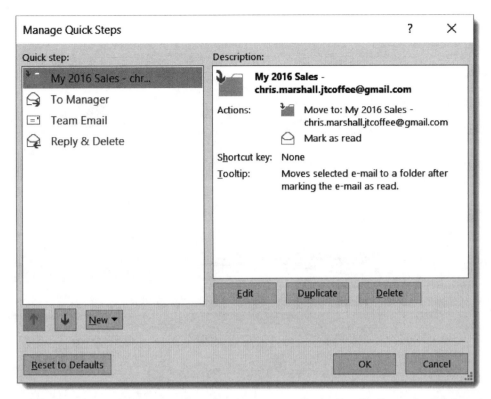

From here, you can create new Quicks Steps, as well as edit, duplicate, and delete them. In addition, you can change their order in the list, and reset to default settings.

Using Quick Steps

Using existing Quick Steps is easy, but the first time you do so, you might be prompted for additional information. For example, to forward a message to your manager, Outlook needs to know your manager's address.

 MOS Outlook Exam Objective(s): 2.4.11

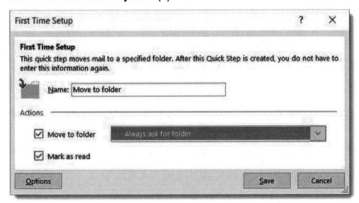

1. Select a message, if necessary.

   For some Quick Steps, you can select multiple messages by pressing and holding **Ctrl**, while others can be applied only to one message at a time.

2. Click the Quick Step you want to apply.

3. If it's the first time you're using the step, you may need to enter necessary information in the **First Time Setup** window, and then click **Save**.

   This won't actually apply the Quick Step, but only save it. To perform the step once it's set up, you'll have to click it again.

Exercise: Using a Quick Step

To complete this exercise, you'll need a partner.

In this exercise, you'll respond to a message by using Quick Steps.

Do This	How & Why
1. Send a message to your partner.	Use a subject and body of your choice.
2. When your partner's message arrives, click **Reply & Delete**.	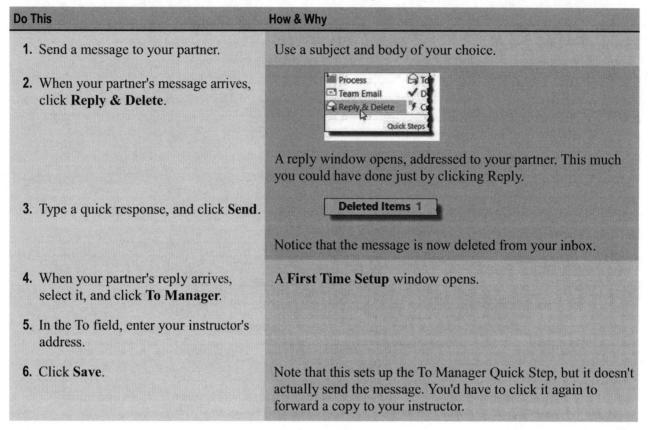 A reply window opens, addressed to your partner. This much you could have done just by clicking Reply.
3. Type a quick response, and click **Send**.	Notice that the message is now deleted from your inbox.
4. When your partner's reply arrives, select it, and click **To Manager**.	A **First Time Setup** window opens.
5. In the To field, enter your instructor's address.	
6. Click **Save**.	Note that this sets up the To Manager Quick Step, but it doesn't actually send the message. You'd have to click it again to forward a copy to your instructor.

Managing Quick Steps

To edit or rearrange your Quick Steps, open the Quick Steps gallery, and click **Manage Quick Steps**, or click the Quick Steps group's launcher button. Using either method opens the **Manage Quick Steps** window.

MOS Outlook Exam Objective(s): MOS 77-884 2.2.4, 2.2.6

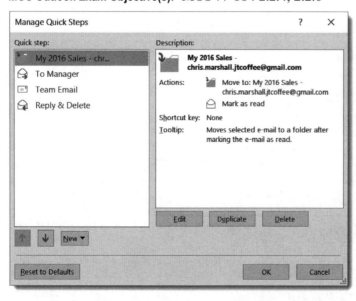

- Clicking a Quick Step displays the actions it performs, the ToolTip displayed when you point to it, and the shortcut key assigned to it, if any.

- To change the order in which a Quick Step is displayed, select it, and click the **Up** or **Down** buttons to move it to the position desired.

- To edit a Quick Step, select it, and click **Edit**.

- To create a new Quick Step modeled on an existing one, click **Duplicate**.

- To create a new Quick Step, click **New**, then select from a list of starting points.

- To delete a Quick Step, select it, and click **Delete**.
    You won't be prompted to confirm your deletion, so be careful not to delete a Quick Step by mistake.

- To reset all Quick Steps to their default settings, click **Restore to Defaults**, then click **Yes** to confirm.

The Edit Quick Step window

Whether you're editing an existing Quick Step or creating a new one, you'll be doing so in the **Edit Quick Step** window. From here, you can view and change all of the Quick Step's properties. Clicking **Show Options** displays all available options related to an action.

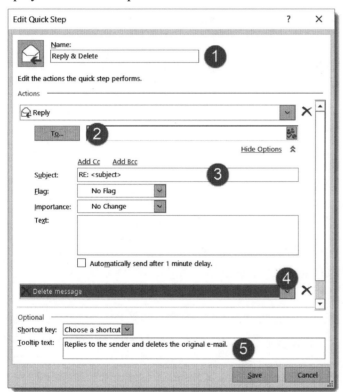

① The *Name* section holds both the Quick Step's name and its icon. These determine its appearance in the gallery.

② The *Actions* section contains one or more actions. You can choose each action from a list, sorted by category.

③ Some actions have a *Show Options* link you can use to see additional settings. For example, actions that respond to a message let you set message options and contents.

④ The *Delete* button removes an action from the Quick Step.

⑤ The *Optional* section contains two fields: the Shortcut Key list lets you choose a key combination for the Quick Step, and the ToolTip text appears when you point to it in the gallery.

In addition, when you're creating or editing a Quick Step, the Edit Quick Step window will often contain an *Add Action* button, which allows you to further refine the Quick Step's function. Each time you click it, the action of your choice is appended to the existing set of actions.

Editing Quick Steps

You can edit an existing Quick Step's properties from the **Manage Quick Steps** window.

1. Select the Quick Step, or right-click it in the gallery.
2. Click **Edit**.
3. Make any changes you wish.
4. Click **Save**.

Duplicating Quick Steps

Duplicating a Quick Step is just like editing one. The only difference is that it is saved as a new Quick Step with a new name.

1. In the **Manage Quick Steps** window, select the Quick Step, or right-click it in the gallery.
2. Click **Duplicate**.
3. Make any changes you need.
   By default, the duplicate's name will be prefixed with "Copy of," but you can change it to whatever you want.
4. Click **Save**.

Creating Quick Steps

If none of your existing Quick Steps is a good starting point for what you want to make, you can create a new one from scratch. The quickest way to do so is provided in the Quick Steps gallery, by clicking **Create New**. This opens a blank **Edit Quick Step** window, where you can set whatever properties you like.

 MOS Outlook Exam Objective(s): 2.4.11

You can also choose from a selection of starting points with popular actions. Doing so opens a **First Time Setup** window, in which you can make further changes.

1. In the gallery, click **New Quick Step**; or, in the **Manage Quick Steps** window, click **New**.

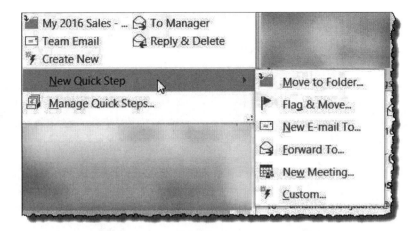

2. Click the type of action you want to perform.

   You can always add additional actions if you need to, so if you're making a complex Quick Step, start with the first one you wish to make.

   When creating your first Quick Step, a **First Time Setup** window appears, with the options necessary for the action you chose.

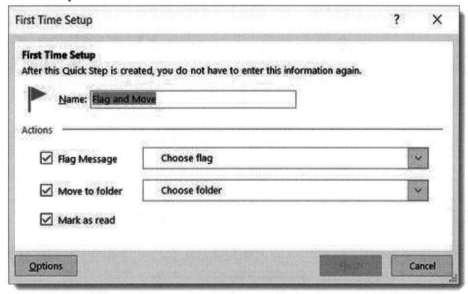

3. Choose a name for the Quick Step, and set any required options.

4. Click **Finish**.

   If you want to add more steps or set more details, click **Options** to open an **Edit Quick Step** window.

Exercise: Managing Quick Steps

For this activity, you'll need to have email addresses for at least two partners. You'll edit and create Quick Steps from the **Manage Quick Steps** window.

Do This	How & Why
1. In the Quick Steps group, open the gallery, and click **Manage Quick Steps**.	You can also click the launcher button. The **Manage Quick Steps** window opens.
2. Add your partners' addresses to the Team E-Mail Quick Step:	
a) Click **Team E-Mail**.	
b) Click **Edit**.	The **Edit Quick Step** window opens.
c) In the To field, type your partners' addresses.	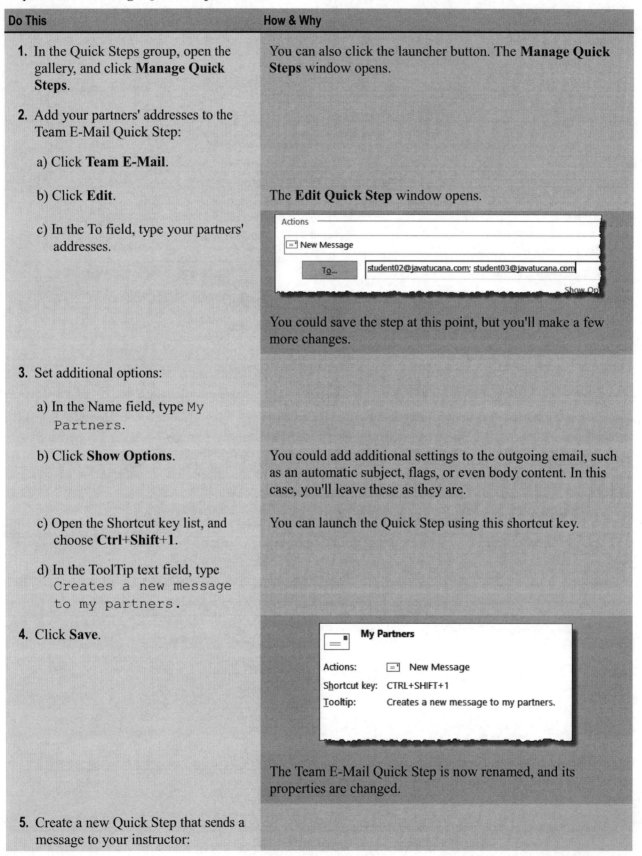
	You could save the step at this point, but you'll make a few more changes.
3. Set additional options:	
a) In the Name field, type My Partners.	
b) Click **Show Options**.	You could add additional settings to the outgoing email, such as an automatic subject, flags, or even body content. In this case, you'll leave these as they are.
c) Open the Shortcut key list, and choose **Ctrl+Shift+1**.	You can launch the Quick Step using this shortcut key.
d) In the ToolTip text field, type Creates a new message to my partners.	
4. Click **Save**.	
	The Team E-Mail Quick Step is now renamed, and its properties are changed.
5. Create a new Quick Step that sends a message to your instructor:	

Do This	How & Why
a) Click **New > New E-Mail To:**	The **First Time Setup** window opens, with a New Message action.
b) In the Name field, type My Instructor.	
c) In the To field, type your instructor's address.	If you wanted to set more options or add more actions, you could click **Options**.
d) Click **Finish**.	The new step is added to the list.
6. Click **OK**.	The new Quick Steps are added to the gallery.

Assessment: Quick Steps

1. Quick Steps allow you to _____. Choose the best way to complete the sentence.

   - Automatically perform commands on messages as they arrive.
   - Easily perform commands that are otherwise buried in obscure menus.
   - Perform multiple commands on a message with a single button click.
   - Perform one command on items in multiple folders.

2. True or false? Not all the default Quick Steps included with Outlook are ready to use as-is.

   - True
   - False

3. True or false? Creating, duplicating, and editing Quick Steps are actions that all use very much the same procedure.

   - True
   - False

4. True or false? When you make a Quick Step, Outlook gives it a ToolTip that describes the steps it performs.

   - True
   - False

Summary: Organizing Outlook

You should now know:

- How to add and configure POP3, IMAP, and Microsoft Exchange accounts

- How to create folders, and move and copy items between them

- About color categories, and how to use them to sort and find items

- How to use Outlook's search features, including the Search tab, Advanced Find, filters, and search folders

- How to use, edit, and create Quick Steps

Synthesis: Organizing Outlook

For this exercise, you'll need to have uncategorized messages from both your instructor and your partner.

In this exercise, you'll practice using tools to organize your Outlook items.

1. View your account settings. Change the mail account name to one of your choosing.
   To change the account name, you'll have to click **More Settings**.

2. Create a new folder, and copy all messages from your partner to it. Move the folder to a location in which it will be easy to find.

3. Categorize any messages or contacts that haven't already been assigned categories.

   - Use at least two categories, and set up new categories as needed.

   - If you don't have contacts for your instructor and partner, create them.

   - If you can't think of better ways to categorize items, imagine that your partner and instructor work with you on different projects in different parts of your company.

4. Experiment with different ways of searching for the items you've categorized, and compare the benefits and drawbacks of each. Try these options:

   - The Scope and Refine groups

   - Advanced Find

   - Filters

   - Search folders

5. Create a new Quick Step that requests a meeting with some of your contacts.

Chapter 8: Managing your mail

You will learn:

- About junk mail settings
- How to use rules
- How to clean up your mailbox

Module A: Managing junk mail

Junk email, also known as spam, is familiar to anyone who's used email. At its most benign, spam crowds your inbox with unwanted messages and wastes your time. Other junk messages will attempt to defraud you or even infect your computer with malware. Outlook provides tools to help you find and remove junk email before it can cause you problems.

You will learn:

- About junk email options
- How to mark messages as junk or not junk
- How to block and allow senders
- How to configure Outlook's junk email filter

The Junk Email folder

Outlook scans all of your incoming email for suspected junk. If a message is junk, it isn't deleted; instead, it goes to the Junk Email folder rather than your Inbox. That way you can review it later, in case it was placed there by mistake. Messages you manually mark as junk also go to the Junk Email folder.

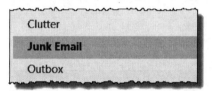

Ideally you want Outlook to catch every junk message you receive, but never place something you want to read into the Junk Email folder. You can't expect this automated process to be perfect, but with a little configuration and some corrections over time, you can refine Outlook's ability to keep unwanted—and only unwanted—messages out of your way.

Be aware that Outlook isn't the only way to scan for junk. Many email providers also automatically scan your incoming email, and either block suspected junk or place it in a spam folder, even before it arrives on your computer. Depending on your account and how it's configured, this can be a separate folder in Outlook, or you might have to log onto your provider's web mail interface to review the messages it's filtered.

Junk email options

You can change your junk email settings either by marking individual messages or by accessing the **Junk E-mail Options** window. The first is more convenient in a lot of cases, but either way, your changes are applied in that window's settings. To configure these settings, it's important to know what the terms mean and what options are available to you.

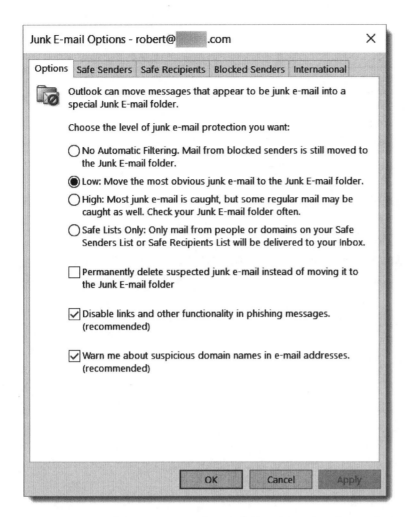

Automatic junk e-mail filter   The *automatic junk e-mail filter* determines how stringent Outlook is when looking for signs that a message might be junk. By default, it uses a low level of protection, but you can set it to high protection, turn it off, or even classify all email as junk until proven otherwise. Whatever option you choose, Outlook still checks to see if other rules have specifically allowed or blocked a message. Remember that although high protection might sound better, it also can mean more good messages mistakenly marked as junk.

Phishing links   Some junk messages are designed for *phishing*, a type of social engineering attack in which a malicious message or website pretends to be a legitimate one. For example, a phishing message might pretend to be an urgent message from your bank, with a link to log into your account on their website. In truth, the link leads to a fake page the attacker will use to steal your login credentials. Outlook can mark a message as suspected phishing even if it's not placed in the Junk E-mail folder, so this option helps keep you from following fake links without realizing it.

Suspicious domain names   Some phishing or other fraudulent messages will use domain names that look very similar to recognizable brands or sites. When this option is checked, Outlook will warn you when a message might be impersonating a different domain name.

Safe Senders List   *Safe senders* are addresses or domain names whose messages will never be treated as junk. This is useful if Outlook is mistakenly marking messages from some senders as suspicious. They're stored in a list on the Safe Senders tab, where you can add or edit them. By default, your contacts are also treated as safe senders.

Safe Recipients List   *Safe recipients* are a little more complicated than safe senders. Junk messages are typically sent to large numbers of people at once, so it's likely your address will be in the Cc or Bcc field of the message rather than the To field. Automatic filters look for this as a sign of junk email, so if you frequently receive copies of messages sent to friends, coworkers, or distribution lists, you can add those addresses or domain names to the Safe Senders list.   **Continued...**

Blocked Senders List *Blocked senders* are addresses and domain names whose messages will always be treated as junk. When Outlook fails to automatically recognize a message as junk, you can add its sender to the Blocked Senders list and stop future messages.

Blocked Top-Level Domain List *Top-level domains* are the highest level of domain name, including two-letter codes for countries or territories, such as ".uk," ".us," or ".de." If you consistently get junk messages from a top-level domain from which you never receive legitimate messages, you can block it on the International tab.

Blocked Encodings List Message text always uses some kind of *character encoding* appropriate to the language and writing style it's in. For example, a message might be encoded in ASCII, Roman, Cyrillic, or Chinese. If you receive a lot of junk messages encoded for languages you can't read and in which you don't communicate, you can block them on the International tab.

Blocking senders

When Outlook fails to catch a junk message, you can simply delete it, but marking it as junk will also block further email from that sender.

 MOS Outlook Exam Objective(s): 2.1.6

1. Select or open a message.

2. In the Delete group, click **Junk > Block Sender**.

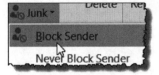

A window will notify you that the sender has been blocked, and the message moved to the Junk E-mail folder.

Marking safe senders and recipients

Whether a message has been marked as junk or not, you can still add its sender or domain to the Safe Senders group. You can also add a group or distribution list to the Safe Recipients list. You can do either of these in the **Junk E-mail Options** window, but it's usually quicker to use the Junk menu in the Delete group.

 MOS Outlook Exam Objective(s): 2.1.6

1. Select or open a message.

2. Add the address or domain to the safe list.

   - Click **Junk > Never block Sender** to add the sender's address to the Safe Senders list.

   - Click **Junk > Never block Sender's Domain** to add the sender's entire domain to the Safe Senders list.

   - Click **Junk > Never block this Group or Mailing List** to add a mailing list to the Safe Recipients list. You're also asked whether to add the sender to the Safe Senders list.

Reviewing junk email

Periodically, you should review your Junk E-mail folder for messages placed there by mistake. If you find one, you can just drag it back to your inbox, but that won't keep the problem from repeating itself the next time you get a similar message from the same sender. Instead, you can mark it as Not Junk to return it to your Inbox and add the sender to your Safe Senders list in a single step.

 MOS Outlook Exam Objective(s): 2.1.6

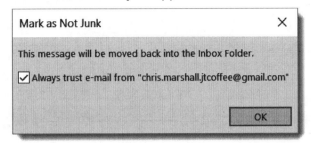

1. Select or open a message in the Junk E-mail folder.
2. In the Delete group, click **Junk > Not Junk**.

   The **Mark as Not Junk** window appears.

3. If you don't want to add the sender to the Safe Senders list, clear the check box.
4. Click **OK**.

After you've restored the messages you want to keep, you might want to empty your Junk E-mail folder. To do so, right-click it, and click **Empty Folder**.

Configuring junk email settings

 MOS Outlook Exam Objective(s): 2.1.6

To change your settings using the options window:

1. When viewing a mail folder or message, in the Delete group, click **Junk > Junk E-mail Options**.

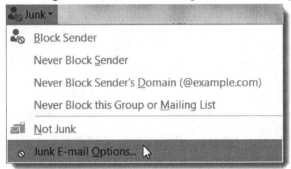

2. In the **Junk E-mail Options** window, configure your settings:
   - Use the Options tab to choose protection level and other options.
   - Use the Safe Senders, Safe Recipients, and Block Senders tabs to access their respective lists. You can add or remove addresses, or even import and export lists of addresses.
   - Use the International tab to access the Blocked Top-level Domain List and Blocked Encoding list.
3. Click **OK** to save your settings.

Exercise: Managing junk email

To complete this exercise, you'll need a partner. You'll mark your partner's messages as junk, then as safe.

Do This	How & Why
1. Block messages from your partner.	
a) Select a message from your partner.	
b) Click **Junk > Block Sender**.	You can find the Junk menu in the Delete group, or in the context menu.
c) Click **OK**.	Your partner is added to the blocked sender list, and the message is moved to the Junk E-mail folder.
2. Send a message to your partner.	When your partner's message arrives, it doesn't appear in your inbox.
3. Click the **Junk E-mail** folder.	The folder contains both messages from your partner: the one you marked as junk, and the one you just received.
4. Mark the original message as not junk.	
a) Select the message.	
b) Click **Junk > Not Junk**.	The **Mark as Not Junk** window appears. The "Always trust email from" box is checked.
c) Click **OK**.	Your partner is added to your Safe Senders list, and the message is returned to your inbox. The other message is left in the Junk E-mail folder.
5. Send a message to your partner.	Because your partner is in your Safe Senders list, this time the message arrives in your inbox.
6. Remove your partner from the Blocked Senders list.	Your partner is now actually both in your Safe Senders and Blocked Senders list. Because the Safe Senders list has precedence, this isn't a problem, but you'll still fix this.
a) Click **Junk > Junk E-mail Options**.	The **Junk E-mail Options** window opens. The Options tab is visible.

Do This	How & Why
b) Click the **Blocked Senders** tab.	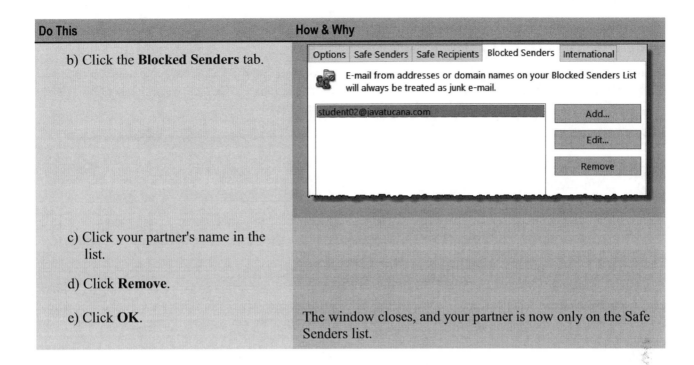
c) Click your partner's name in the list.	
d) Click **Remove**.	
e) Click **OK**.	The window closes, and your partner is now only on the Safe Senders list.

Assessment: Managing junk mail

1. A phishing email typically tricks recipients into _____. Choose the best way to complete the sentence.

   - Buying products from an unfamiliar and untrustworthy vendor.

   - Clicking a fake link to what appears to be a trustworthy site.

   - Performing "security fixes" that actually make their computer vulnerable or non-functional.

   - Viewing an attachment that contains malware.

2. True or false? You should always set your automatic filtering to a high sensitivity level.

   - True

   - False

3. What's the best action to take when an important message from a colleague has been mistakenly marked as junk? Choose the best single response.

   - Add the sender to the Safe Senders list.

   - Add your address to the Safe Recipients list.

   - Drag it back to your Inbox folder.

   - Mark it as Not Junk.

Module B: Using rules

Even after you've eliminated the junk email, you might find yourself surprised at how much mail you're receiving after you've used an account for a while. To make sorting your mail easier, you can use Outlook's rules feature to scan incoming messages and perform automatic actions on them.

You will learn:

- About rules
- How to create rules
- How to manage rules

About rules

Rules are automated processes Outlook performs on incoming messages. A rule could be something as simple as a notification sound that plays when a message arrives, or its being assigned to a category. It could also be something more involved, such as an automatic forward or reply, the launching of an application, or the running of a script. You can even have rules that perform multiple steps, or apply multiple rules to the same message.

You can define a rule that affects all incoming mail, but more commonly, rules only act on messages meeting certain criteria, such as those from specific senders or with specific subject terms. For example, you could have Outlook play a specific alert sound whenever you receive a message from your manager.

One common use of rules is to address graymail. *Graymail* is a term for bulk messages you've opted to receive, such as sales, social media notifications, and mailing lists. They're not spam, as you've chosen to receive them and could opt out if you wanted, but they're seldom urgent and can easily overwhelm your inbox. Moving graymail to other folders for later review makes it easier to recognize and act on the more personal and urgent messages you receive.

Creating simple rules

To quickly create a simple rule based on an existing message, use the **Create Rule** window.

 MOS Outlook Exam Objective(s): 2.1.3

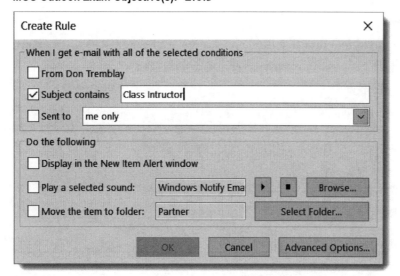

1. Select a message.

   If you want the rule to apply to messages from a specific sender, it must be a message from that sender.

2. In the Move group, click **Rules** > **Create Rule**.

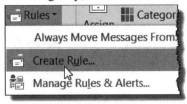

The **Create Rule** window opens.

3. In the top section, enter criteria for the rule.

- You can apply the rule to messages from that sender, messages with specific terms in the subject header, or messages addressed to you or other specific people.

- If you check multiple criteria, the rule applies only to messages that meet all of them.

- If you want to add criteria not in the list, click **Advanced Options** to switch to the Rules Wizard interface.

4. In the bottom section, select the actions you want to perform.
   As with criteria, if you don't see the action you want, click **Advanced Options**.

5. Click **OK**.
   The **Success** window might appear, showing that the rule was created. If you haven't chosen the option to apply the rule to existing messages, you're prompted to do so now.

6. Choose whether to apply the rule on existing items in the current folder, then click **OK**.

Exercise: Creating a rule

To complete this exercise, you'll need a partner. You'll create a rule to move all messages from your partner to a new folder.

Do This	How & Why
1. Select a message from your partner.	
2. In the Move group, click **Rules** > **Create Rule**.	The **Create Rule** window opens.
3. Configure the rule to move all messages from your partner to a Partner folder.	
a) Below "When I get e-mail with all the selected conditions," check the first box.	You'll set this rule to apply to all messages from your partner. 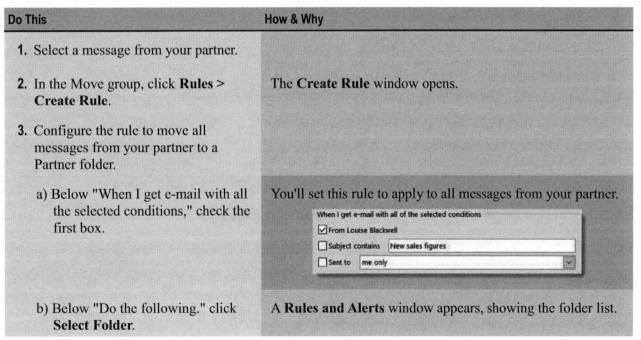
b) Below "Do the following." click **Select Folder**.	A **Rules and Alerts** window appears, showing the folder list.

Do This	How & Why
c) In your Inbox, create a `Partner` folder.	Click **New** to open the **Create New Folder** window, then select the Inbox folder and type its name. ▲ Inbox **2** 　My 2016 Sales 　New Coffee Projects 　**Partner**
d) Click **OK**.	☑ Move the item to folder: `Partner`　[Select Folder...] When you define the folder, the action is automatically checked.
4. View the Rules Wizard interface.	Your rule is finished, and at this point you could simply click **OK**, but first you're going to view some more advanced options.
a) Click **Advanced Options**.	Rules Wizard Which condition(s) do you want to check? Step 1: Select condition(s) ☑ from <u>Louise Blackwell</u> ☐ with <u>Fwd: New sales figures</u> in the subject The **Rules Wizard** window appears. The first screen is a list of criteria for the rule. The one you set is already checked. At the bottom of the window is a description of the full rule you've defined.
b) Click **Next**.	To view the full list of actions you can take. Again, you'll keep the ones you just set.
c) Click **Next**.	To view exceptions that will prevent the rule from being run.
d) Click **Next**.	To view the last page of the Rules Wizard. Here you can rename the rule, choose whether to turn it on, and whether to run it on existing messages.
e) Click **Finish**.	The Wizard closes, and the rule is applied.
5. Send a message to your partner.	**Partner 1** Your partner's message is immediately placed in the Partner folder.

The Rules and Alerts window

The central place for managing your rules is the E-mail Rules tab of the **Rules and Alerts** window. To open it, in the Move group, click **Rules > Manage Rules & Alerts**.

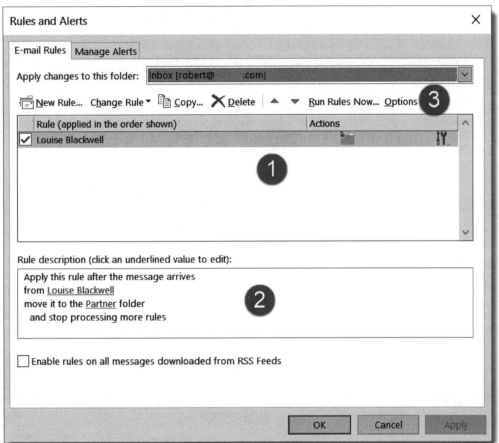

The E-Mail Rules tab of the window has three primary sections.

1 The *rules list* shows the rules you have configured. Each can be checked and active, or cleared and inactive. When a message arrives, all active rules are applied in order.

2 The *rule description* gives a full description of the currently selected rule. Underlined terms are links you can use to configure variables, such as sender names or folders.

3 The top menu allows you to create, change, copy, and delete rules; to run existing rules; and to change the order rules are run in.

Creating rules

 MOS Outlook Exam Objective(s): 2.1.3

When you create or edit a rule from the **Rules and Alerts** window, you'll use the **Rules Wizard** interface. This method gives you full access to all rule options. You can either choose to begin with one of several common templates and modify it, or create a new rule from scratch.

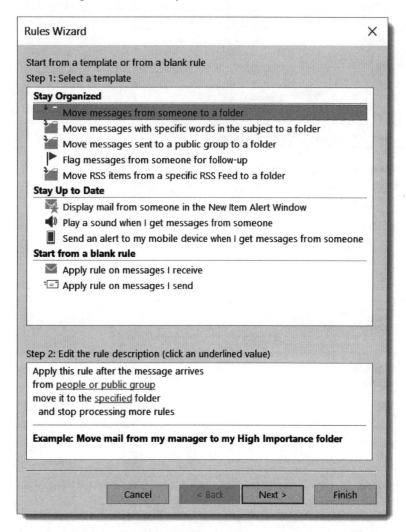

When you work in the **Rules Wizard** window, the lower pane shows a description of the rule as it presently stands. As in the **Rules and Alerts** window, an underlined term is a link with options you need to set.

1. Click **Rules > Manage Rules and Alerts**.

    To open the **Rules and Alerts** window.

2. Select a template, or start from a blank rule.

    Starting from a blank rule is exactly like clicking **Advanced Options** in the **New Rule** window.

3. Set one or more starting conditions for the rule, then click **Next**.

    • If you started with a template, some conditions will be checked already.

    • Check conditions in the list to add them to the rule description.

    • If a condition has an underlined term, click it in the description to set its options.

4. Set one or more actions for the rule to perform, then click **Next**.

    • Like with conditions, you'll need to configure options for some actions.

- If the **Stop processing more rules** action is checked, Outlook won't apply any other rules to the current message. Setting or clearing this option can be very important when multiple rules might apply to a single message.

5. Set any exceptions you want for the rule, then click **Next**.

   - Unlike conditions and actions, exceptions are optional.

   - Exceptions let you avoid overly broad rules. For example, you could move newsletters and sales messages to a folder, but create an exception to ensure important account alerts stay in your inbox.

6. Finalize the rule setup, and click **Finish**.

   - Type a name for the rule.

   - If you want to apply it to messages already in the current folder, check **Run this rule now**.

   - If you don't want the rule to become immediately active, clear **Turn on this rule**.

Editing rules

You can edit or rename a rule in the **Rules and Alerts** window by selecting it and clicking **Change Rule**.

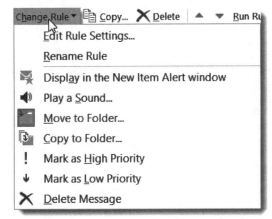

- To rename the rule, click **Rename Rule**. Then type the new name, and click **OK**.
- To add an action listed on the menu, click it. You may be prompted to configure additional options.
- Actions already in the rule are highlighted. To remove one, click it.
- To edit the rule in the Rules Wizard, click **Edit Rule Settings**.

Managing rules

You can also use the **Rules and Alerts** window to arrange, copy, delete, and run rules.

 MOS Outlook Exam Objective(s): 2.1.3

- Click a rule to select it. Its description is shown in the lower section of the window.
- Clear or check the first column of a rule in the list to disable or enable it.
- Use the ▲ or ▼ arrow buttons to change the selected rule's place in the list.
- Click **Copy** to copy the selected rule to a different mailbox.
- Click **Run Rules Now** to run selected rules in a folder of your choice.
- Click **Options** to import or export rules to and from previous versions of Outlook.
- Click **Delete** to delete a rule.

Exercise: Editing a rule

You'll need to have finished the Creating a Rule exercise above. You'll edit an existing rule.

 MOS Outlook Exam Objective(s): 2.1.3

Do This	How & Why
1. Click **Rules > Manage Rules and Alerts**.	The **Rules and Alerts** window opens, with the E-mail Rules tab active.
2. Observe the existing rules.	*Rule (applied in the order shown)* ☑ Louise Blackwell ☑ Clear categories on mail (recommended) There are two rules set. One is the rule you created earlier. The other is included with Outlook by default to clear other people's categories from incoming mail.
3. Move the rule you created to the bottom of the list. a) Select the rule. b) Click ⏷	
4. Edit the rule using the Rules Wizard. a) Click **Change Rule > Edit Rule Settings**.	The **Rules Wizard** window opens. You'll change the rule to apply to messages from your instructor instead.
b) In the lower part of the window, click your partner's name.	*Step 2: Edit the rule description (click an underlined value)* Apply this rule after the message arrives from Louise Blackwell move it to the Partner folder An address book window appears.
c) In the From field, enter your instructor's address, and click **OK**.	Don't forget to delete your partner's address. Apply this rule after the message arrives from Outlook Instructor move it to the Partner folder The rule description is updated, but you also want to rename the rule.
d) Click **Next** three times.	You don't need to change the actions or exceptions for the rule.
e) In the "Specify a name" field, type `Class notifications`.	
f) Click **Finish**.	Next, you'll delete the rule.
5. Click **Delete**.	Outlook asks you to confirm the deletion.
6. Click **Yes**.	The Class notifications rule is removed from the list.

Do This	How & Why
7. Click **OK**.	To close the **Rules and Alerts** window.

Assessment: Using rules

1. Which of the following is an appropriate example of a rule? Choose all that apply.

    -   Flag all messages from your manager for follow-up.

    -   Forward any message you assign to a certain category.

    -   Move all messages from a known spammer to your Junk Email folder.

    -   Move all new messages addressed to your project team into a Project Team folder.

    -   Play a specific sound when a high-priority message arrives.

2. True or false? Even if a message meets the conditions for multiple rules, only one rule can ever act on it.

    -   True

    -   False

3. True or false? You can run a rule on messages already in your mailbox.

    -   True

    -   False

Module C: Cleaning up your mailbox

Even with the help of automated tools, in time you'll find your mailbox will grow larger and larger. Whether your problem is gigabytes of data using up your quota, or just thousands of messages making it hard to find what you need, there are many ways you can clean up your mail folders.

You will learn how to:

- View folder sizes
- Clean up conversations
- Clean up folders
- Archive mail

Mailbox size

Even if you carefully sort all your messages into manageable folders, you probably shouldn't just let your mailbox grow forever. Your email provider probably has set a *quota*, or maximum amount of space your account can use on the server. Although these limits are often more generous than they once were, it's still possible to meet them, especially if you have an IMAP or Microsoft Exchange account that stores copies of all your messages on the server. Additionally, if you configure any new devices to use that account, it will take them more time and bandwidth to download older messages or headers.

Even if server quota isn't a concern, local space might be, especially if you're using an older computer or a portable device with limited storage, like a tablet. Larger mailboxes also make for larger backups, longer searches, and even slower overall performance. Non-mail items such as contacts and calendar entries take space in your data file as well, but they're only likely to be large if you attach a lot of files to them.

Although you can view the total size of your Outlook data file by looking on your hard drive or the size of an individual message by pointing at it and reading the Tooltip, the **Folder Size** window provides a folder-by-folder list of the currently selected data file's size.

Using Mailbox Cleanup

The **Mailbox Cleanup** window has a number of commands to help manage your mailbox size.

MOS Outlook Exam Objective(s): 2.4.5

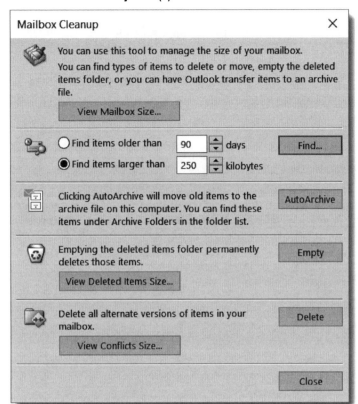

1. To open the window, in Backstage view, click **Cleanup Tools > Mailbox Cleanup**.

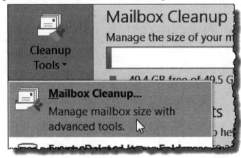

2. Use cleanup options.

   - To open the **Mailbox Size** window, click **View Mailbox Size** for all folders, or **View Deleted Items Size** for just the Deleted Items folder.

   - To launch an Advanced Find for large or old messages, set options for one or the other, then click **Find**.

   - To run AutoArchive with current settings, click **AutoArchive**.

   - To empty the Deleted Items folder, click **Empty**.

Cleaning up conversations

You might find a lot of the messages in your inbox are lengthy conversations comprised of replies by you and others to an original message. Further, each message will usually quote all the messages that came before, so most of the messages are entirely redundant. The **Clean Up Conversation** command allows you remove those redundant messages, and leave just the most recent message for your reference.

To clean up a selected folder, or the folder and its subfolders, you can use **Clean Up Folder**, in the Folder tab's Clean Up group.

 MOS Outlook Exam Objective(s): 2.4.5

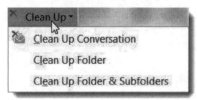

By default, Clean Up Conversation doesn't delete categorized, flagged, or signed messages. It also checks for conversations in which the original message was changed or deleted, rather than simply added to. You can change these and other options in the Mail section of the **Outlook Options** window.

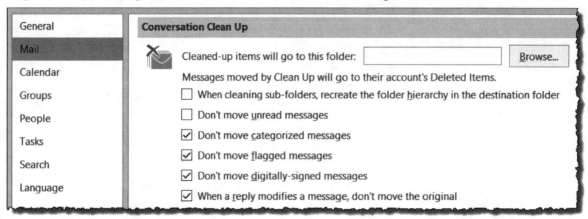

You can also clean up conversations in an entire folder at once, or even a folder and its subfolders. The commands are slightly different, but the process is the same.

1. Select the conversation you want to clean up.
2. In the Delete group, choose the command for what you want to clean up.
   - For the selected conversation, click **Clean Up > Clean Up Conversation**.
   - For the selected folder, click **Clean Up > Clean Up Folder**.
   - For the selected folder and its subfolders, click **Clean Up > Clean Up Folder & Subfolders**.

3. In the **Clean Up Conversation** (or **Clean Up Folder**) window, click **Clean Up**.

Ignoring conversations

Sometimes you might find you don't need to read any of a conversation, but you keep getting included as part of a list or by people simply including your name in the reply list. Instead of deleting each reply as it arrives, or asking to be removed, you can simply ignore it. By ignoring a conversation, you send all of its messages to the Deleted Items folder. Any new replies to the conversation are immediately sent to Deleted Items as well.

 MOS Outlook Exam Objective(s): 2.4.8

1. Select any message in a conversation.
2. Click **Ignore**.
3. In the confirmation window, click **OK**.

Manually cleaning folders

Automated tools can be a big help for cleaning up your mailbox, but you might find it helps to simply delete messages you no longer need. In particular, attachments can take a lot of space, so deleting them can make a big difference.

- If you won't need a message, delete it after reading. This is especially useful for messages with large attachments.
- If you've saved or don't need a message attachment, but want to keep the message itself, right-click the attachment, and click **Remove Attachment**.
- If you want to save an individual message as an external file, in Backstage view, click **Save As**.

Emptying deleted items

Deleting messages you don't need is easy enough, and you can do it in multiple ways. Remember that they'll still take space in the Deleted Items folder until you empty it.

- When viewing the Deleted Items folder, on the Folder tab, click **Empty Folder**.
- Right-click the Deleted Items folder, and click **Empty Folder**.
- In the **Mailbox Cleanup** window, click **Empty**.
- In Backstage view, **Cleanup Tools > Empty Deleted Items Folder**.

Exercise: Cleaning up your inbox

You'll need a partner and the Product List document. You'll use various cleanup tools on your inbox.

Do This	How & Why
1. Send `Product list.docx` to your partner as a message attachment.	`Product List.docx` is in the default data location. Type a subject and body of your choice.
2. Check your mailbox size.	
a) In Backstage view, click **Cleanup Tools > Mailbox Cleanup**.	The **Mailbox Cleanup** window opens.
b) Click **View Mailbox Size**.	Your mailbox won't exactly match the image, but notice the size of your Inbox folder.

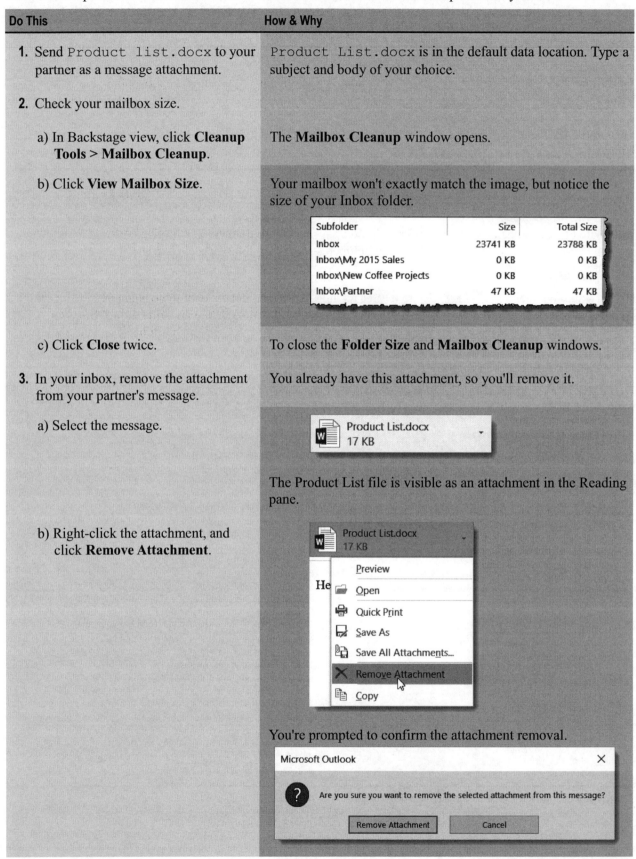

c) Click **Close** twice.	To close the **Folder Size** and **Mailbox Cleanup** windows.
3. In your inbox, remove the attachment from your partner's message.	You already have this attachment, so you'll remove it.
a) Select the message.	

The Product List file is visible as an attachment in the Reading pane.

b) Right-click the attachment, and click **Remove Attachment**.	

You're prompted to confirm the attachment removal.

Do This	How & Why
c) Click **Remove Attachment**.	To confirm the deletion. The message remains in your Inbox, but the attachment is removed.
4. Create a conversation from your partner's message.	You'll need to reply both to your partner's original message and to the reply the partner made to your message.
a) Send a reply to your partner's message.	In the body, type something like `Thanks, but I have the file already.`
b) When you receive your partner's reply, reply to it in turn.	In the body, type something like `I'll let you know if I get any updates.` There should now be two conversations in the folder, one for the message you originally sent, and one for your partner's reply.
5. Clean up your Inbox folder.	
a) In the Delete group, click **Clean Up > Clean Up Folder**.	A **Clean Up Folder** window appears.
b) Click **Clean Up Folder**.	Any redundant messages in the folder are sent to Deleted Items.
c) Expand the conversation your partner started.	It's still a conversation with multiple messages, but only because your reply is in Sent Items. Only the most recent message in the Inbox is still there.
d) Click the **Deleted Items** folder.	The other message from your partner is now in Deleted Items.
6. Click **Empty Folder**, then click **Yes**.	To empty the Deleted Items folder.
7. Check your mailbox size again.	In Backstage view, click **Cleanup Tools > Mailbox Cleanup**, then click **View Mailbox Size**.

Subfolder	Size	Total Size
Inbox	18991 KB	19038 KB
Inbox\My 2015 Sales	0 KB	0 KB
Inbox\New Coffee Projects	0 KB	0 KB
Inbox\Partner	47 KB	47 KB
Journal	0 KB	0 KB

Your Inbox is smaller than when you started, though since you've added messages but only deleted one, the difference might not seem very dramatic.

Do This	How & Why
8. Click **Close** twice.	To close the **Folder Size** and **Mailbox Cleanup** windows.

Archiving mail

Once you've cleaned up the messages you really don't need, you still might have a lot left. If you still want to make your mailbox smaller, you can *archive* your old messages by saving them to a different data file in case you need them. This frees up space in your main mailbox, while still leaving the old messages accessible.

Outlook supports multiple archiving methods.

- At any time, you can manually create an archive by moving old data to a file of your choice.

- By enabling the *AutoArchive* function, you can have Outlook automatically clean up or archive your items at regular intervals. You can also archive mail using your default AutoArchive settings from the **Mailbox Cleanup** window.

- If you have an account with Microsoft Exchange 2010 (or newer), or an Exchange Online Archiving subscription for Office 365, your administrator can configure an online *archive mailbox*, which archives your mail on the server.

Configuring AutoArchive defaults

 MOS Outlook Exam Objective(s): 2.4.12

You can configure AutoArchive settings individually for each folder, or just configure the default to use for all folders. You'll also need to modify the default settings to automatically run AutoArchive.

1. In Backstage view, click **Options**.

2. In the left pane of the **Outlook Options** window, click **Advanced**.

3. Click **AutoArchive Settings**.

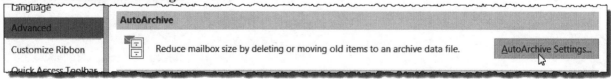

4. Check **Run AutoArchive every**.

   Even if you only want to use AutoArchive manually from Mailbox Cleanup, you can't edit the default settings without checking the box. You can uncheck it later, if you want.

5. Configure settings. By default, AutoArchive:

   - Runs every 14 days.

- Prompts you before it runs.

- Deletes messages that have an expiration date set. If you want to archive them instead, you'll need to change this.

- Archives messages to an archive folder which appears in your folder list.

- Cleans out items older than six months.

- Archives to a file named archive.pst. You can change the file name, or choose to permanently delete old items instead.

6. If you want to override any specific folder settings, click **Apply these settings to all folders now**.

7. Click **OK** twice.

Configuring AutoArchive by folder

If you want to specify AutoArchive settings for a particular folder, you can do so on the AutoArchive tab of the **Folder Properties** window.

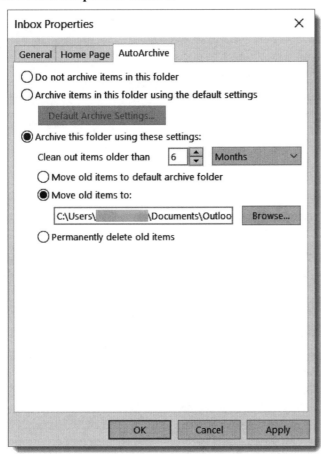

1. Select a folder in the Navigation Pane.

2. On the Folder tab, click **AutoArchive Settings**.

3. In the **Folder Properties** window, configure settings.

- You can choose not to archive a folder, to archive it by the default settings, or to archive by folder-specific settings.

- Unless you've already clicked **Apply these settings to all folders now** in default settings, the folder default will be not to archive.

- If you choose individual folder settings, you can specify options such as how long you want to keep items before cleaning them up, whether to archive or delete items, and what archive file to move them to.

4. Click **OK**.

Manually archiving items

You can also manually archive items at any time, without changing your AutoArchive settings.

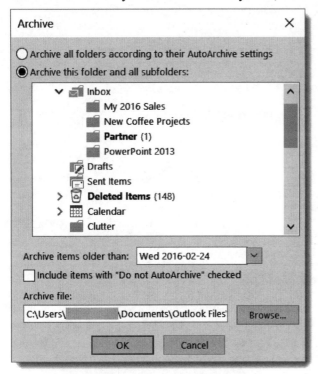

1. In Backstage view, click **Cleanup Tools > Archive**.

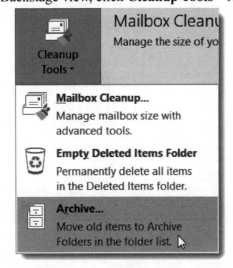

2. Select a folder, or the root folder if you want to archive a whole data file.

All subfolders in the folder you select will also be archived.

3. Set the criteria for the archive.

- Set the date. By default, items over three months old will be archived.

- Check the box if you even want to archive items that are set not to be AutoArchived.

4. Choose the archive file, if necessary.

5. Click **OK**.

Exercise: Configuring AutoArchive

In this exercise, you'll configure and run AutoArchive.

Do This	How & Why
1. Open the **AutoArchive** window.	
a) In Backstage view, click **Options**.	To open the **Outlook Options** window.
b) In the left pane, click **Advanced**.	
c) Click **AutoArchive Settings**.	

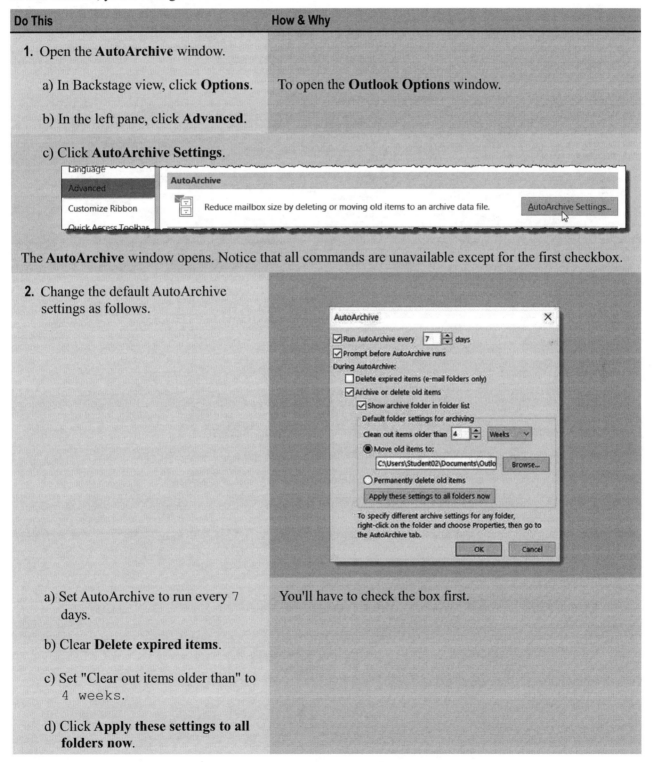

The **AutoArchive** window opens. Notice that all commands are unavailable except for the first checkbox.

2. Change the default AutoArchive settings as follows.	
a) Set AutoArchive to run every 7 days.	You'll have to check the box first.
b) Clear **Delete expired items**.	
c) Set "Clear out items older than" to 4 weeks.	
d) Click **Apply these settings to all folders now**.	

Do This	How & Why
3. Click **OK** twice.	To close the **AutoArchive** and **Outlook Options** windows.
4. Perform a manual archive using your AutoArchive settings.	You don't want to wait a week to see the results, so you'll run this now.
a) In Backstage view, click **Cleanup Tools > Archive**.	The **Archive** window opens. You could manually archive items in any folder by date.
b) Select **Archive all folders according to their AutoArchive settings**.	
c) Click **OK**.	To perform the archive.
5. Switch to Folder List view.	You'll have to leave Backstage view first. In the Navigation pane, the Archives data file is now visible below your existing folders.
6. Expand the Archives data file.	Unless you have items older than six months, the folders will be empty, but AutoArchive recreated your entire folder structure, including subfolders.

Assessment: Cleaning up your mailbox

1. True or false? Even when server limits aren't an issue, you might want to clean up your mailbox regularly.

   - True
   - False

2. What happens when you clean up a conversation? Choose the best response.

   - All messages in the current folder, except the latest reply, are deleted.
   - All messages in the current folder, except the original message and latest reply, are deleted.
   - All messages older than a certain point are deleted.
   - The conversation is moved to a Conversations subfolder.

3. True or false? You can customize which folders to AutoArchive, but all folders must be archived to the same file.

   - True
   - False

Summary: Managing your mail

You should now know how to:

- Eliminate unwanted email by configuring Outlook to recognize junk messages without deleting important ones
- Use rules to sort incoming mail
- Clean up your mailbox by deleting or archiving old messages

Synthesis: Managing your mail

To complete this exercise, you'll need a partner.

In this exercise, you'll exchange a series of messages with your partner, and then clean up your mailbox.

1. Plan a project name with your partner. Choose something distinct and unique.
2. Create a rule to move all messages including the project name to a custom project folder.
3. Exchange several messages with your partner, including the project name for each.
   Create at least two conversations, and reply to each other more than once for each. You don't need to make very lengthy replies.
4. Clean up your project folder.
   Only the most recent reply of each conversation should be left.
5. Add your partner to the Safe Recipients list.
   In Junk E-mail settings.

Chapter 9: Advanced email settings

You will learn:

- About message options
- How to format message appearance

Module A: Message options

A message is more than just subject, body, and recipients: you can add a number of other properties to a message to change how it is delivered and instruct recipients how to act on it. Outlook provides features for message importance, sensitivity, tracking, and delivery options.

You will learn how to:

- Set message tags
- Use voting buttons and tracking options
- Set delivery options

The message properties window

When composing a new message, you can access a variety of properties from the Options tab, and the Tags group on the Message tab, but many of them you'll need to actually set in the **Properties** window. You can open this window by clicking the launcher button on the Message tab in the Tags group, or on the Options tab in the Tracking or More Options groups.

The Properties window for a message being composed

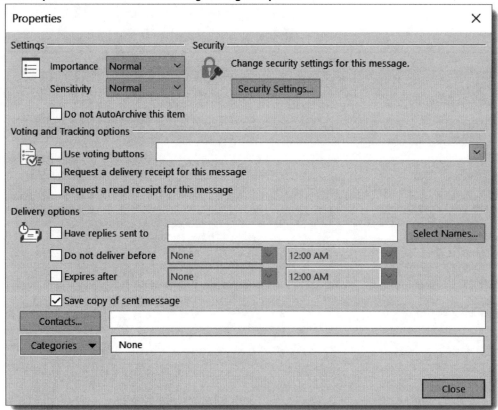

Settings	Contains settings for Importance, Sensitivity, and whether to AutoArchive the message.
Security	Lets you add security features to the message, like encryption or a digital signature. To use these, you and the recipients will need to have Outlook configured to use security certificates.
Voting and Tracking options	Lets you add voting buttons or request delivery or read receipts for the message.

Delivery options   Lets you set a reply address, delivery date, expiration date, and properties for the copy saved in your Sent Messages folder.

You can also view properties on messages you receive by clicking the launcher button in the Tags group. On a message you receive, the **Properties** window contains the same sections, but you can't edit most options. Additionally, there is an Internet headers section, which shows the full header text of the email if you need it for troubleshooting purposes.

The Properties window for a newly received message

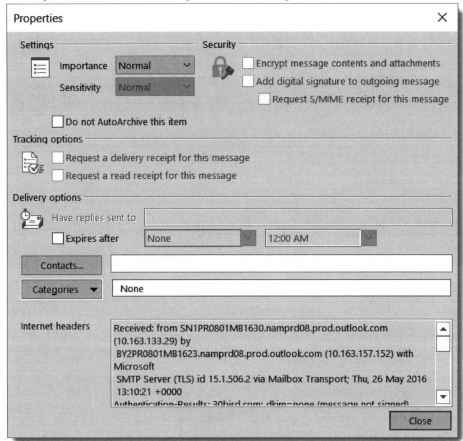

Setting importance and sensitivity

Importance and sensitivity are indicators that you can add to a message you're composing; they advise the recipient about how urgent the message is, and how private or personal its content is. Neither indicator is binding: a recipient can respond to or share the message the same way, however its indicator is set. Think of the indicator as a notification and communication tool you can use in conjunction with the message's content.

    MOS Outlook Exam Objective(s): 2.2.8

Importance can be set to High, Normal, or Low, and is the more commonly used of the two indicators. When you receive a message of Low or High importance, it will have a notice in the InfoBar at the top of the message body, but will also have a distinctive icon in the message list.

Sensitivity can be Normal, Personal, Private, or Confidential. Sensitivity doesn't appear in the message list, but any sensitivity other than Normal is shown in the InfoBar.

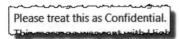

- To simply set importance on a message, on the Message tab of the Tags group, click **High Importance** or **Low Importance**.

- To set sensitivity, or to clear an importance setting, click the launcher button in the Tags group to open the **Properties** window. You can then choose importance and sensitivity in the Settings section.

Flagging messages for follow-up

If you want more flexibility in how you mark a message, you can also set a flag for it. Although you can't make a To-do item from a message for others directly, as you can for yourself, you can set a custom flag for message recipients. Much as with an importance setting, this flag appears as an icon in the message list, with text of your choosing in the InfoBar of the message. You can even set a reminder time.

 MOS Outlook Exam Objective(s): 2.4.7

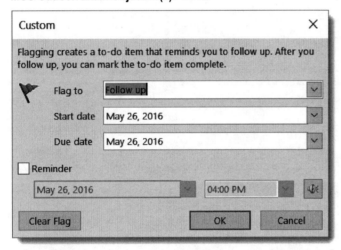

1. In a new message window, in the Tags group, click **Follow Up > Custom**.

2. In the **Custom** window, check **Flag for Recipients**.

By default, the message will also flag the message as a To-do item. If you don't want to do so, clear **Flag for Me**.

3. In the Flag to field, choose the flag message, or type one in of your choosing.

4. Optionally, check **Reminder**, then set a date and time for follow-up.

5. Click **OK**.

About voting buttons

It can be harder than it sounds to ask people simple questions by email. They might give unclear answers, and if you're asking questions of a lot of people, it can be extra work keeping track of who's said what. You can simplify this by adding *voting buttons* to encourage simple replies from a predefined list of contacts.

When you receive a message with voting buttons, they'll appear at the top of the message: in the InfoBar, if you're reading it in the Reading Pane; or in the Respond group, if you open the message. Either way, choosing the option automatically creates a response to the sender with your answer.

Voting buttons in the InfoBar

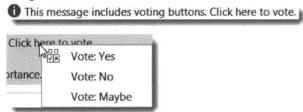

When you send a message with voting buttons, Outlook tracks responses and lets you view them in the original message.

Adding voting buttons

You can set voting options in the **Properties** window, or from the ribbon, using the Tracking group on the Options tab.

 MOS Outlook Exam Objective(s): 2.2.4

Properties window voting and tracking options

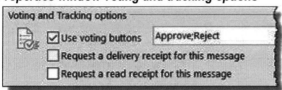

The Tracking group on the ribbon

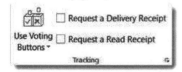

1. In a message composition window, click the **Options** tab.

2. In the Voting and Tracking Options section, click **Use Voting Buttons**.

3. Select from the list of response options, or click **Custom** to write your own.

    If you choose Custom, write out your options in the **Properties** window, with each option separated by a semicolon.

Replying using voting buttons

1. Preview or open the message.

2. Choose your response.

    • If the message is in the Reading Pane, click the InfoBar to view response options.

    • If the message is open in its own window, in the Respond group, click **Vote** instead.

3. In the confirmation window, choose whether to send the response immediately, or first edit it.

4. Click **OK**.

If you choose to edit the response, a reply window opens, and you still need to edit and send the message.

Requesting message receipts

If you don't need a particular response but need to verify that a message arrived or was read, you can request a receipt for the message. There are two types of receipts.

 MOS Outlook Exam Objective(s): 2.2.6

A *delivery receipt* is sent when the message arrives in the recipient's mailbox. Although it can be useful for troubleshooting, you probably won't need this very often: many Internet email providers block delivery receipts because of junk email issues, and when a message isn't delivered at all, you'll usually get an error message.

A *read receipt* is sent when the recipient actually reads the message and requires permission from the recipient.

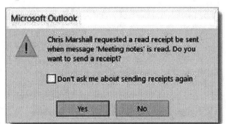

You can also configure messages to automatically request delivery or read receipts on the Mail tab of the **Outlook Options** window. This isn't usually a good idea unless you need to: because recipients might get tired of all your messages requesting responses, they're more likely to actually approve them if you only use them occasionally, for important messages.

1. When composing a message, click the **Options** tab.

    You can also open the **Properties** window and set them there.

2. In the Tracking group, check one or both receipt options.

    • **Request a delivery receipt**

    • **Request a read receipt**

Tracking votes and receipts

When you receive a poll reply, read-message receipt, or delivery receipt, it will arrive as a simple message in your Inbox. Sometimes that might be all you need, but especially if you have a lot of recipients, you might rather check the compiled responses in the original message.

To quickly view voting results, click in the InfoBar of a response, then click **View voting responses**.

You can instead view voting results and receipts by opening the original message and displaying tracking results manually.

1. In the Sent Items folder, open the original message.

2. In the Show group, click **Tracking**.

    The reply totals are shown in the InfoBar, with a list below, arranged by user. If a message has both voting buttons and receipts, these will display in different columns.

Exercise: Using message options

For this exercise, you'll need a partner. You'll explore message properties.

Do This	How & Why

1. Create a new message to your partner.
 	
  a) In the Subject field, type `New Logo Revision`.
 	
  b) In the body, type `As requested, I tweaked the new logo colors. Should we keep this one?`
 	
  c) From the data folder, attach `logo.png`.
	Don't send it just yet.

2. Set the message properties. a) In the Tags group, click the launcher button.	The **Properties** window opens.
b) From the Importance list, choose **High**.	
c) From the Sensitivity list, choose **Confidential**.	
d) Under Voting and Tracking options, check **Use voting buttons**.	The default response options are Approve and Reject. You'll keep those.

Do This	How & Why
e) Check **Request a read receipt for this message**.	
f) Click **Close**.	**You added voting buttons to this message.**
	The High Importance button on the ribbon is highlighted, and the InfoBar notifies you the message has voting buttons.
3. Send the message.	When your partner's message arrives, it has a red high importance icon in the message list.
4. Respond to your partner's message.	
a) Double-click the message in your Inbox.	Microsoft Outlook Robert ___ requested a read receipt be sent when message 'New Logo Revision' is read. Do you want to send a receipt? ☐ Don't ask me about sending receipts again Yes No
	You're asked whether to send a read receipt.
b) Click **Yes**.	When the message opens, the InfoBar informs you of the importance, sensitivity, and voting settings. Additionally, a Vote command appears in the Respond group. **Please treat this as Confidential.** **This message was sent with High importance.**
c) In the Respond group, click **Vote > Approve**.	You're asked whether to send the response immediately or first edit it.
d) Click **OK**.	To accept the default of sending immediately. The InfoBar now shows that you responded Approve.
e) Close the message window.	You receive a read receipt and a vote response from your partner.
5. View both responses from your partner.	Both are just automated replies to your message. The read receipt tells you the time the message was read, and the vote response shows your partner's choice in both the subject and InfoBar.

Do This	How & Why
6. In the message body Approve response, click the **Infobar**, then click **View voting responses**.	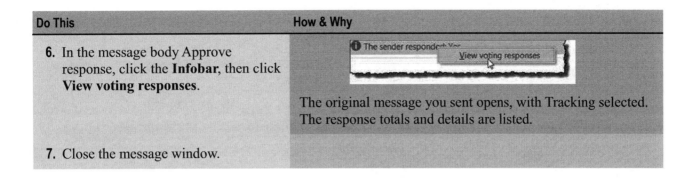
	The original message you sent opens, with Tracking selected. The response totals and details are listed.
7. Close the message window.	

Delivery options

You can change how a message is delivered, and what Outlook does with the sent copy, in the Delivery Options section of the **Properties** window.

You can also perform some of the same tasks from the ribbon's Options tab, in the More Options group.

Redirecting replies

Sometimes you'll want to send a message from one address but have replies go to another—either from a different account of yours or that of a coworker. You can change the reply address in delivery options.

1. When composing a message, in the More Options group, click **Direct Replies To**.
   If the **Properties** window is already open, just check **Have replies sent to**.

2. In the highlighted field, enter the address or addresses you want to receive replies.
   You can also click **Select Names** to choose from your contacts.
   Click **Close**.

Delaying message delivery

If you don't want a message to be delivered immediately, you can instruct Outlook to hold it in the Outbox folder until a specified time.

1. When composing a message, in the More Options group, click **Delay Delivery**.
   If the **Properties** window is already open, just check **Do not deliver before**.

2. Use the date and time fields to set the time of delivery.

3. Click **Close**.

Recalling a sent message

 MOS Outlook Exam Objective(s): 2.2.9

In some cases, you can recall or retract a message you've sent in Outlook. However, not all sent items can be recalled. A sent item can only be recalled if it hasn't yet been opened by the recipient. Another important requirement is that you and the recipient both share the same Microsoft Exchange server, as would be typical if you both work at the same company. If that's not the case, and/or the recipient has already opened the message, then it can no longer be recalled.

 Note: Clearly, it wouldn't be a good idea to rely on this feature, as its requirements are fairly specific. Thus, success in recalling sent items isn't guaranteed!

1. In the Sent Items folder, open the sent message you wish to recall.

In Mail view. Double-click the message to open it.

2. On the Message tab, click **Actions > Recall This Message**.

In the Move group.

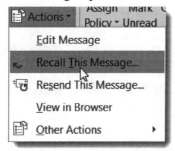

In the **Recall This Message** window, **Delete unread copies of this message** is selected by default, as this is the more commonly used option. However, you can instead select **Delete unread copies and replace with a new message**. It's a good idea to leave **Tell me if recall succeeds or fails for each recipient** selected, as it will provide you with some confirmation if the action is successful.

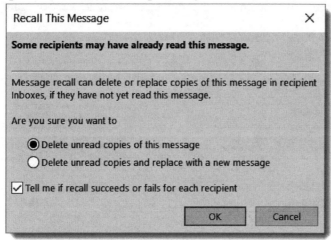

3. Click **OK**.

Specifying sent item options

Normally, whenever you send a message, Outlook saves it in a default location. For most accounts this will be your Sent Items folder. If you want to change the location where a message is saved—or not save it at all—you can use the Options tab's More Options group.

You can also use the **Properties** window to specify not to save a copy, or to apply a category to the sent message, but you can't use it to save a copy to a different folder.

1. In the More Options group, click **Save Sent Item To**.

   On the Options tab

2. Select where you want the message saved.

   • **Use Default Folder** sends the message and saves a copy to the default sent items folder for that account.

   • **Do Not Save** sends the message, but doesn't save a local copy.

   • **Other Folder** opens a **Select Folder** window, where you can choose any folder you like.

Exercise: Using delivery options

For this exercise, you'll need a partner. You'll send a message with custom delivery options.

Do This	How & Why
1. Create a message to your partner, but don't send it yet.	Use whatever subject and body you like.
2. On the Options tab, click **Save Sent Item To > Do Not Save**.	
3. Direct replies to this message to your instructor.	
a) Click **Direct Replies To**.	The **Properties** window opens, with **Have replies to** checked and the address field highlighted. Also note that "Save copy of sent message" is now cleared.
b) Type your instructor's address.	If your instructor is in your contacts, you can instead click **Select Names**.
4. Set the message to wait five minutes before delivery.	
a) Check **Do not deliver before**.	In the Delivery Options section.

Do This	How & Why
b) Edit the time field to a few minutes from now.	
c) Click **Close**.	The **Properties** window closes.
5. Send the message.	Outbox [1] The message isn't sent immediately, but instead is left in the Outbox folder.
6. When the message is finally sent, check in your Sent Items folder.	There are copies of all the other messages you've sent recently, but not that one.
7. When your partner's message arrives, select it, and click **Reply**.	Your instructor's address is in the To field.
8. Close the message window without sending.	

Assessment: Message options

1. Which of the following are valid message importance settings? Choose all that apply.

   - Confidential
   - High
   - Normal
   - Personal
   - Urgent

2. True or false? Voting and receipt results can all be viewed in the same place.

   - True
   - False

3. Which of these actions can you perform only from ribbon commands, not from the Properties window? Choose the best response.

   - Add voting buttons.
   - Delay delivery.
   - Flag a message for follow-up.
   - Set message sensitivity level.

Module B: Customizing message appearance

You can format an HTML or Rich Text message however you like, but manually formatting all your messages can be time-consuming. Outlook includes styles, themes, and stationery that you can use to create consistent and visually appealing messages.

You will learn:

- The differences between themes, styles, and stationery
- How to apply and customize themes
- How to apply and customize styles
- How to apply and customize stationery

Styles, themes, and stationery

Styles, themes, and stationery all provide ways to format your messages in a consistent and unified fashion. Because they have overlapping functions, the differences among the three can seem confusing at first, but each is distinct, and all three might be useful to you in different circumstances.

A *style* is a predefined combination of font or paragraph formatting attributes that you can apply to specific text in a message. For example, you can use styles to mark headers or emphasize text. Unlike ordinary text formatting, when you modify a style, it automatically changes all text formatted with that style. Additionally, styles are grouped into *style sets*. By changing the style set, you can change font and paragraph formatting for all styles at once to give your message a consistent and professional feel.

A *theme* is similar to a style, but applies to a message's overall appearance. Usually themes don't dramatically change paragraph formatting as do style sets; instead, they define the fonts and colors used in the message, and the visual effects used for elements such as charts or SmartArt graphics. By changing themes, you can adjust the feel of your entire message with a single click.

Stationery is also a set of unified design elements such as fonts, colors, bullet styles, and background images, but is used as a default setting for new messages. You don't change stationery to reformat an existing message; instead, you set it to apply to messages you'll create in the future. Most stationery features apply only to new messages you create, though you can change the default font for your replies and forwarded messages as well.

 Note: Although Outlook gives you nearly all the formatting features of a word processing application like Word, remember that not all email clients will display messages the same way. The more complex your formatting is, the more likely it is that your recipients could have problems reading your emails. Additionally, many users expect messages to be simple and to the point. When in doubt, keep your message formatting easily readable, and consider attaching Word or PDF documents when complex formatting is important to your message.

The Styles gallery and Styles pane

When you're composing a message, you can apply or modify styles from either the Styles gallery or the Styles pane. Some tasks can be performed from only one or the other; for others, it's just a matter of which you find more convenient to use.

The Styles gallery is located on the Format Text tab, in the Styles group. It contains a partial list of available styles, as well as additional commands. It doesn't have all available options, but it's convenient to use. Additionally, you can see a live preview of how a style will look by simply pointing to it in the gallery.

Clicking the launcher button in the Styles group opens the Styles pane. It can show more available styles than the gallery, and includes command buttons for creating and managing styles. You can also show or hide the Styles pane by pressing **Ctrl**+**Alt**+**Shift**+**S**.

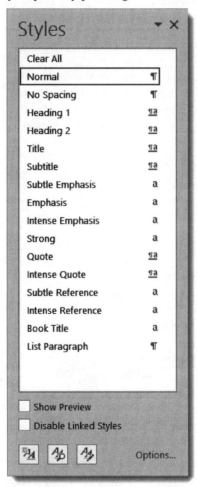

 Note: You're most likely to use styles or themes when composing messages, but you can also use them in most other items that have a body or Notes field you can edit, such as appointments or contacts.

Applying styles

There are three types of styles: character, paragraph, and linked. Once you understand their differences, applying them is easy.

 MOS Outlook Exam Objective(s): 2.3.3

- *Character styles* contain only font formatting elements, but not paragraph formatting elements. This means you can apply them to any amount of text, from a single character to an entire message.

- *Paragraph styles* can contain both font formatting elements and paragraph formatting elements. You can only apply a paragraph style to entire paragraphs, not to part of one.

- *Linked styles* can also contain both font and paragraph formatting elements, but can behave as either character or paragraph styles, depending on how you apply them. If you apply a linked style to an entire paragraph, it will create a paragraph style, but if you apply it to only part of a paragraph, only its character elements are applied.

If you're not sure what type a given style is, you can quickly check by looking at the symbol next to its name in the **Styles** window.

1. Select the text to which you'd like to apply the style.

   - Character styles will apply only to the text you've selected. If you simply place the insertion point in a word, the style will apply only to that word.

   - Paragraph styles will apply to any paragraph included in your selection, even if you've selected only part of the paragraph. You can affect a whole paragraph just by clicking within it.

   - Linked styles will apply as character or paragraph styles, depending on whether you select parts of a paragraph, or entire paragraphs at a time.

2. Click the style name in the Styles gallery or **Styles** window. Click **Clear Formatting** or **Clear All** to remove existing formatting.

   In the gallery, you can point to the style name first to view a Live Preview.

Creating styles

You can create new styles from either the Styles gallery or the Styles pane. In either case, the style will initially be based on whatever text you have selected, so you might want to select something that will make a good starting point. Otherwise, the **Create New Style from Formatting** window contains options to reformat the new style in whatever way you like.

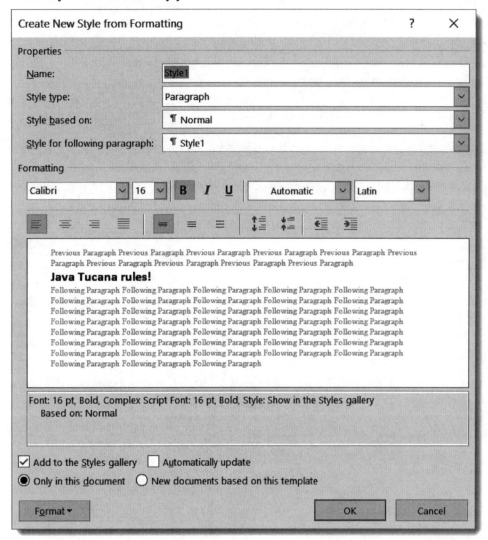

1. Place the insertion point in the text on which you want to base the style.

   It doesn't really matter whether you select words or paragraphs: the new style will be based on the beginning of your selection.

2. Open the **Create New Style from Formatting** window.

   - In the Styles pane, click 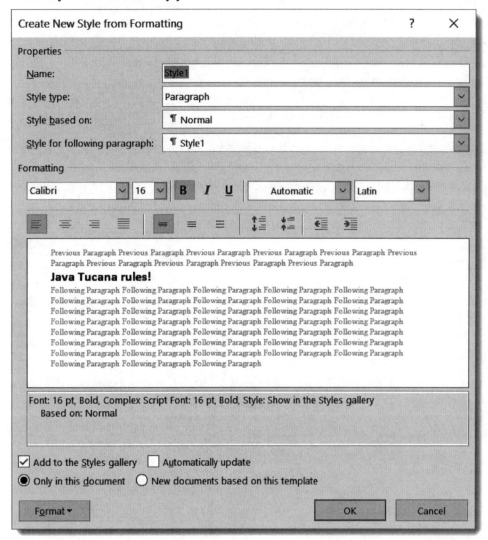 (New Style). This will create a paragraph style by default.

   - In the Styles gallery, click **Save Selection as a New Quick Style**. This will create a linked style by default.

     If you use the Styles gallery, the window will at first be simpler, with just a preview of the style. If you want to change more than the name, you need to click **Modify** to continue.

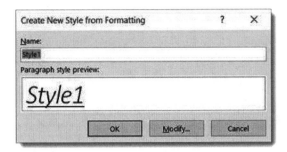

3. Type a name for your style.

4. Optionally, change other elements, such as style type, formatting, and whether to add it to the Quick Style list.

   More detailed settings can be found in the Format menu at the bottom of the window.

5. Click **OK**.

Modifying styles

When you modify an existing style, it automatically updates any text already using that style. You can update a style to match selected text, such as some you've already manually formatted. You can also modify it in the **Modify Styles** window, which is almost exactly like the **Create New Style from Formatting** window.

- To update a style based on existing text, such as some you've manually modified already, right-click the style name, and click **Update <Name> to Match Selection**.

- To update a style in the **Modify Styles** window, right-click the style name in either the gallery or **Styles** window, and click **Modify**.

Changing style sets

By changing style sets, you can change all standard styles at once in a unified manner. The Change Styles menu allows you to change style sets, as well as colors, fonts, or paragraph spacing.

1. In the Styles group, click **Change Styles**.

2. Choose one of the submenus.

   - **Style Set** shows a list of predefined style sets, which can change font, color, and formatting.

   - **Colors** changes theme colors, while retaining other formatting elements.

   - **Fonts** changes theme fonts but not other formatting.

   - **Paragraph Spacing** adjusts how tightly packed your paragraphs are. It can be set to No Paragraph Space, Compact, Tight, Open, Relaxed, or Double.

- **Set as Default** allows you to set your selection as the default.

3. In the presented list, click your selection. You can point to any option to see a Live Preview.

Changing themes

The Themes menu is located on the Options tab. The Themes group also contains galleries for the three elements of each theme: Colors, Fonts, and Effects. Each gallery works the same way: it displays a list of all current themes, and whichever one you select applies to entire documents. You might notice that the Colors and Fonts lists are the same as those in the Change Styles menu.

 MOS Outlook Exam Objective(s): 2.3.3

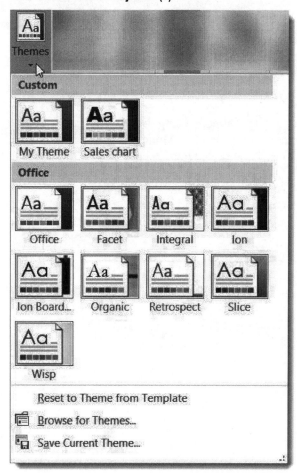

1. Open the gallery.

- **Themes** changes the entire theme.

- **Colors** changes the theme color set. Each set has ten colors: two text, two background, and six accent.

- **Fonts** changes the theme font set. Each one consists of a heading font, and a body font.

- **Effects** changes the line and fill effects used by graphical elements like shapes and SmartArt.

2. Click the theme you want to apply.

As with other galleries, you can point to see a Live Preview, but due to the size and placement of the gallery on the ribbon, it might obscure most or all of the message.

Creating themes

You're not limited to the themes included with Outlook. You can mix and match individual elements of a theme, and even create your own custom color and font sets. If you create a combination of formats you want to keep, you can even save it as a new theme.

- To create a new theme color set, click **Colors** > **Customize Colors**.

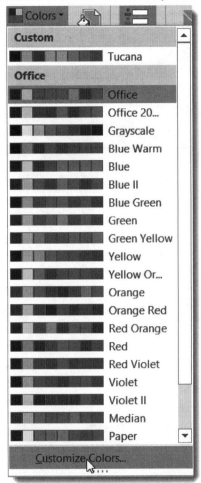

This opens the **Create New Theme Colors** window, where you can choose a name and colors.

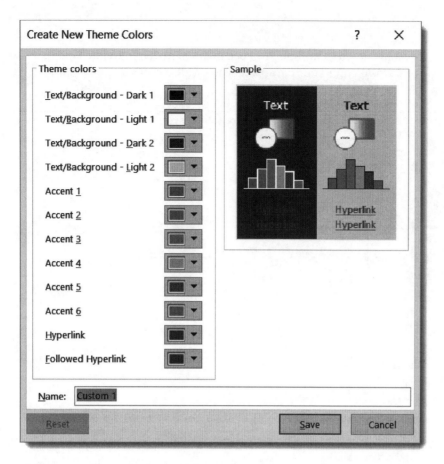

- To create a new theme font set, click **Fonts > Customize Fonts**.

  This opens the **Create New Theme Fonts** window, where you can choose a name, heading font, and body font.

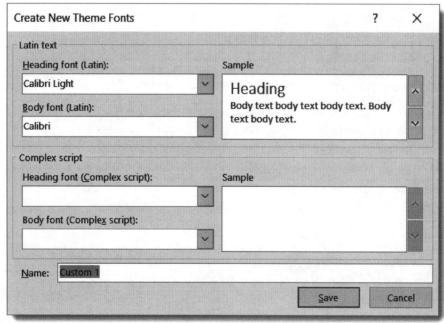

- To save the current theme, click **Themes > Save Current Theme**.

  This opens a **Save As** window. By default, themes are saved in your Office Templates folder.

Exercise: Using styles and themes

You'll need to have Microsoft Word installed. You'll apply styles and themes to a message.

Do This	How & Why
1. Open a new message window.	You don't need an address or subject, you're just displaying formatting.
2. Paste the contents of `About Us.docx` into the message body.	Rather than typing out a message to format, you'll paste one from a Word document.
a) Open `About Us.docx` from the data folder.	
b) Select the entire document.	Press **Ctrl+A**.
c) Copy the text.	Press **Ctrl+C**.
d) Paste the text into the message body.	Press **Ctrl+V**. The text was pasted using Outlook's default theme and styles, so it looks different in the message window. That's okay, as you'll be changing it anyway.
3. Format the two coffee categories in the Heading 2 style.	They've been manually formatted using font and paragraph controls, so you'll match them with the rest of the message.
a) Select **Single-region South American coffees**.	
b) In the Styles gallery, click **Heading 2**.	On the Format Text tab. The font, color, and alignment now match the second-level headings above.
c) Apply **Heading 2** to "Java Tucana's blends."	Select the text, and click **Heading 2.**
4. Apply the Modern style set to the message.	
a) On the Format Text tab, in the Styles group, click **Change Styles > Style Set**.	To display the list of style sets. Before applying one, you'll preview a few.
b) Point to each style set in turn.	As you point to a style, a Live Preview affects the entire text. Some of the changes can be very dramatic, but notice that they don't affect the graphic.

Do This	How & Why
c) Using the ToolTips to view the name of each style set as you hover over it, find and click **Casual**.	To apply the style set. Notice that all styles in the document have been changed.
5. Apply the Urban theme to the message.	
a) On the Options tab, click **Themes**.	To open the gallery.
b) Preview the available themes.	Don't worry if the text in the Smart Art graphic doesn't fit right in the preview. It will resize once you select a final result. While the text formatting doesn't change, the fonts and colors do. So do the line and fill effects of the graphic.
6. Create a custom theme.	
a) In the Theme group, click **Colors**, and select theme colors of your choice.	There's a color scheme corresponding to each theme.
b) Select theme fonts of your choice.	Click **Fonts**.
c) Choose a theme effects setting.	Only the graphic is affected.
7. Save your custom theme.	
a) Click **Themes > Save Current Theme**	The **Save Current Theme** window opens, showing the `Document Themes` folder.
b) In the File name field, type `My Theme`.	
c) Click **Save**.	
8. Click **Themes**.	Your new theme is shown in the Custom section. You can apply it to future messages.
9. Close the message.	If you're prompted, don't save it as a draft.

Stationery settings

Stationery settings are located on the Personal Stationery tab of the **Signatures and Stationery** window.

 MOS Outlook Exam Objective(s): 2.1.1

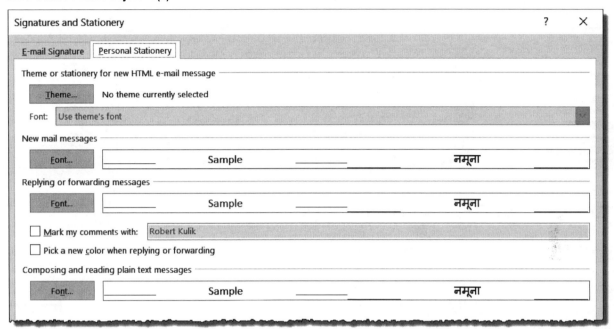

From this window, you can set a *stationery theme*. Each theme can contain formatting elements such as fonts, colors, bullet formats, and background colors or images. Stationery themes shouldn't be confused with Office themes; even though they have some overlapping features, the two function differently. In particular, stationery themes are applied only to new messages you compose, and can't be set on existing messages.

In addition to setting stationery themes, you can also set the default font used by your new messages, or for your forwards and replies. You can even set the font Outlook uses to display plain text messages, even if that doesn't affect the message itself.

Changing stationery

You can change stationery settings in the **Theme or Stationery** window.

 MOS Outlook Exam Objective(s): 2.1.1

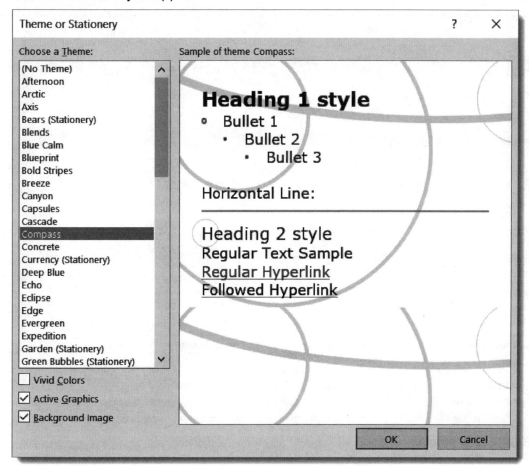

1. Open the **Signatures and Stationery** window.

   • In Backstage view, click **Options**, then **Stationery and Fonts**.

   • On the Message tab of a new message window, in the Include group, click **Signature > Signatures**.

   Note: Stationery changes don't apply to the current message, only to future ones you create.

2. On the Personal Stationery tab, click **Theme**.

3. Choose a theme.

   • For most themes, you can check or clear **Vivid Colors**, **Active Graphics**, and **Background Image**.

   • If the theme is labeled as "(Stationery)," the additional options are unavailable.

4. Click **OK** three times.

Setting stationery for individual messages

Whether you set a permanent stationery or not, you can also use it for individual messages.

1. On the Home tab, click **New Items** > **E-mail Message Using** > **More Stationery**.

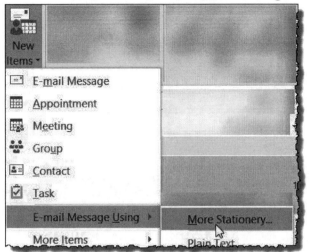

2. In the **Theme or Stationery** window, choose a theme.

3. Click **OK**.

   A new message window opens, using the selected theme.

Exercise: Using stationery

You'll need a partner. You'll choose stationery settings, then exchange messages with your partner.

Do This	How & Why
1. Send a message to your partner.	Use whatever subject and content you like.
2. Open the **Signatures and Stationery** window.	
a) In Backstage view, click **Options**.	The **Outlook Options** window opens.
b) In the left pane, click **Mail**, if necessary.	
c) In the right pane, click **Stationery and Fonts**.	

> 🔤 Use stationery to change default fonts and styles, colors, and backgrounds.   [Stationery and Fonts...]

The **Signatures and Stationery** window opens.

3. Choose a stationery theme.	
a) Click **Theme**.	To open the **Theme or Stationery** window.
b) Choose a theme from the list.	Make sure to choose a different theme from your partner.

Do This	How & Why
c) Click **OK** three times.	To close all three windows.
4. Compose a message to your partner.	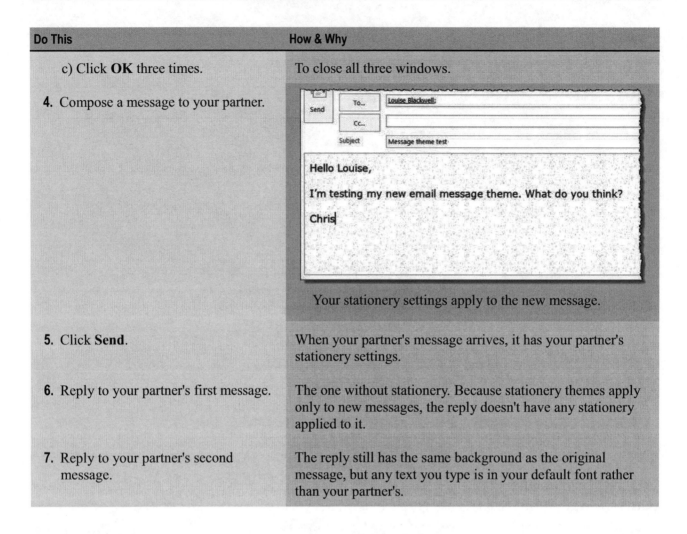 Your stationery settings apply to the new message.
5. Click **Send**.	When your partner's message arrives, it has your partner's stationery settings.
6. Reply to your partner's first message.	The one without stationery. Because stationery themes apply only to new messages, the reply doesn't have any stationery applied to it.
7. Reply to your partner's second message.	The reply still has the same background as the original message, but any text you type is in your default font rather than your partner's.

Assessment: Customizing message appearance

1. What would you change to quickly adjust all text formatting in a message? Choose the best response.

   - Stationery
   - Styles
   - Style Sets
   - Themes

2. Which of these is *not* a theme element? Choose the best response.

   - Colors
   - Effects
   - Fonts
   - Paragraph spacing

3. True or false? It's not difficult to only use stationery for occasional messages.

   - True
   - False

Summary: Advanced email settings

You should now know how to:

- Set advanced message properties, including importance and sensitivity, voting buttons, receipts, and delivery options

- Customize message appearance using styles, style sets, themes, and stationery

Synthesis: Advanced email settings

For this exercise, you'll need a partner.

In this exercise, you'll experiment with formatting and message options.

1. Create a new message to your partner.

2. Paste the contents of `Lunch Menu.docx` into the message body.

3. Using styles, format the message.
   Try using different levels of heading to mark categories or menu item names, or character styles to make specific text stand out.

4. Using themes and style sets, change the overall appearance of the message.
   If you like, try modifying some individual styles once you've settled on a style set.

5. Add voting options to the message.

6. Add your instructor to the reply list.
   Don't remove yourself from the list, just add your instructor.

7. Send the message to your partner.

8. When you receive your partner's message, vote for it. In your reply, leave a comment for additional feedback.

9. Remove your default stationery.

10. Send a brief message to your partner, using custom stationery.

Chapter 10: Notes and Journal entries

You will learn how to:

- Create and manage notes
- Track activity with the Journal

Module A: Notes

Tasks, appointments, and contacts let you store a lot of information for your own use, but they're not always the most appropriate way of quickly marking useful information. Notes provide a quick, versatile way of storing important ideas and reminders, then having them conveniently at hand while you work.

You will learn:

- How to create notes
- How to manage notes
- About note views
- How to change note color and size

About notes

It's best to think of notes as Outlook's equivalent to ordinary "sticky" notes you might use around the home or office. They're small and easy to create and drag around your screen. They're best suited for short notes that don't have to be formally recorded in your tasks, contacts, or calendar folders.

Notes are simpler and more limited than most other items. They open as small windows without a ribbon. They show plain text and the last update time. Although you can categorize a note, you can't format it, add graphics, or attach files to it. Notes don't even have separate subjects and bodies; in the Notes folder, each appears simply as the first part of its text.

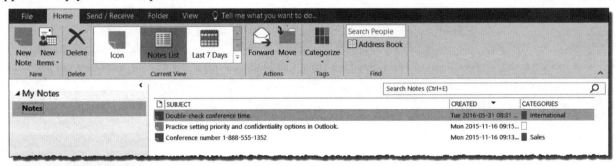

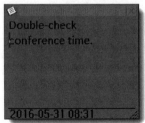

As with many Outlook elements, how much you'll use Notes depends on your work environment and organizational style, but they're simple to use, even if you have only occasional need for them.

Creating notes

Because notes have fewer properties than other items, creating them is very simple. There are two options for doing so: the Home tab's **New Note** command and the keystroke shortcut **Ctrl+N**. In order for the New Note option to be available, Outlook must be in Notes view. On the other hand, you can create new note using the keystroke shortcut from any Outlook view.

MOS Outlook Exam Objective(s): 3.4.2

1. In the Navigation options, click , and then click **Notes**.

   Clicking the overflow Navigation option displays additional view options.

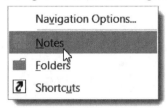

2. In Notes view, click **New Note**.

3. Type or paste content into the note.

4. Close the note.

   The note will be automatically saved, as long as you've entered something into it. You don't actually need to save it as you would other items.

Managing notes

Managing notes is likewise simple. You can edit a note only after opening it, but all other commands can be performed either by selecting it in the folder or in the open note itself. Because there's no ribbon in a note window, you instead need to click the upper left icon to open a menu.

MOS Outlook Exam Objective(s): 3.4.2

- To edit a note, open it and make changes.

  Just like creating a new note, your changes are automatically saved, along with the current time.

- To delete a note, click **Delete**.

  If you delete an open note from the ribbon, the note window will stay open until you close it. Then it won't be saved.

- To forward a note as a message attachment, click **Forward**.

- To categorize, click **Categorize** and choose a color.

  When you categorize a note, its whole color changes to match the category.

Note views

Like other folders, you can change the appearance of Notes view in the Home tab's Current View gallery. However, more icon size options are available in the View tab's Arrangement group. By default, notes are shown in Icon view, which looks a bit like a whiteboard with your notes stuck to it. When you create a new note, it's placed at the end of the list, but you can drag them around to whatever position you like.

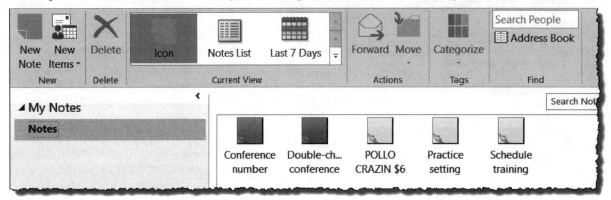

If you want a more detailed listing, in the Home tab's Current View gallery, you can click **Notes List** to view all your notes, or **Last 7 Days** to view only recent ones.

Printing notes

Printing notes is much like printing other Outlook items. The important difference is that to print a list of all notes in a folder, you have to actually select them all.

1. Select one or more notes.

    You can select multiple notes by pressing and holding down **Ctrl** or **Shift**.

2. In Backstage view, click **Print**.

3. Select your print settings.

    • **Memo Style** prints each note on its own page.

    • **Table Style** is only available if you selected multiple notes. It prints a list of all selected notes, formatted just as in Notes List view.

    • If you don't want to use the default printer, select a different one from the list.

    • Click **Print Options** for additional settings.

4. Verify your settings in the Print Preview pane on the right.

5. Click **Print**.

Changing note color and size

You can change the color of individual or multiple selected notes, as well as their window sizes. However, by default, all new notes are yellow with 11 point Calibri text.

To change the color of a note, if it's open, click the note menu, then click **Categorize** and select the color; if it's closed, right-click it, then click **Categorize**, and select the color. To change the size of an open note, drag its window handles as you would with any other window.

Exercise: Taking notes

For this exercise, you'll need a partner. If you don't have one, you can just skip the forwarding step. You should also have a Sales category defined.

In this exercise, you'll practice creating notes.

Do This	How & Why
1. Switch to Notes view.	In the Navigation options, click `•••` , and click **Notes**.
2. Create a note.	
a) On the Home tab, click **New Note**.	A blank note opens.
b) Type `Conference number 1-888-555-1352`.	
c) Close the note.	It appears in the folder.
3. Add to the note.	
a) Double-click the note.	To open it.
b) Press **Enter** twice, then type `Password 64572`.	You can't use formatting controls in a note, but you can still add lines and tabs.
c) Move the note window out of the way.	It's updated as you edit it, so you don't need to deliberately save changes.
4. Create a new reminder note about an Outlook feature you should practice more.	Click **New Note**, then type the reminder.
5. Assign the Sales category to the Conference number note.	
a) In the Notes folder, select the note.	

Do This	How & Why
b) On the Home tab, click **Categorize** > **Sales**.	If you haven't assigned a Sales category, pick an unassigned category, and name it `Sales`. 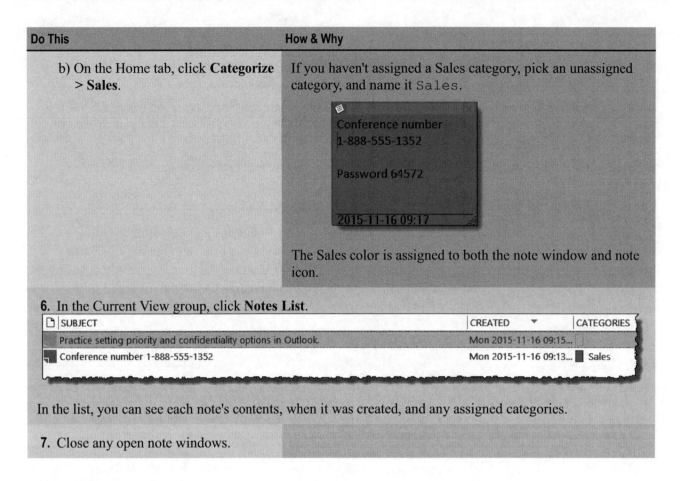 The Sales color is assigned to both the note window and note icon.

6. In the Current View group, click **Notes List**.

☐	SUBJECT	CREATED ▼	CATEGORIES
	Practice setting priority and confidentiality options in Outlook.	Mon 2015-11-16 09:15...	
	Conference number 1-888-555-1352	Mon 2015-11-16 09:13...	■ Sales

In the list, you can see each note's contents, when it was created, and any assigned categories.

7. Close any open note windows.

Assessment: Notes

1. True or false? Compared to other Outlook items, notes have far fewer properties to set.

   • True

   • False

2. True or false? You can change the font settings for individual notes.

   • True

   • False

3. A note's color indicates its _____. Choose the best answer.

   • Age

   • Category

   • Importance

   • Size

Module B: Using the Journal

Outlook's Journal is designed to track your interactions with your contacts. It can track Outlook items such as messages and meetings, files that you use in other Microsoft Office applications, and even other activities, such as phone conversations or paper correspondence.

You will learn:

- How to enable the Journal
- About automatic tracking of Outlook activities
- How to create manual journal entries
- How to manage your journal entries

About the Journal

If your Calendar and Tasks folders keep track of things you need to do, the Journal keeps track of what you've already done. Journal entries were originally intended to track Outlook items associated with your communications—for example, email messages, meeting or task requests, or phone calls you've made outside of Outlook. However, beginning with Outlook 2013, automatic journaling is no long supported. Thus, you can still record, share, and open shared journal entries—even if they were created in earlier versions of Outlook—but you must do so manually.

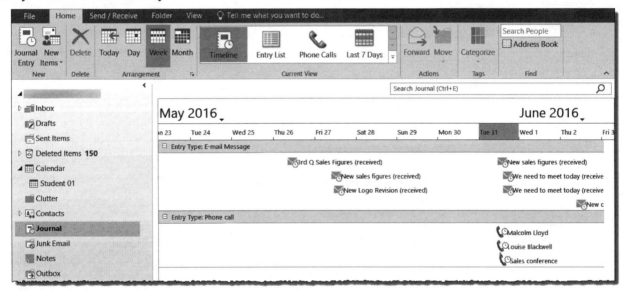

Viewing the Journal

By default, the Journal button is displayed only on the Home tab in Folders view.

1. In the Navigation pane, open the overflow options, and click **Folders**.

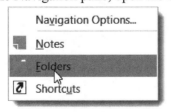

2. In Folders view, click the **Journal** folder.

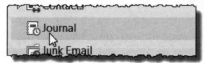

Journal view is displayed, and the Journal Entry button appears in the Home tab's New group.

Creating journal entries from emails and contacts

You can create journal entries from existing Outlook items, such as emails and contacts.

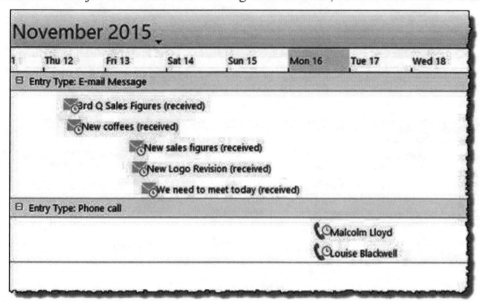

- To create a journal entry for an email:

a) In the Mail view item list, right-click the email, and in the context menu, click **Move > Copy to Folder**.

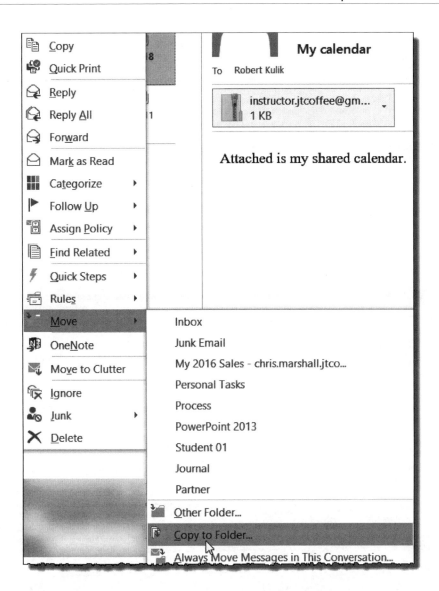

b) In the **Copy Items** window, click **Journal**, then click **OK**.

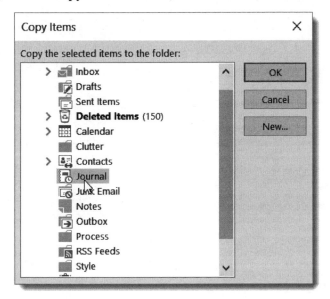

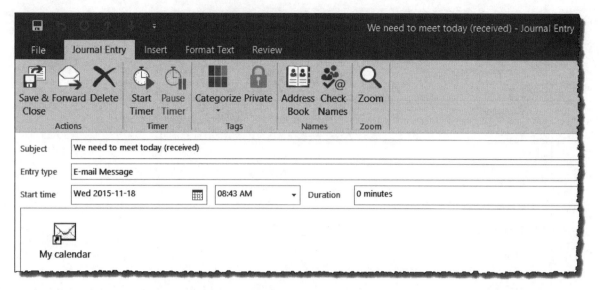

c) In the Journal Entry window, click **Save & Close** to complete the entry.

• The steps for creating a journal entry for contact information is exactly the same, once you've displayed your contacts in People view: right-click the contact; in the context menu, click **Move > Copy to Folder**; and so on.

Creating manual journal entries

You can manually create journal entries from scratch. The **Journal Entry** window is very similar to that of most other item types, though as usual, the specific fields and ribbon commands are specific to the item type.

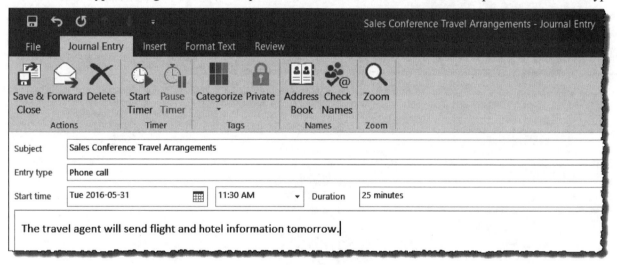

Like most items, a journal entry has a subject and body. As with an appointment, it has a start time and duration, though not a separate end time. Unique to journal entries is the "Entry type" field. This can be any of the item or file types you can automatically track; it can also be a non-Outlook communication such as a phone call, conversation, letter, or remote session.

1. On the Home tab, click **Journal Entry**.

   If you're not in the Journal, you can click **New Items > More Items > Choose Form**. In the **Choose Form** window, select **Journal Entry**, and click **Open**.

2. Set the journal entry's properties.

   • By default, the start time is right now.

- You can either enter a duration, or click **Start Timer** and **Pause Timer** to time an ongoing entry like a phone call.

- To associate the entry with a contact, click **Address Book**, and select one or more contacts.

3. Click **Save & Close**.

   The new entry is displayed in the Journal folder.

Managing journal entries

Finding and editing journal entries is similar to working in the Calendar.

The Journal's Home tab

- Use the Current View gallery to change views.

  - **Timeline** view is similar to Schedule view in the Calendar, with a horizontally oriented timeline. By default, entries are grouped by entry type.

  - **Entry List** view is a list view with properties for each entry.

  - **Phone Calls** and **Last 7 Days** are like Entry List view, but filtered to show only those entries.

- In Timeline view, the Home tab's Arrangement group is visible.

  - Click **Day**, **Week**, or **Month** to change the scale of the calendar.

  - Click **Today** to move to the present.

  - To move to another day, scroll along the calendar, or click the **launcher** button and specify a date.

- Depending on your journal settings, double-clicking an entry opens either the entry or the item to which it refers. You can then edit or otherwise act on it, as usual.

  - Regardless of your option settings, you can instead right-click the entry, then click **Open Journal Entry**, or **Open Item Referred To**.

  - Automatic journal entries embed the referred item as an object, so you can double-click that object when the entry is open in order to view it.

  - Even if a journal entry is automatic, you can edit its time, name, and associated contacts.

- To remove an entry, select it, and click **Delete**.

Exercise: Using the Journal

To complete this activity, you'll need to have a partner who is also defined as a contact. You'll create journal entries from existing items, and create on from scratch.

Do This	How & Why
1. Display Folders view, then display the Journal folder.	
a) In the Navigation pane, open the overflow options, and click **Folders**.	
b) In Folders view, click the **Journal** folder.	
2. Create journal entries for at least two existing emails.	
a) Display Mail view by clicking the **Mail** Navigation option.	
b) In the item list, right-click the email, and in the context menu, click **Move > Copy to Folder**.	
c) In the Copy Items window, click **Journal**, then click **OK**.	
d) In the Journal Entry window, click **Save & Close** to complete the entry.	
3. Create a journal entry for at least one contact.	Use the same method you used in step 2, but first display your contacts list by clicking the **People** Navigation option.
4. In the Journal, click **Journal Entry**.	A **Journal Entry** window opens.

5. Set the entry's properties as follows:

- Subject: `Sales Conference Travel Arrangements`
- Entry Type: `Phone call`
- Company: `Southwind Travel`
- Duration: `15 minutes`

If you were making a real phone call, you could use the Timer group on the ribbon to track how long it took.

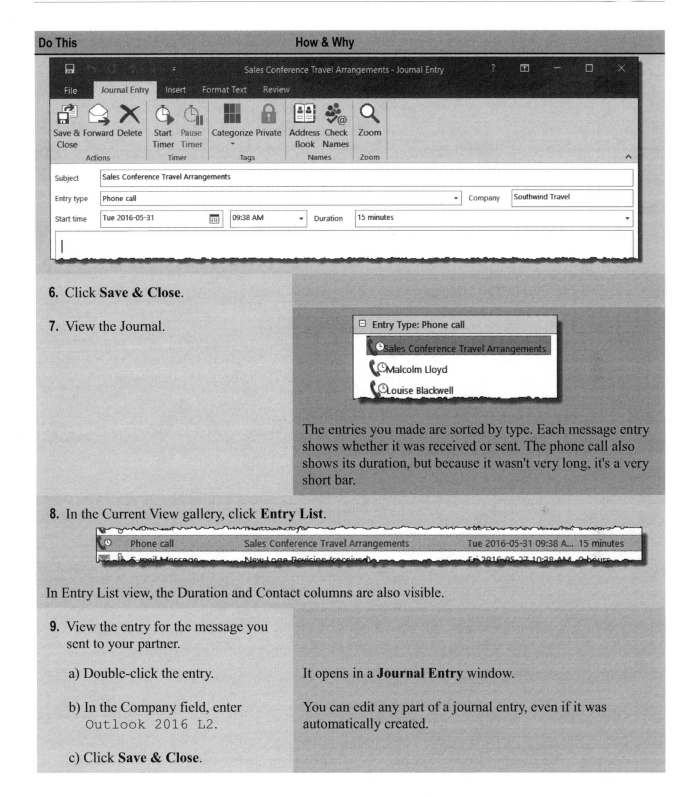

Do This	How & Why

6. Click **Save & Close**.

7. View the Journal.

The entries you made are sorted by type. Each message entry shows whether it was received or sent. The phone call also shows its duration, but because it wasn't very long, it's a very short bar.

8. In the Current View gallery, click **Entry List**.

In Entry List view, the Duration and Contact columns are also visible.

9. View the entry for the message you sent to your partner.

    a) Double-click the entry.

    It opens in a **Journal Entry** window.

    b) In the Company field, enter `Outlook 2016 L2`.

    You can edit any part of a journal entry, even if it was automatically created.

    c) Click **Save & Close**.

Assessment: Using the Journal

1. True or false? You can create journal entries only from existing email messages.

    - True
    - False

2. True or false? You can change the start time of a journal entry later, should you need to.

    - True
    - False

Summary: Notes and journal entries

You should now know how to:

- Use notes to conveniently store simple information in Outlook
- Create journal entries for emails and contacts

Synthesis: Notes and journal entries

For this exercise, you'll need to have a partner who is saved as a contact. You should also have completed the Using the Journal activity.

1. Create separate journal entries for several emails and at least one contact.
2. Arrange a meeting for next week with your partner.
     One of you should pick a time and send the invitation, and the other should reply.
3. Open `Coffee varieties.docx` in Word.
4. Using your web browser, look up some of the coffee regions referred to in the document.
5. In Outlook, save a few website addresses or quotes from your search as notes.
6. Close Word.
7. Email your partner about an interesting fact that you've found, and reply to your partner's email.
8. Create a journal entry for your partner's new email.
9. Review the items created in the Journal since the beginning of this exercise.

Chapter 11: Collaboration

In this chapter, you'll learn how to:

- Perform mail merges
- Share items and work with multiple calendars
- Integrate Outlook with other applications and social media networks

Module A: Performing mail merges

When you need to send the same message to a lot of people, you could simply address the same message to all of them. If you also have Word 2013 installed, you can instead create a mail merge. Unlike an ordinary group message, a mail merge creates a separate, personalized message addressed to each recipient.

In this module, you'll learn:

- When to use mail merges
- How to initiate a mail merge in Outlook
- How to use mail merge fields in Word

Planning mail merges

The difference between a mail merge and an ordinary email sent to many recipients is in the message itself. Instead of exactly the same message going to each recipient, each recipient of a mail merge will get a slightly different message. Typically this means that at least their individual name and address will be in the message's header. It may also contain other information, such as a company name, position, or any other field appropriate to that contact.

A mail merge being composed.

Hello «First_Name»,

Java Tucana's tenth anniversary is coming up, and we're celebrating by introducing a whole new line of premium coffees and teas from all over the world. Since we never would have made it here without loyal customers like «Company», we'd like to offer you an exclusive sample pack along with your next order.

The same mail merge as seen by a recipient.

Hello Robin,

Java Tucana's tenth anniversary is coming up, and we're celebrating by introducing a whole new line of premium coffees and teas from all over the world. Since we never would have made it here without loyal customers like Choi Flowers, we'd like to offer you an exclusive sample pack along with your next order.

Before you send a mail merge, it's important to make sure you have everything you need.

Because the fields in a mail merge come from your contacts, you'll obviously need to have a contact created for each recipient. In addition, each contact must be set up with all the fields you plan to use. For example, if you want to include a company name field, each recipient needs to have a company name set; otherwise, some will receive a message that clearly looks wrong.

Additionally, you can't perform a mail merge with Outlook alone; you need the matching version of Microsoft Word to edit the message itself. If you installed Office 2016 in one go, this shouldn't be a problem, but if you installed only Outlook, or have one version of Outlook and a different version of Word, you can't use this feature.

Finally, and most importantly, you should make sure that your mail merge is both appropriate and in keeping with applicable laws. No one wants to receive junk email, and the line between junk mail and a wanted message as the recipient sees it can be hard for the sender to guess. Also, although Outlook is capable of sending mail merges, they're not intended for large, regular mailings. If you're distributing something like a newsletter or sale flyer to a large number of people on a regular basis, look into an application or service intended specifically for mass mailings.

Avoiding junk mailings

In most countries, unsolicited commercial email is against the law, and even allowed bulk mailings are subject to legal restrictions. For example, in the United States, the CAN-SPAM Act of 2003 requires commercial mailings to adhere to the following rules:

- Mail can't be sent to addresses "harvested" from other listings. Existing customers, people who have signed up for commercial mailings, or people who have inquired about company products or services are valid recipients.

- The sender's identity must be accurately presented: the From lines must be present and accurate, and the sender's physical mailing address must be included.

- The message subject must be accurate and relevant to the content. If the message contains adult content, it should be clearly labeled as such.

- Each message must have a clear and working "unsubscribe" mechanism, and unsubscribe requests must be honored within 10 days.

Some content is exempt from commercial restrictions, such as religious or political messages. However, it may still be subject to other rules.

Even if your messages comply with such laws, or are exempt from them, consider how your message will be received. Customers and coworkers alike might be annoyed by form letters if they're frequent or not relevant to them. Additionally, some content might trigger spam filters on your recipients' email servers or clients.

Beginning mail merges

Before you can actually generate a mail merge, you need to set it up using the **Mail Merge Contacts** window.

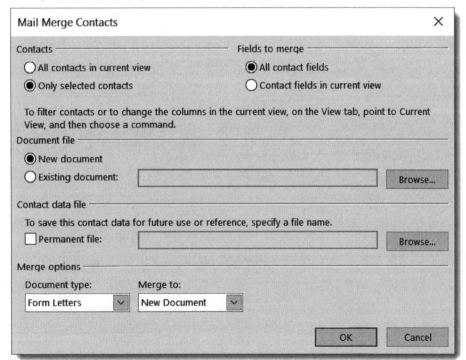

1. Choose the contacts you want to include in the mail merge. You can do this either of two ways.

  - Select the contacts you want to include.

  - Choose a view that displays only the contacts you want to include. You can use folders or filters.

2. In the Home tab's Actions group, click **Mail Merge** to open the **Mail Merge Contacts** window.

3. Choose the contacts and fields to include.

   • Under Contacts, choose the option that corresponds with how you chose contacts at the outset.

   • Under Fields to merge, choose whether to include all contact fields, or only those fields in the current view.

   If you're in a non-list contacts view (e.g. Business Card view), you can choose only **All contact fields**.

4. If you want to base the mailing on an existing Word document, choose **Existing document**, then browse for the file.

5. If you want to save the contact data for future mailings, check **Permanent File**, then click **Browse** to choose a location.

6. From the "Merge to" list, select **E-mail**.

   Merging to New document or Printer is more suited to paper mail merges.

7. Enter a message subject line for the mailing.

8. Click **OK**.

   The mail merge document opens in Word.

Inserting merge fields

Once Word opens, you can compose your message as you would any other, at least for the parts that will be the same for every message. For the parts you want to personalize, you can use *merge fields*, placeholders that will be replaced by data from each contact file. Rather than typing these out, you can use the **Insert Merge Field** button on the Mailings tab. You can do this either of two ways.

   • Click the lower half of the button to open a menu, then select the field you want to add.

- Click the upper half of the button to open the **Insert Merge Field** window. Then select a field and click **Insert**.

Reviewing merges

Before you actually finalize a mail merge, you should make sure you're sending to the right recipients, and that the final result looks appropriate. You can do this using the Mailings tab in Word.

- Click **Edit Recipient List** to open the **Mail Merge Recipients** window.

  It will show all recipients and fields in the merge. Although you can't edit them directly, you can clear the check box by a contact to remove it from the merge.

- Click **Highlight Merge Fields** to display merge fields more clearly in the document.

- Click **Preview Results** to show the results of the merge, using the data from the first person on the list.

  You then use the arrow buttons and number field to move through the list and look for any mistaken or unnatural-looking results.

- Click **Auto Check for Errors** to specify how you'd like to handle any errors in the merging process.

Finalizing merges

Once you've finished your merge in Word, you need to send it back to Outlook to mail it.

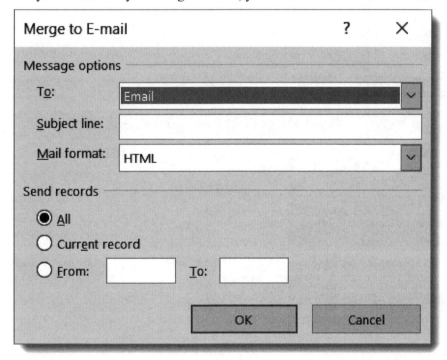

1. In the Finish group, click **Finish & Merge > Send Email Messages**.

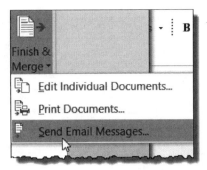

2. In the **Merge to E-mail** window, specify options.

   • From the To: list, choose the contact property with the recipient's address. By default, this is Email.

   • If necessary, edit the subject line.

   • Choose the mail format for the message: HTML, Attachment, or plain text.

   • Choose which contacts in the merge list to which you want to send it. You can choose all contacts, the current one, or a range of them.

3. Click **OK**.

   Outlook automatically sends the messages.

4. Close Word.

Exercise: Performing a mail merge

For this activity, you'll need at least three partners. You'll also need to have Microsoft Word 2016 installed. You'll perform a mail merge to some of your classmates.

Do This	How & Why
1. Set up all of your partners for this activity as contacts.	Make sure each has a first name, last name, company name, and job title. You can each make up details for yourselves, if you like.
2. Set up a mail merge to your partners.	
a) Select all your partners' contacts.	Press **Ctrl** and click each in turn.
b) In the Actions group, click **Mail Merge**.	Mail Merge The **Mail Merge Contacts** window opens.
c) View the default options.	The mail merge will be sent to the contacts you've selected, merging all contact fields. You'll keep that, but change some of the rest.
d) Under Document File, click **Browse**.	This also automatically selects the **Existing document** radio button.

Do This	How & Why
e) In the data folder for the module, select `Survey email.docx`, and click **Open**.	
f) From the Merge to list, select **E-mail**.	The Message subject line field appears.
g) In the Message subject line field, type `Customer Survey`.	
h) Click **OK**.	The survey message opens in Word, with the Mailings tab active. The insertion point is at the top of the document.
3. Compose a greeting using the recipient's name as a merge field.	You could type this manually, but the **Greeting Line** command lets you create an automated version.
a) In the Write & Insert Fields group, click **Greeting Line**.	The **Insert Greeting Line** window opens.
b) Observe the default options.	
	You can change the format of the greeting, specify what will be shown if a recipient lacks a valid name, and preview how each message in the list will look.
c) Click **OK**.	«GreetingLine»
	The Greeting Line field is added to the message.
4. Add merge fields to the message.	The generic part of the message body is already there, so you can just add the fields.
a) Click right before the period at the end of the second sentence.	Right after the word "as."

Do This	How & Why
b) Click the lower half of **Insert Merge Field**.	To display a list of fields.
c) Click **Job_Title**.	position as «Job_Title» Please
	The field is inserted.
d) In the last sentence, place the insertion point between "from" and "you'll."	
e) Insert the Company merge field.	Click **Insert Merge Field > Company**.
f) Make sure there's one space on each side of the Company merge field.	
5. Preview the results of the merge.	
a) Click **Preview Results**.	To show the message as it will be sent to your first partner. The greeting line, job title, and company fields are all filled in with your partner's contact information.
b) Click the **Next Record** button.	
	To show your next partner's information.
c) Preview the rest of your partners' messages.	Click **Next Record** for each.
6. Finalize the mail merge.	
a) In the Finish group, click **Finish & Merge > Send Email Messages**.	The **Merge to E-mail** window opens.

Do This	How & Why
b) View the default settings.	It will be sent as an email with the subject line you specified earlier, in HTML format, and it will be sent to all records.
c) Click **OK**.	The messages are sent through Outlook.
7. Close Word.	Don't save changes.
8. In Outlook, view the messages from your partners.	Each has your contact information inserted in place of the merge fields, and you're the only listed recipient. There's nothing directly in the messages to indicate they weren't written for and sent to you alone.

Assessment: Performing mail merges

1. What do you need to perform a mail merge in Outlook? Choose all that apply.

   - A matching version of Microsoft Word.
   - An account with a mass mailing service.
   - Word 2007 or later.
   - All recipients configured as contacts.

2. True or false? Before performing a mail merge, you should consider any potential legal and professional issues.

   - True
   - False

3. True or false? It's easy to edit contact fields in Word while composing a mail merge.

   - True
   - False

Module B: Sharing items

Although it's easy to email an item to another person, you might want to give someone access to your contacts, calendar, or other items. If you're both using accounts on the same Microsoft Exchange server, you can easily share folders with each other. If you're not, your options are more limited, but you can still send your calendar to a friend or coworker to let them know when you'll be available.

In this module, you'll learn how to:

- Share items in a Microsoft Exchange environment

- Share calendar details via email

- Use multiple calendars

About shared folders

One of the primary advantages of using Microsoft Exchange accounts with Outlook is access to Exchange sharing features. When someone shares a folder with you, you can access it without the other person having to specifically send you each item.

Sharing a folder isn't the same thing as marking it open to anyone, though. You can choose who can access a folder, and just what permissions they have to view, edit, or create items in it. You can even set different permissions for each person with access to the folder.

Permissions settings for a shared folder

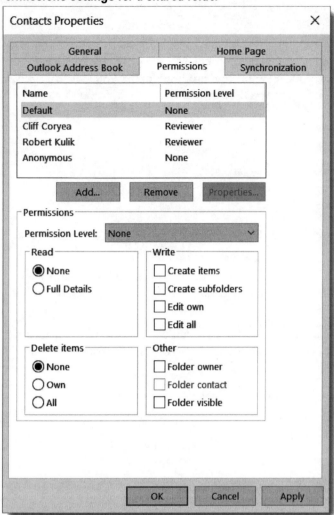

Permissions allow you to set just how a given user can access the folder. You can separately set permissions for whether they can read items in it, create new ones, edit existing ones, delete items, or see the folder in the first place. You can even give ownership of a folder to someone else.

Although you can set permissions piece by piece, you might find it easier to choose a *permission level* with a default set of permissions. For example, if you share a Contacts folder, it by default assigns the other users Reviewer permissions. They can view all items in the folder but not make changes, create, or delete items. If you wanted to give someone more permissions, you could set them as Author, Editor, or even Owner, among others.

Sharing folders

You can share most folders, but the process is simplest for folders that aren't used for mail or calendar items. You can share Contacts, Tasks, Notes, and Journal folders by using the Share group on the ribbon's Folder tab. For Contacts, the Share group is also on the Home tab.

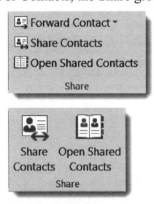

The icons and names are slightly different, depending on the folder type, but the procedure to share a Contacts folder is the same.

1. Select the folder, and click **Share Contacts**.

    A message window opens, with sharing information in the header.

2. In the To field, add whichever users with whom you want to share the folder.

3. Click **Send**.

4. In the confirmation window, click **Yes**.

The recipient receives your message with a link that will open the shared folder.

Changing sharing permissions

 MOS Outlook Exam Objective(s): 2.4.13

If you want to change permissions for a folder you've shared, you'll need to use the Permissions tab of the **Folder Properties** window.

1. Select the folder.
2. Click **Folder Permissions**.
3. Select the user whose permissions you want to change.
4. Choose a permission level, or set custom details.
   - If you're setting calendar details, the detail level is in the Read group.
   - If you just want to remove the user from the list, click **Remove**.
5. Click **OK**.

Opening shared folders

You can open a shared folder using the Share group, or by using Backstage view. If you don't already have access to the folder, you can ask permission from the owner.

1. In Backstage view, click **Open & Export**.

2. Click **Other User's Folder**.
3. In the **Open Other User's Folder** window, specify the user and folder type you want to open.

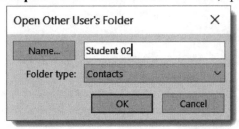

4. Click **OK**.

   If you have permission, the folder will open. If you don't, a confirmation window will open.

5. In the **Microsoft Outlook** window, click **Yes**.

   A **Sharing request** message window opens, addressed to the owner.

6. Edit the message, if necessary, and click **Send**.

   The owner will receive a message with your request, and will need to click **Allow** to send you an invitation in response. You can't access the folder until permission is granted.

Exporting Outlook items

 MOS Outlook Exam Objective(s): 1.2.4, 1.2.5

You can export Outlook items using the Import/Export wizard in Backstage view. Exporting Outlook data as a .pst file preserves formatting and other features.

1. Run the Import/Export wizard.

   a) Click **File > Open & Export**.

   b) Click **Import/Export**.

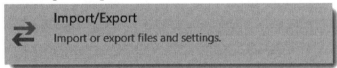

   The **Import and Export Wizard** window options.

2. Click **Export to a file**.
   In the "Choose an action to perform" list.

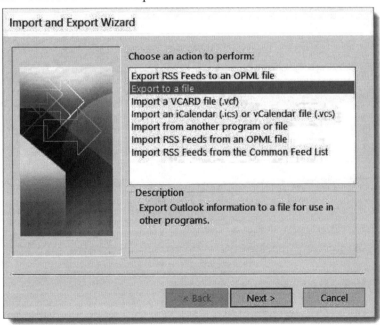

3. Click **Next**.
   To advance to the next screen.

4. Click **Outlook Data File (.pst)**.

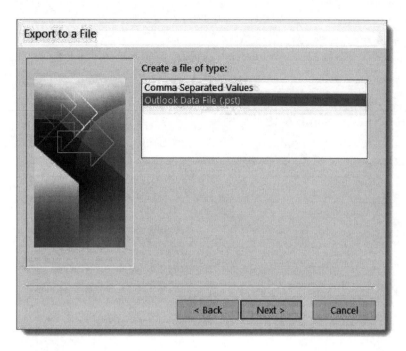

5. Click **Next**.

6. In the **Export Outlook Data File** window, select the folder of the email account you wish to export from. Check **Include subfolders** to include all items in all folders below the level of the selected folder.

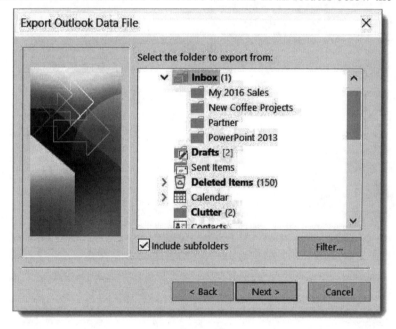

7. Click **Next** to advance to the last screen of the wizard.

   You're prompted to name the file (currently "backup.pst").

8. Name the file.

   If you wish to navigate to another folder, click **Browse**.

   Under Options, **Replace duplicates with items exported** is selected by default. You can instead choose to **Allow duplicate items to be created**, or choose **Do not export duplicate items**.

9. When you're done, click **Finish**.

Sharing calendars via Exchange

 MOS Outlook Exam Objective(s): 3.1.9

Sharing a calendar is like sharing most other folders, except that you must also specify the calendar's *detail level*. You can choose **Full Details**, which allows the recipient to see everything; **Limited details**, which shows the time and subject of each appointment; or **Availability only**, which displays whether you are "free," "busy," "tentative," or "out of office."

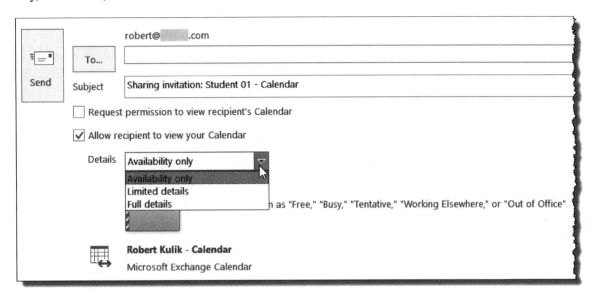

1. While viewing your calendar, in the Share group, click **Share Calendar**.

2. In the To field, enter recipients.
3. From the Details list, choose a detail level.
   By default, **Availability only** is selected.
4. Click **Send**.
5. In the confirmation window, click **Yes**.

Sending calendars via email

Exchange isn't the only way to share content. You can integrate Outlook with SharePoint or social media services to share your contacts or calendar. You can also publish your calendar to Office.com or to a WebDAV server. All of these methods still require both you and everyone with whom you want to share to have access to the hosting service.

If you don't have such a service to share, you can also send your calendar via email in iCalendar format. This isn't quite as powerful as sharing a folder, because it's a one-time exchange. Although any updates you make to a shared calendar are immediately visible to the other user, when you send a calendar by email, you're just sending a snapshot of how your calendar looks right now. If you change it later, you'll need to send it again.

Because you're sending rather than sharing, you can instead send only the part of your calendar that's relevant, such as for a given day or the upcoming month. You can also restrict it to show only appointments within your working hours. Doing so not only prevents you from unintentionally sharing more details than you want, but it can affect message size when you have a lot of calendar items.

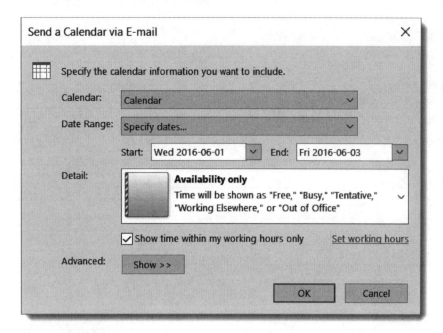

1. In the Share group, click **E-mail Calendar**.

A blank message window and the **Send a Calendar via E-mail** window open.

2. From the Date Range list, choose a range.

   If you choose **Specify Dates**, you'll also need to specify start and end dates. Otherwise, they'll be automatically chosen.

3. Choose the detail level.

4. Click **OK**.

5. In the message window, specify recipients.

6. Click **Send**.

Exercise: Sending a calendar

To complete this exercise, you'll need to have a partner and some items on your calendar. You'll send a copy of your calendar to your partner via email.

Do This	How & Why
1. Review your calendar for the upcoming week. If you don't have at least two appointments or meetings in that time, create some.	
2. In the Share group, click **E-mail Calendar**.	The **Send a Calendar via E-mail** window opens, with a new message window behind it.
3. Specify how much of your calendar to send.	

Do This	How & Why
a) From the Date Range list, select **Next 30 days**. b) From the Details list, choose **Full details**.	 **Availability only** Time will be shown as "Free," "Busy," "Tentative," "Working Elsewhere," or "Out of Office" **Availability only** Time will be shown as "Free," "Busy," "Tentative," "Working Elsewhere," or "Out of Office" **Limited details** Includes the availability and subjects of calendar items only **Full details** Includes the availability and full details of calendar items You'll share everything with your partner for this exercise.

c) Under Advanced, click **Show**.

There are additional details you can specify, but you won't use them now.

Send a Calendar via E-mail   ✕

Specify the calendar information you want to include.

Calendar: Calendar

Date Range: Next 30 days

Wed 2016-06-01 through Thu 2016-06-30

Detail: **Full details**
Includes the availability and full details of calendar items

Advanced: Hide <<

☐ Include details of items marked private

☐ Include attachments within calendar items

E-mail Layout: Daily schedule

OK   Cancel

Do This	How & Why
d) Click **OK**.	The calendar is shown in the message body, and also as a message attachment.
4. In the To field, enter your partner's address.	
5. Click **Send**.	

Do This	How & Why

6. When your partner's message arrives, view it.

The next 30 days are highlighted on the calendar.

Robert Kulik Calendar
Robert@▮▮▮▮.com
June 1, 2016 – June 30, 2016
Time zone: (UTC-05:00) Eastern Time (US & Canada)
(Adjusted for Daylight Saving Time)

June 2016

Su Mo Tu We Th Fr Sa

			1	2	3	4
5	6	7	8	9	10	11
12	13	14	15	16	17	18
19	20	21	22	23	24	25
26	27	28	29	30		

■ Busy ▨ Tentative ☐ Free
■ Out of Office ▨ Working Elsewhere ▨ Outside of Working Hours

June 2016

▲ Jun 1 – Jun 3

▨ Before 08:00 AM Free

☐ 08:00 AM – 05:00 PM Free

▨ After 05:00 PM Free

You can view your partner's calendar in the email body, or click at the top to open it as a calendar. You won't do that just yet, though.

Multiple calendars

Usually in Outlook, you view one folder at a time, and if you really need to view two at once, you open them in separate windows. A notable exception is in Calendar view, where you can open as many calendars as you like and display them side by side in the same window.

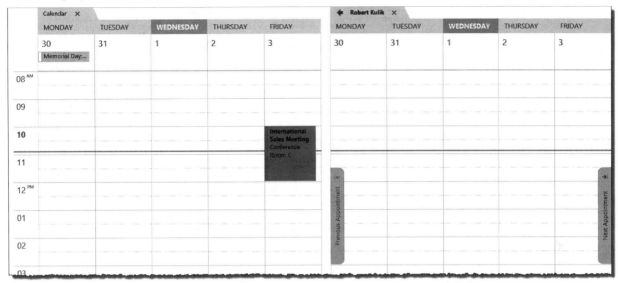

Viewing multiple calendars allows you to compare them easily, and even navigate them in unison to look for conflicts or open times. This is especially useful when you're viewing a shared calendar, so you can coordinate times with your team members.

Schedule view is a great tool for viewing multiple calendars, and especially when you need to find free times during which to schedule meetings. It features a horizontal format that makes comparing calendars convenient, and a combined timeline bar at the top shows times when any displayed calendar is busy. Schedule view is automatically selected when you view five or more calendars at a time, but you can choose it for any number.

Adding calendars

 MOS Outlook Exam Objective(s): 3.1.1

By default, you just have one calendar. If someone shares their calendar with you, the sharing invitation message has a link you can click to add it to your list. You can also click **Open Calendar** in the ribbon's Manage Calendars group to access or create calendars.

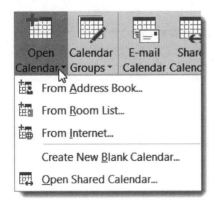

- To open calendars for users or rooms on your Exchange server, click **From Address Book**, **From Room List**, or **Open Shared Calendar**. As usual, if you don't already have access, you'll have to request it from the owner.

- To open an Internet calendar, click **From Internet**, then enter its URL.

- To create a new calendar of your own, click **Create New Blank Calendar**.
  This opens the **Create New Folder** window.

Viewing multiple calendars

Viewing multiple calendars is very similar to viewing a single one. The available views are the same, and the navigation controls move all open calendars to the same point in time. Still, there are additional commands specific to multiple calendar views, and others that are available for single calendars but more useful when you're viewing more than one.

 MOS Outlook Exam Objective(s): 3.1.6, 3.1.8

- To hide or show calendars, check or clear them in the Folder pane.

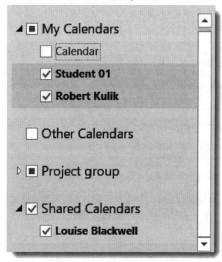

- By default, multiple calendars use different colors, but you can change the color for any calendar by selecting its tab and opening the Color menu on the View tab or context menu.

- You can create appointments and meetings on your own calendar, as usual, but if you double-click a shared calendar, you create a meeting invitation addressed to that calendar's owner.

- To display multiple calendars in a single window, on the View tab, in the Arrangement group, click **Overlay**.

  You can also click the arrow button in the tab for each calendar. Click again to view them side by side.

  Appointments for each calendar will appear in that calendar's color in the overlaid view.

Deleting a calendar

 MOS Outlook Exam Objective(s): 3.1.4

You can quickly delete an undesirable calendar from the Folder pane.

1. In the Folder pane, right-click the name of the calendar you wish to delete, and click **Delete Calendar**.

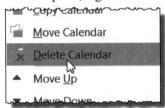

You're prompted to confirm the deletion.

2. Click **Yes**.

Creating calendar groups

If you commonly work with a particular set of calendars, you can put them in a *calendar group*. Then, instead of viewing or hiding each of those calendars individually, you can show and hide the whole group at once. Normally, calendars are automatically part of either the My Calendars or Shared Calendars groups, but you can create additional groups.

 MOS Outlook Exam Objective(s): 3.1.7

You can create a calendar group from calendars you're already viewing, or by adding calendars for people in your address book.

1. Open the **Create New Calendar Group** window.

    • If you're already showing the calendars you want to add to the group, in the Manage Calendars group, click **Calendar Groups > Save As New Calendar Group**.

    • If you want to create a group from scratch, click **Calendar Groups > Create New Calendar Group**.

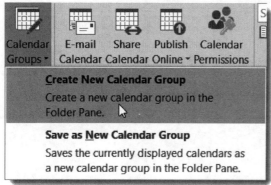

2. Type the new group's name, and click **OK**.

    If you're saving the existing view as a new calendar group, it will be created and selected. If you're creating a new group, the **Global Address List** window will open.

3. In the **Global Address List** window, select the desired contacts, and click **Group Members** to add them. When you're done adding contacts, click **OK**.

    To create the group without immediately adding any calendars to it, you can click **Cancel**.

After you've created a group, you can drag existing calendars into it in the Folder pane.

Scheduling meetings in Schedule view

 MOS Outlook Exam Objective(s): 3.1.2

Schedule view doesn't just allow you to compare multiple calendars to find free times for a meeting; rather, it also lets you quickly schedule the meeting itself.

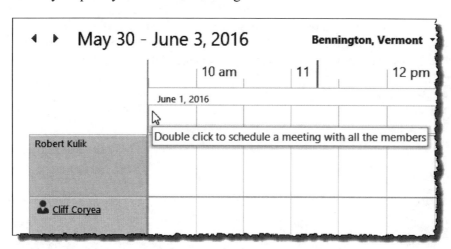

• To schedule a meeting with all visible participants, double-click the timeline row at the top of Schedule view.

    A new meeting request window will open.

- If you want to mark out a time period before creating the meeting request, click once in the timeline bar to select a time, then drag in either direction to change the duration.

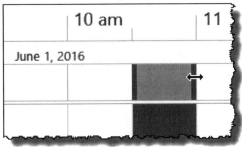

Exercise: Viewing shared calendars

To complete this activity, you'll need to have completed the **Sending a calendar** exercise. You'll view the calendar your partner sent.

Do This	How & Why
1. Add your partner's shared calendar.	
a) At the top of the message, click **Add Calendar**.	A confirmation window appears.
b) Click **Yes**.	Your partner's calendar is now displayed alongside your own in Calendar view.
2. Create an item on each calendar by double-clicking it.	
a) Double-click your own calendar.	A new **Appointment** window opens.
b) Double-click your partner's calendar.	A new **Meeting Request** window opens, addressed to your partner.
c) Close both the new windows without saving.	
3. Navigate through the calendar.	
a) Using the Date Navigator, move to different days or months.	Wherever you navigate, the same time range appears on both calendars.
b) On the View tab, click **Day**, **Week**, and **Month**, in turn.	The calendar view changes for both.
c) Navigate to the present month.	There should be appointments visible on both calendars.

301

Do This	How & Why
d) In the Arrangement group, click **Overlay**.	The selected calendar fills the whole pane, but appointments on the other calendar still appear in its color.
4. Schedule a meeting with your partner using Schedule view.	
a) Click **Schedule View**.	Now both calendars are shown one above the other.
b) Navigate to a point where one or the other of the calendars shows an appointment.	Whenever either of you are busy, there's a horizontal bar in the top row of the pane.
c) In the timeline row, double-click a time when you and your partner will both be free.	A new meeting request opens, addressed to your partner.
d) Enter a subject and location for the meeting.	
e) Click **Send**.	The meeting now appears on your calendar. If this calendar were shared through Exchange rather than via email, you'd be able to see it on your partner's calendar, once the invitation was accepted.
5. Clear the check box next to your partner's calendar.	It's no longer displayed, and your calendar automatically reverts to Day view.

Assessment: Sharing items

1. Most of Outlook's sharing features assume that you have a(n) _____ account. Choose the best response.

   - IMAP
   - Office.com
   - Microsoft Exchange
   - Microsoft SharePoint

2. When you share a folder, what is its default permission level? Choose the best response.

   - Author
   - Contributor
   - Editor
   - Reviewer

3. What feature allows you to coordinate multiple calendars? Choose the best response.

   - Calendar groups
   - Microsoft Exchange
   - Schedule view
   - SharePoint

Module C: Outlook integration

In addition to Microsoft Exchange, you can integrate Outlook with a number of other network services. These include social media sites, messaging applications, and web application services.

In this module, you'll learn:

- About installing add-ins for Outlook
- How to connect to social networks using the Outlook Social Connector
- About integrating Outlook with SharePoint or other services

Outlook Add-Ins

Outlook is designed to integrate with other Microsoft Office applications, as well as Microsoft Exchange, but you can also integrate it with other applications and services. One way to do so is by using *add-ins*, components you can install to help Outlook connect to those applications. Some add-ins are included when you install Outlook, such as the Microsoft Outlook Social Connector or the Microsoft Exchange add-in. Others you'll need to install separately, or they'll be installed along with other applications designed to synchronize with Outlook, such as Skype or iCloud.

You can view your installed add-ins in the Add-Ins section of the **Outlook Options** window.

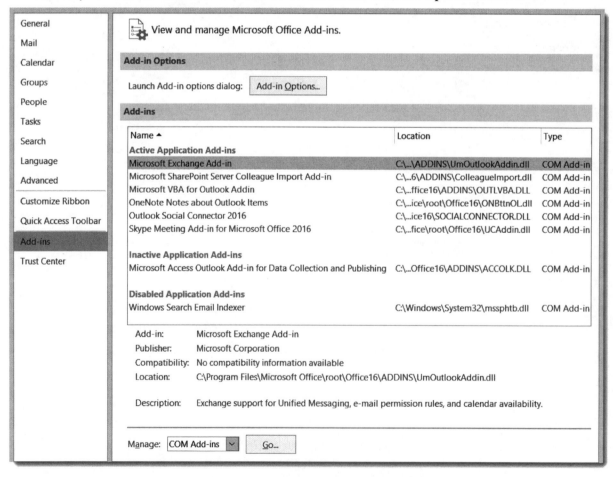

Configuring add-ins

How you install and use add-ins depends entirely on what they are. They might enable or enhance built-in Outlook functions or add entirely new ones. They also might have additional configuration options available either in the application or in Outlook.

For an example, if you use the Skype Meeting add-in, any phone calls you make to Outlook contacts go through Skype. You can also address IMs to your contacts. Likewise, you can configure additional options, such as having Skype automatically show you as "away" when your Outlook calendar shows a meeting, marking Skype calls you make in the Journal, or scanning your messages to recognize phone numbers and allowing you to call them with a simple click. Keep in mind that to use the Skype Meeting add-in, you need a Skype for Business account and you must be signed into that account.

Many add-ins have their controls on the ribbon's Add-Ins tab. This may include access to further configuration options specific to the add-in.

More generically, you can manage your add-ins from the **COM Add-ins** window. You generally can't configure the add-ins themselves this way; rather, you control which ones Outlook uses.

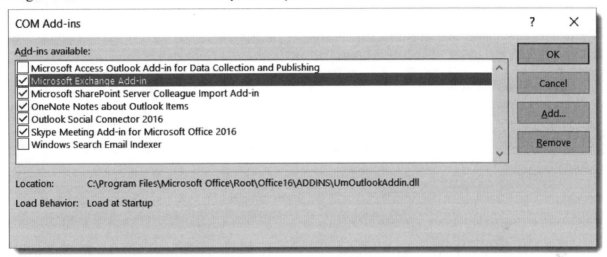

1. In Backstage view, click **Options**.
2. In the left pane of the **Outlook Options** window, click **Add-Ins**.
3. Under Manage, make sure that **COM Add-ins** is selected, and click **Go**.

4. Set add-in options.

   • To enable or disable an add-in, check or clear it.

   • To remove an add-in, select it and click **Remove**. You might not be able to do this with some built-in add-ins.

   • To add a new add-in you already have in executable file format, click **Add**, and select its program file.

5. Click **OK**.

SharePoint integration

Microsoft SharePoint is another service commonly integrated with Outlook. It's most commonly used by midsized or larger businesses with a dedicated IT staff, but Microsoft's new cloud-based SharePoint Online service is making it more accessible for other businesses.

You're likely to use SharePoint with Outlook only if your organization does so, and its configuration and use is beyond the scope of this course. If your organization does use SharePoint, you can use it to connect to Outlook and synchronize your online and offline tasks, contacts, and calendars, viewing them in Outlook even when you're not connected to the network. Once you initiate it from your SharePoint site, the process is similar to connecting to any other folder.

Connecting to social networks

You can use the Outlook Social Connector to connect to social networks and view information related to your contacts, or to anyone else on those networks who sends you email messages. The connector installed by default allows you to connect to your organization's SharePoint site, but you'll have to download and install connectors for other social media networks, such as Facebook. Once you've installed a connector, you can configure it from Outlook.

It's important to know, however, that certain social networks, such as Facebook, are no longer supported and updated by Outlook. You might still be able to use your Facebook account through Outlook, but Outlook does not keep track of your Facebook account or its settings. In addition, LinkedIn is no longer available as an Outlook social network account.

1. On the View tab, click **People Pane** > **Account Settings**.

2. Configure the account.

   • To enable a new account, check it. You'll be prompted for login information, which might include user name, password, and site URL, depending on the service.

   • To configure an existing account, click .

   • To delete an account, click 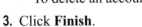 .

3. Click **Finish**.

Exercise: Using integration tools

In this exercise, you'll view add-in and Outlook Social Connector settings.

Do This	How & Why
1. View your installed add-ins.	
a) In Backstage View, click **Options**.	The **Outlook Options** window opens.
b) In the left pane, click **Add-ins**.	On the right, you can see a list of add-ins. They're sorted by status: "active," "inactive," and "disabled."
c) Click any add-in.	Its information is displayed below the list, including name, publisher, file location, and description.
	Add-in:　Microsoft Outlook Social Connector Publisher:　Microsoft Corporation Compatibility:　No compatibility information available Location:　C:\Program Files\Microsoft Office\Office14\SOCIALCONNECTOR.DLL Description:　Connects to social networking sites and provides people, activity, and status information.
d) Click **Go**.	To open the **COM Add-ins** window. Here you can add, deactivate, or remove add-ins.
e) Click **OK**.	To close the window.
2. Examine your Outlook Social Connector settings.	
a) On the View tab, click **People Pane** > **Account Settings**.	A **Microsoft Outlook** window opens, showing your available networks. Only the My Site network is installed.

Do This	How & Why
b) Check **My Site**.	If your company had a SharePoint server, you could connect to it to follow your colleagues through Outlook. 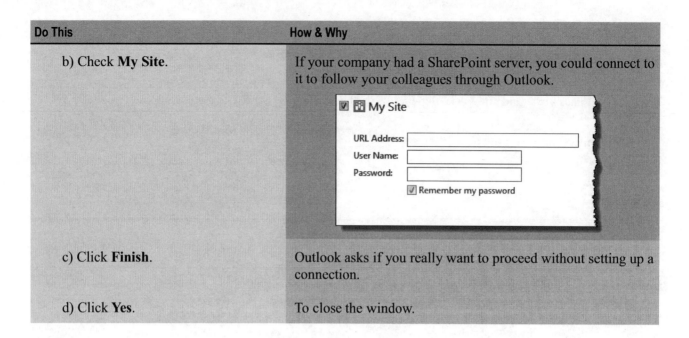
c) Click **Finish**.	Outlook asks if you really want to proceed without setting up a connection.
d) Click **Yes**.	To close the window.

Assessment: Outlook integration

1. True or false? Outlook uses an add-in to integrate with Microsoft Exchange.

    *   True
    *   False

2. True or false? Using the Outlook Social Connector, you can connect to a supported social network by entering its name and your user credentials.

    *   True
    *   False

3. True or false? If your organization uses SharePoint, Outlook lets you synchronize SharePoint content to view it when you're not connected to the network.

    *   True
    *   False

Summary: Collaboration

In this chapter, you learned how to:

- Use mail merges to create personalized messages to a list of your contacts

- Share your items with other users on an Exchange server, send your calendar via email, and work with multiple calendars and calendar groups

- Integrate Outlook with other applications using add-ins, and connect to social media networks, using the Outlook Social Connector

Synthesis: Collaboration

For this exercise, you'll need to have three partners.

In this exercise, you'll schedule a group meeting, using shared calendars.

1. Create a few appointments for yourself over the next week. Make sure to leave most of your schedule open.

2. Send your calendar for the next week to your partners by email.

3. Using Schedule view, invite your partners to a meeting at some time you're all available.
   If for some reason there aren't any times everyone is free, choose a time when as many people as possible can make it.

4. Create a calendar group for you and your partners, then close it.

5. Using a web search, find out if any social media networks you use have Outlook Social Connector. If time allows, download and install one.

Alphabetical Index